Living on Borrowed Time

The Imminent Return of Jesus

Living on Borrowed Time
The Imminent Return of Jesus

For the grace of God has appeared, bringing salvation to all men, instructing us to deny ungodliness and worldly desires and to live sensibly, righteously and godly in the present age, looking for the blessed hope and the appearing of the glory of our great God and Savior, Christ Jesus . . . — Titus 2:11-13

Dr. David R. Reagan

LAMB
& LION
MINISTRIES

McKinney, Texas

Dedicated to

Bob & Grace Wallace

in appreciation for their encouragement
and support.

First edition, 2013
Second printing, 2015
Third printing, 2019

Copyright © 2013 by Lamb & Lion Ministries

ISBN: 978-0-945593-21-8

Library of Congress Control Number: 2013907987

Lamb & Lion Ministries
P.O. Box 919
McKinney, Texas 75070
lamblion@lamblion.com
www.lamblion.com

Cover design by Trey Collich.
Cover photo by Photos.com.

All scripture quotations are from the New American Standard
Version, © 1995 by the Lockman Foundation.

Printed in the United States of America.

Contents

Part 3 — The Key Signs

Contents

Books by Dr. David R. Reagan

The Christ in Prophecy Study Guide (McKinney, TX: Lamb & Lion Ministries, 1987). Second edition in 2001. Third edition in 2006.

Trusting God: Learning to Walk by Faith (Lafeyette, LA: Huntington House, 1987). Second edition by Lamb & Lion Ministries in 1994. Third edition in 2015.

Jesus is Coming Again! (Eugene, OR: Harvest House, 1992).

The Master Plan: Making Sense of the Controversies Surrounding Bible Prophecy Today (Eugene, OR: Harvest House, 1993).

Living for Christ in the End Times (Green Forest, AR: New Leaf Press, 2000). Second edition in 2015.

Wrath and Glory: Unveiling the Majestic Book of Revelation (Green Forest, AR: New Leaf Press, 2001). Second edition in 2015.

America the Beautiful? The United States in Bible Prophecy (McKinney, TX: Lamb & Lion Ministries, 2003). Second edition in 2006. Third edition in 2009.

God's Plan for the Ages: The Blueprint of Bible Prophecy (McKinney, TX: Lamb & Lion Ministries, 2005).

Eternity: Heaven or Hell? (McKinney, TX: Lamb & Lion Ministries, 2010).

Jesus: The Lamb and The Lion (McKinney, TX: Lamb & Lion Ministries, 2011).

The Man of Lawlessness: The Antichrist in the Tribulation (McKinney, TX: Lamb & Lion Ministries, 2012).

A Prophetic Manifesto (McKinney, TX: Lamb & Lion Ministries, 2012)

Living on Borrowed Time: The Imminent Return of Jesus (McKinney, TX: Lamb & Lion Ministries, 2013).

The Jewish People: Rejected or Beloved? (McKinney, TX: Lamb & Lion Ministries, 2014)

Preface

When Jesus ascended into Heaven from the Mount of Olives, "two men in white clothing" appeared to His disciples and said, "This Jesus, who has been taken up from you into heaven, will come in just the same way as you have watched Him go into heaven" (Acts 1:11). In other words, the promise was made that Jesus would one day return bodily and visibly.

The last words Jesus spoke on this earth are recorded in Revelation 22:20. He spoke the same promise to the Apostle John that one day He would return: "I am coming quickly." This repeated promise was made 65 years after Jesus ascended into Heaven. He had returned to the island of Patmos, off the coast of modern day Turkey, for the purpose of ministering encouragement to John, and through him, to churches that were suffering from Roman persecution.

The promise to one day return to this earth to reign in glory and majesty was made by Jesus many times during His brief ministry of a little over three years. A good example can be found in Matthew 16:27 where Jesus is recorded as having said, "For the son of Man is going to come in the glory of His Father with His angels; and will then recompense every man according to his deeds."

The world scoffs at the idea of Jesus' return. To them, the whole concept is utterly absurd. Some professing Christians take the startling position that His promise to return was fulfilled in 70 AD when God's wrath was poured out on Jerusalem and the Jews through the Romans. The vast majority of Christendom — both Catholics and Protestants — argues that Jesus will never return to this earth. To them, the so-called "Second Coming" will simply be an appearance of Jesus in the sky to call believers off the earth, returning with them to Heaven.

So, what about it?

Do the biblical prophets promise a Second Coming of
Jesus to this earth?
Did the heavenly host make such a promise?
Did Jesus Himself make such a promise?
And if such a promise was made, why has it not yet
been fulfilled — after 2,000 years?

Further questions also come to mind —

Does the Bible hint at a date for the Lord's return?
If not, why not?
And, if so, then are there any signs we are to watch
for?
And if there are signs, are any on the scene today?

It will be my thesis in this book that both the biblical prophets and Jesus made a very definite promise that He would return, and that the Bible gives us definite signs to watch for that will identify the season of His return. Further, I will contend that the signs are all around us today, pointing to the fact that Jesus is at the very gates of Heaven, waiting for His Father's command to return. In short, the theme of this book will be the proclamation that we are living on borrowed time.

And the crucial question for you is whether or not you are ready for Jesus to break from the heavens.

Maranatha!

Spring of 2013

Living on Borrowed Time
Part 1
Scriptural Principles

The Promise to Return   1
Believing in a rock solid guarantee.

The Bible specifically promises that Jesus will return to this earth a second time. This promise is found in Hebrews 9:28 where it says, ". . . so Christ also having been offered once to bear the sins of many, shall appear a second time for salvation without reference to sin, to those who eagerly await Him."

The Bible also promises that when Jesus returns, He will reign over all the world from Jerusalem for one thousand years, bringing peace, righteousness and justice to all the nations of the world.

These promises can be found throughout the Scriptures, in both the Old and New Testaments. Below is an outline summary of the key biblical passages that speak of the Lord's return and His reign.

Jesus is going to return and reign on the earth because the Old Testament prophets say so.

1) The Psalms

- Psalm 2:6-9 — David says the Messiah will reign over "the very ends of the earth" (v. 8) from Mount Zion in Jerusalem.

- Psalm 22:27-31 — David again affirms that the Messiah will be given dominion over "the ends of the earth" (v. 27) at the time when He "rules over the nations" (v. 28).

- Psalm 47 — The sons of Korah rejoice over the day

when the Lord will be "a great King over all the
earth" (v. 2), and they state that this will take place
when the Lord subdues the "nations under our feet"
(v. 3).

- Psalm 67 — An unidentified psalmist speaks prophetically of the time when the nations of the world will
"be glad and sing for joy" (v. 4). This will be when
the Lord comes to "judge the peoples with upright-
ness" (v.4). At that time the Lord will "guide the
nations on the earth" (v. 4) so that "all the ends of the
earth may fear Him" (v. 7).

- Psalm 89:19-29 — The psalmist, Ethan, speaks of the
Davidic Covenant and proclaims that it will be
fulfilled when God makes His "first-born the highest
of the kings of the earth" (v. 27).

- Psalm 110 — David says a time will come when God
will make the enemies of the Messiah a footstool
under His feet (v. 1). This will occur when the Messiah stretches forth His "strong scepter from Zion" (v.
2). At that time He will "rule in the midst of His
enemies" (v. 2), "for . . . He will shatter kings in the
day of His wrath, He will judge among the nations"
(vs. 5-6).

- Psalm 132:13-18 — An unnamed psalmist speaks of
God's fulfillment of the Davidic Covenant. He says
this will occur at a time when "the horn of David"
springs forth to reign from Zion (v. 17). He says "His
crown will shine" (v. 18), and He will make Zion His
"resting place forever" (v. 14), for He will dwell
there.

2) Isaiah

- Isaiah 2:1-4 — Isaiah says that "in the last days" (v. 2) the Messiah will reign from Mount Zion in Jerusalem and the entire world will experience peace (v. 4).

- Isaiah 9:6-7 — The Messiah will rule from the throne of David (v. 7), giving the world a government of peace, justice, and righteousness. (Note: The throne of David is not in Heaven. It is located in Jerusalem — see Psalm 122. Jesus is not now on the throne of David. He sits at the right hand of His Father on His Father's throne — see Revelation 3:21.)

- Isaiah 11:3b-9 — The Messiah will bring "righteousness" and "fairness" to the earth when He returns to "slay the wicked" (v. 4). At that time, the curse will be lifted and the plant and animal kingdoms will be restored to their original perfection (vs. 6-9).

- Isaiah 24:21-23 — When the Messiah returns, He will punish Satan and his demonic hordes in the heavens and will punish "the kings of the earth, on earth" (v. 21). He will then "reign on Mount Zion and in Jerusalem" for the purpose of manifesting His glory (v. 23).

3) Jeremiah

- Jeremiah 23:5 — "'Behold, the days are coming,' declares the Lord, 'when I shall raise up for David a righteous Branch; and He will reign as king and act wisely and do justice and righteousness in the land.'" (Note: The term, "Branch," is a Messianic title.)

- Jeremiah 33:6-18 — A day will come when the Lord will regather the dispersed of both Judah and Israel and will save a great remnant. At that time the Lord "will cause a righteous Branch of David to spring forth; and He shall execute justice and righteousness on the earth" (v. 15).

4) Ezekiel

- Ezekiel 20:33-44 — The Lord says a day will come when He will regather the Jews to their land and will "enter into judgment" with them (v. 35). He says that at that time "I shall be king over you" (v. 33). He then adds that "the whole house of Israel, all of them, will serve Me in the land" (v. 40).

- Ezekiel 37:24-28 — The Lord says that He will dwell in the midst of Israel after a remnant of the Jews is regathered to the land and saved (v. 27), and He promises that "David My servant shall be their prince forever" (v. 25).

- Ezekiel 39:21-29 — The Lord says that following the battle of Armageddon (vs. 17-20), "I will set My glory among the nations; and all the nations will see My judgment which I have executed, and My hand which I have laid on them" (v. 21).

- Ezekiel 43:7 — While being given a tour of the future Millennial Temple, Ezekiel is told by the Lord: "Son of man, this is the place of My throne and the place of the soles of My feet; where I will dwell among the sons of Israel forever."

5) Daniel

- Daniel 7:13-14,18,27 — Daniel says he was given a vision in which he saw the Messiah, the "Son of Man," being given dominion over all the earth by God the Father, "the Ancient of Days." And then he adds in verses 18 and 27 that the kingdom is shared "with the saints of the Highest One," and they are allowed to exercise sovereignty with Him over "all the kingdoms under the whole heaven."

6) Hosea

- Hosea 3:4-5 — The Jews will be set aside "for many days" (v. 4), but a time will come "in the last days" when they "will return and seek the Lord their God and David their king" (v. 5).

7) Joel

- Joel 3:14-17,21 — Joel says that following the battle of Armageddon (verses 14-16), the Lord will dwell "in Zion, My holy mountain" (v. 17). He repeats this in verse 21. And in verse 17 He identifies Zion as the city of Jerusalem.

8) Micah

- Micah 4:1-7 — Micah repeats in greater detail the prophecy contained in Isaiah 2. Like Isaiah, he says the Lord will make Jerusalem the capital of the world. The world will be flooded with peace and prosperity. All believing Jews will be regathered to Israel, and "the Lord will reign over them in Mount Zion" (v. 7).

9) Zephaniah

- Zephaniah 3:14-20 — This entire book is devoted to a description of the day the Lord will return to the earth in vengeance. The prophet says that at the end of that day, when the Lord's enemies have been destroyed, the Jewish remnant will shout in triumphant joy because "the King of Israel, the Lord," will be in their midst (v. 15).

10) Haggai

- Haggai 2:20-23 — The Lord says that a day will come when He will "overthrow the thrones of kingdoms and destroy the power of the kingdoms of the nations" (v. 22). Then, using Zerubbabel, governor of Judah, as a type of the Messiah, the prophet adds:

"'On that day,' declares the Lord of hosts, 'I will take you, Zerubbabel, son of Shealtiel, my servant,' declares the Lord, 'and I will make you like a signet ring, for I have chosen you,' declares the Lord of hosts" (v. 23). The reference to the signet ring means the Father will grant His Son ruling authority.

11) Zechariah

- Zechariah 2:10-13 — The Lord says that when He comes, He will "dwell in the midst" of the Jews (v. 10), possessing Judah as "His portion in the holy land" and again choosing Jerusalem (v. 12).

- Zechariah 6:12-13 — When the Messiah ("the Branch") returns, He will build a temple and "rule on His throne" (v. 13), and the offices of priest and king will be combined in Him. Thus, "He will be a priest on His throne" (v. 13).

- Zechariah 8:2-3 — The Lord promises that when He returns to Zion, He will "dwell in the midst of Jerusalem," and Jerusalem will be called "the city of Truth" (v. 3).

- Zechariah 9:10 — The Messiah will bring peace to the nations and "His dominion will be from sea to sea" (v. 10).

- Zechariah 14:1-9 — The Messiah will return to the Mount of Olives (v. 4). The Mount will split in half when His foot touches it, and the Jewish remnant left alive in Jerusalem will flee the city and hide in the cleavage of the Mount (vs. 4-5). Verse 9 says that on that day, "the Lord will become king over all the earth."

Jesus is going to return and reign on the earth because the New Testament prophets say so.

1) **Peter**

- Acts 3:21 — In his sermon on the portico of Solomon, Peter says Jesus must remain in Heaven "until the period of the restoration of all things about which God spoke by the mouth of His holy prophets from ancient time." The period of restoration spoken of here will occur during the Millennium when the curse is partially lifted and nature is restored (Romans 8:18-23).

2) **Paul**

- 2 Thessalonians 1:7-10 — Paul says that when Jesus returns "dealing out retribution to those who do not know God and to those who do not obey the gospel" (v. 8), He will also come for the purpose of being glorified before His saints (v. 10). The return of Jesus to be glorified before His saints and all the nations of the world is one of the persistent themes of Old Testament prophecy (Isaiah 24:23, Isaiah 52:10,13, Isaiah 61:3, and Psalm 46:10).

- 2 Timothy 2:12 — Paul says "if we endure, we shall also reign with Him."

3) **John**

- Revelation 12:5 — John sees a vision in which a sun clothed woman (Israel) gives birth to a male child (Jesus) "who is to rule all the nations with a rod of iron."

- Revelation 19:15-16 — In his description of Jesus returning to earth, John says He bears the title, "King of kings and Lord of lords" (v. 16), and John says He will "rule the nations with a rod of iron" (v. 15).

- Revelation 20:1-7 — John says that after the return of Jesus to the earth, He will reign with His saints ("those to whom judgment has been given") for a thousand years. And this promise of a reign lasting one thousand years is repeated six times in these seven verses.

Jesus is returning to earth to reign because the Heavenly Host say so.

1) Gabriel

- Luke 1:26-38 — When the archangel Gabriel appeared to Mary, he told her that she would bear a son named Jesus who would be called "the Son of the Most High" (v. 32). He then added three promises that are yet to be fulfilled: "the Lord God will give Him the throne of His father David; He will reign over the house of Jacob forever; and His kingdom will have no end" (vs. 32-33).

2) The Four Living Creatures and the 24 Elders

- Revelation 5:9-10 — When John is raptured to Heaven and finds himself standing before the throne of God (Revelation 4), he hears "the four living creatures" (special angelic creatures called seraphim in Isaiah 6) and "the twenty-four elders" (probably representative of the redeemed) singing a song of praise to Jesus. In this song they say that Jesus is a Worthy Lamb who has made His redeemed a kingdom, "and they will reign upon the earth" (v. 10).

3) The Angels of God

- Revelation 11:15 — Voices from Heaven make a proleptic proclamation in the midst of the Tribulation: "The kingdom of the world has become the kingdom of our Lord, and of His Christ; and He will reign forever and ever." (Note: A proleptic statement is one that speaks of a future event as if it has already occurred. This is a common form of expression in prophecy because all future events are settled in the mind of God as if they had already happened in history.)

4) The Tribulation Martyrs

- Revelation 15:3-4 — At the end of the Tribulation, right before the final pouring out of God's wrath in the form of the bowl judgments, all the Tribulation martyrs who are in Heaven join together in singing "the song of Moses . . . and the song of the Lamb" (v. 3). In that song, they declare the Lamb (Jesus) to be the "King of the nations" (v. 3), and they proclaim that "all the nations will come and worship before Thee" (v. 4).

> **Jesus is returning to reign on the earth**
> **because Jesus said so.**

- Matthew 19:28 — Jesus said that during "the regeneration" (the same time as "the period of restoration" referred to by Peter in Acts 3:21), He will "sit on His glorious throne," and the Apostles will join Him in judging the twelve tribes of Israel.

- Matthew 25:31-32 — Jesus said that when He returns in glory, "the Son of Man . . . will sit on His glorious throne. And all the nations will be gathered before Him" for judgment. The throne of Jesus is the throne of David which has always been located in only one place — in Jerusalem (see Isaiah 9:6-7 and Psalm 122).

- Acts 1:3-6 — Luke says that Jesus spent 40 days teaching His disciples about the kingdom of God. Then, as He was ready to ascend into Heaven, one of the disciples asked, "Lord is it at this time You are restoring the kingdom to Israel?" (V. 6). The question indicates that Jesus taught a time would come when the kingdom would be restored to Israel. Jesus' response to the question indicated the same thing. He did not rebuke the question. Rather, He simply said it was not for them to know the times and seasons when the kingdom would be restored to Israel (v. 7).

• Revelation 2:26-27 — Jesus says that He has a special reward for any "overcomer" who keeps His deeds until the end: "To him I will give authority over the nations; and he shall rule them with a rod of iron."

• Revelation 3:21 — Jesus makes it clear that the overcomers will reign jointly with Him: "He who overcomes, I will grant to him to sit down with Me on My throne, as I also overcame and sat down with My Father on His throne." Again, the throne of Jesus is the throne of David (Luke 1:32 and Revelation 3:7). The throne of David is in Jerusalem, not in Heaven (Psalm 122). Jesus currently shares His Father's throne. He is not sitting on His own throne and will not do so until He returns to this earth. Then He will allow the redeemed to share His throne with Him.

Summary

And so we have the testimony of the Old Testament prophets, the New Testament prophets, the Heavenly Host, and Jesus Himself — all promising that one day the Messiah will return to this earth and reign over all the world from Jerusalem. The only way to avoid this conclusion is to spiritualize the promises into meaning something other than what they say.

And yet, that is exactly what most Christians have done, as we shall see in the next chapter.

The Challenge to the Return   2

Denying that Jesus will ever return to this earth.

Is Jesus returning to this earth to reign over all the nations of the world? Most professing Christians in the world today would answer, "No!" They argue that Jesus will never put His feet on this earth again. They scoff at the very idea that the Lord would even be interested in returning to reign.

Where, then, does the minority view come from? Why do some Christians believe there will be a future, literal, and personal reign of Jesus over all the earth? Are these people victims of wishful thinking? Are they simply harboring a fanciful hope? Or, does their opinion have some basis in Scripture?

Could it possibly be that the majority viewpoint is wrong? If so, then how did the view develop, and what are its scriptural weaknesses and contradictions?

Like Night and Day

The two viewpoints are radically different. For example, the majority view holds that history as we know it will very soon end with the destruction of the earth. In sharp contrast, the minority view looks forward to the continuation of history in a glorious thousand year reign of the Lord here on this earth.

There is no future role for Israel in the majority viewpoint; God has washed His hands of the Jews. The minority view sees the Jews as a nation under discipline, temporarily set aside, but they believe a time is coming very soon when the Church will be taken out of the world, and God will once again focus on the Jews, bringing a great remnant of them to salvation in Yeshua, their Messiah.

The majority view sees no purpose left for this planet. It is polluted and despoiled. When the Lord returns, He will take the redeemed to live with Him forever in Heaven, and the earth will cease to exist, as will all the material universe. Those who hold the minority view believe that God intends to redeem the earth and all of His creation — the plant and animal kingdoms. Further, they believe that the earth will one day be returned to its original perfection and will serve as the eternal abode of the redeemed.

As you can see, the differences are like night and day. An outsider would undoubtedly conclude that the two groups have been reading a different book, for how could people read the same book and come to such totally different conclusions?

The Challenge of Truth Seeking

As the title of this article indicates, I believe the minority viewpoint on this central issue of Scripture is correct, and it is my intention to show you why I believe the Bible teaches that Jesus will return to reign.

I have not come to this conclusion casually. I grew up in a church that taught the majority viewpoint. It was drilled into me at an early age. The road that led me to a different view was a tortuous and painful one. It cost me friends. It brought condemnation upon my head. It finally forced me to leave the church where I had spent 30 years of my life.

But the rewards that come from following the truth of Scripture wherever it might lead are always greater than the disadvantages that may be incurred. Jesus said, "You shall know the truth, and the truth shall make you free" (John 8:32). But He qualified that promise with one condition that is usually overlooked. It is stated in the previous verse: "If you abide in My word" (John 8:31). That's a big "if."

As you read this article, I want to challenge you to put aside all preconceptions and traditions of men. Have an open heart, and test what I have to say by the Scriptures and not by the creed of your particular denomination.

I challenge you to be like the Bereans whom Paul commended as "more noble-minded than those in Thessalonica, for they received the word with great eagerness, examining the Scriptures daily, to see whether these things were so" (Acts 17:11).

The Biblical Statement

In Revelation 20:6 we are told that Jesus is returning to reign together with His saints for a thousand years. Here's how it is stated:

> Blessed and holy is the one who has a part in the first resurrection; over these the second death has no power, but they will be priests of God and of Christ and will reign with Him for a thousand years.

Those who hold the majority viewpoint often try to put down this verse by saying, "But that's the only place in the Bible where a thousand year reign of Jesus is mentioned." That, of course, is not true, as I demonstrated in chapter 1.

But let me make something very clear. If this passage in Revelation 20 were the only one in the Bible to speak of a future earthly reign of Jesus, I would still believe in such a reign. God doesn't have to say something more than once for me to believe it. And God clearly says in Revelation 20 that Jesus will reign on this earth for a thousand years.

The Flow of Events

In chapter 19 of Revelation Jesus returns to the earth and defeats the Antichrist and his false prophet. His next order of business is to bind Satan (Revelation 20:1-3). He then begins His reign with His saints.

Six times in Revelation 20:1-7 we are told that the reign of the Lord will last 1,000 years. Consider Revelation 20:4 for example. The verse says that the saints "came to life and reigned with Christ for a thousand years." What could be clearer? What would God have to do to convince us that He means what He says? Does He have to put the message in the sky with blinking neon lights?

At the end of the thousand years, we are told that Satan will be released "to deceive the nations" (Revelation 20:8). He will rally the majority of Mankind in rebellion against the Lord, and they will march upon Jerusalem to overthrow the Lord's kingdom. Notice that Revelation 20:9 says that all this action takes place "on the broad plain of the earth." This is no ethereal battle between spirit beings in the heavens.

As the millennial rebels approach Jerusalem, they are destroyed by fire from heaven (Revelation 20:9), and Satan is thrown into the lake of fire (Hell) where he "will be tormented day and night forever and ever" (Revelation 20: 10).

Imagination vs. Plain Sense

The message of Revelation 19 and 20 is very clear. A little child could understand it without interpretation. It takes a fanciful flight of imagination to explain away its obvious meaning.

But that is exactly what St. Augustine very successfully accomplished around 400 AD. when he developed the Amillennial interpretation of Revelation 20. He did it by applying his imagination to the passage and spiritualizing it beyond recognition.

When he got through interpreting the events described in these two chapters, Revelation 19 had been transformed into a description of Christ's battle on the Cross, and Revelation 20 had been turned into a description of the Lord's spiritual reign over the world from Heaven through His Church. Satan's binding was attributed to the Cross and not to the Second Coming.

In other words, Augustine argued that the Millennial reign of the Lord began at the Cross and will continue until He returns for His Church. That means that according to the Amillennial viewpoint we are in the Millennium now! It also means that the 1,000 years mentioned six times in chapter 20 really doesn't mean 1,000 years. Rather, it is a symbolic number that stands for an indefinite period of time.

This incredibly imaginative interpretation that conflicts with the plain sense meaning of the passage was immediately adopted by the Roman Catholic Church in 431 A.D. It is still Catholic dogma to this day. It has also been adopted by all the liberal, mainline Protestant denominations. In short, this view of end time events is the one that is held by the vast majority of all professing Christians today.

The Imagination Trap

The basic flaw in the whole Amillennial interpretation of Revelation 19 and 20 is rooted in its denial of the plain sense meaning of the passages.

God knows how to communicate, and He desires to communicate. You do not have to have a Ph.D. in hermeneutics or an active imagination to understand His Word.

The book of Revelation begins with the words, "The revelation of Jesus Christ . . ." (Revelation 1:1). The word, revelation, in the Greek is "apocalypse," which means "an unveiling." The purpose of the book of Revelation is to reveal or unveil the ultimate triumph of Jesus over Satan. If God's purpose is to reveal something so significant, why would He write it in a code language that a person cannot understand unless he has graduated from a seminary? It makes no sense.

Advocates of the Amillennial view usually respond by saying that Revelation is full of symbols. Yes, there is a lot of symbolic language in the book, but symbols have a plain sense meaning. They are not used pell-mell, and the reader does not have the freedom to assign any meaning to them that he pleases.

Furthermore, the fulfillment of First Coming prophecies provides the best rule of thumb for the interpretation of Second Coming prophecies. And any cursory examination of First Coming prophecies will quickly reveal that they were fulfilled in their plain sense meaning.

Take for example the prophecy in the book of Zechariah that says the Messiah will come on a donkey (Zechariah 9:9). If today's Amillennial spiritualizers had lived in Old Testament times, I feel certain they would have denied the plain sense meaning of this verse. "Zechariah is apocalyptic literature," they would have said, "and such literature never means what it says. Therefore, this verse must simply mean that the Messiah will be a humble person." No, the verse meant what it said, and in fulfillment of it, Jesus made His triumphal entry into Jerusalem riding on a donkey.

The bottom line is that when you interpret Scripture imaginatively rather than for its plain sense meaning, you can make it mean whatever you want it to mean, and God's message gets lost in flights of fancy.

Satan's Activity

Another flaw in the Amillennial approach is its contention that the binding of Satan that is mentioned in Revelation 20:1-3 occurred at the Cross.

The first thing that must be kept in mind regarding this point is that Satan has always been bound in the sense that he has never had the freedom to do whatever he pleases. Many scholars consider Job to be the oldest book in the Bible. That book begins with Satan standing before the throne of God requesting permission to touch Job, his family, and his possessions. Satan is not omnipotent. He has always worked within parameters laid down by the Lord.

It is true that Satan was further bound by the Cross. As a result of our Lord's work on the Cross, believers since that time have received the indwelling power of the Holy Spirit (Romans 5:5), and the Scriptures assure us that "greater is He who is in you than he who is in the world" (1 John 4:4). Thus, we now have greater power in resisting the temptations and attacks of Satan than did believers in Old Testament times.

But the binding of Satan that Revelation 20:1-3 says will mark the beginning of the Millennium is a special type of binding that did not occur at the Cross. Revelation says that Satan will be bound in such a way that he will no longer "deceive the nations" (Revelation 20:3).

As you look around the world today and observe the behavior of the nations, can you truly believe that they are no longer deceived? The fact of the matter is that they are terribly deceived. As in the time of David, the nations are "in an uproar," and their rulers continue to "take counsel together against the Lord and against His Anointed" (Psalm 2:1-2).

Satan's Continuing Rule

The third critical flaw in the Amillennial view is the idea that Jesus is reigning today over the nations of the world. This contention is really an insult to the Lord, for if He is ruling, He is doing a very poor job! We live in a world characterized by injustice, poverty, pestilence, and terrorism — to name only a few of our planet's maladies.

The Word says that when the Lord reigns, "the earth will be full of the knowledge of the Lord as the waters cover the sea" (Isaiah 11:9). Is this true today? Has it ever been? Of course not!

We are told in 1 Peter 5:8 that Satan still prowls about "like a roaring lion, seeking someone to devour." And in 1 John 5:19, written long after the Cross, we are told that "the whole world lies in the power of the evil one." The Scriptures make it clear that Satan continues as "the ruler of this world" (John 12:31).

The Cross sealed the fate of Satan. He is a mortally wounded monarch who is desperately clinging to his kingdom. One day soon when the Lord returns, Satan will be crushed under the feet of the redeemed (Romans 16: 20). But the total defeat of Satan is yet future. It is one of the benefits of the Cross that has not yet become a reality in history.

Jesus' Ultimate Triumph

As a result of the Cross, Jesus has won back the dominion over this earth that was lost by Adam and Eve when they sinned against God (Daniel 7:13-14 and Revelation 5:9-10). But, He is not yet exercising that dominion. The writer of Hebrews makes this point. He says that Jesus has been crowned with glory and honor and that God "has put all things in subjection under His feet" (Hebrews 2:7-8), but then he proceeds to observe: "But now we do not yet see all things subjected to Him" (Hebrews 2:8).

Some of the benefits of the Cross are delayed and will not be realized until Jesus returns. For example, the Cross guarantees the salvation of believer's bodies, but that blessing of glorification will not be realized until "the revealing of the sons of God" (Romans 8:19). This phrase is a reference to the resurrection of the saints, something that Paul makes clear a few verses later (Romans 8:23).

In like manner, the Cross guarantees the total defeat of Satan and the ultimate triumph of Jesus as "King of kings and Lord of lords" (Revelation 17:14). But that triumph will not occur in history until the Lord returns. In this regard, Jesus is like David when he was anointed the King of Israel but then had to wait a long time before he took possession of his kingdom.

Jesus' Current Role

Accordingly, Jesus is not portrayed in Scripture as being a reigning king now. Rather, He is pictured as our High Priest before the throne of God (Hebrews 8:1). He is our mediator, our intercessor (Hebrews 9:11-16).

When He came the first time, He came as our Savior. He is now our Mediator. He will return as our Sovereign. Redeemer, Priest, and King — those are the three roles of Jesus — past, present, and future.

Jesus' Future Role

Revelation 19:11 says that when Jesus returns, His initial purpose will be to judge and make war against the enemies of God. But verse 16 reveals that His ultimate purpose will be to serve as "King of kings and Lord of lords."

Long before Revelation was written, the prophet Zechariah had revealed the same thing. In portraying the Lord's return, He pictured the Lord destroying the nations rebelling against God, and when that work is completed, he states "the Lord will be king over all the earth" (Zechariah 14:9).

Revelation 19 and 20 clearly establish the fact that Jesus is going to return to reign — but there are other reasons I believe in such a future reign on this earth.

Summary

The Amillennial viewpoint of end time prophecy — the majority view among Christians — is based on a gross spiritualization of Scripture that denies the clear meaning of many Bible passages that proclaim that Jesus will one day return to this earth to reign from Jerusalem.

Accordingly, the Amillennial view is a classic example of what develops when the golden rule of biblical interpretation is violated. That rule states: "When the plain sense makes sense, don't look for any other sense, lest you end up with nonsense."

A Question

Jesus is definitely returning. The question that naturally arises from that fact is the timing of His return. Can we know when He will return?

Over the centuries since Jesus ascended into Heaven, many people have tried to calculate when He would return. Often, they have set definite dates. Thus far those efforts have proven to be exercises in futility. Which leaves us with the question: "Is there anything we can know about the timing of the Lord's return?"

The Timing of the Return   3

Recognizing the season.

We are in the midst of an epidemic of date setting concerning the return of Jesus, and it is going to get worse the closer we get to the time of His actual return.

Satan knows Bible prophecy (Revelation 12:12). He can look at world events and discern from the signs of the times that Jesus is coming soon.

But Satan does not want anyone else to be aware of the Lord's soon return, so he is doing everything possible to discredit God's Prophetic Word. One ingenious technique he loves to use is to motivate very sincere people to set dates for the day Jesus will return.

A Satanic Trick

This approach appears to be paradoxical on the surface. Why would Satan motivate people to set dates for the return of Jesus if he does not want people to know that Jesus is coming soon? The reason is that he knows the dates will prove to be false because the Bible states that God alone knows when Jesus will return (Matthew 24:36).

Date setting diverts people's attention from Jesus to a date. It builds expectations that will be shattered by disappointment. That disappointment will, in turn, produce embarrassment and disillusionment.

The disillusionment is usually manifested in the development of an attitude of contempt for prophecy. The individual who was "burned" by putting his faith in a date, often backs off from prophecy and decides it is nothing but a playground for fanatics.

Another negative effect of date setting is that it promotes ridicule and scoffing by the world. The media love date setters. They focus their cameras and microphones on the date setter and let him hang himself with his date. When the date comes and passes, the media then laugh and scoff and do their best to paint Christians as fools.

The Numbing Effect

The worst effect of date setting is that it cools people's attitudes toward the Second Coming. It's the old wolf story all over again: If you shout "Wolf!" enough times when there is no wolf, people will stop paying attention to the shout.

Likewise, when there is an epidemic of date setting — as there is now — people stop paying attention to the dates and grow apathetic about the Lord's return. Then, when a responsible prophecy teacher comes along and says, "I don't know the date of the Lord's return; all I know is that we are in the general season of His return" — the apathetic and the burned-out respond by thinking, "Oh sure, I've heard that line before."

And Satan sits on the sidelines and laughs.

Knowing the Season

What we need to keep in mind is that although we cannot know the date of the Lord's return, we can definitely know the season. By season, I don't mean a three month period of time like Spring or Fall. I'm talking about a general time period.

For example, Noah preached for 120 years that the people of his time were living in the season of the pouring out of God's wrath. People mocked him and ridiculed him.

Can you imagine what they must have been saying after fifty years? "Noah is a one issue obsessionist! All he ever preaches about is the pending wrath of God. Why, he's been preaching the same sermon for fifty years, and nothing's happened yet!" Some continued to laugh and scoff until they could tread water no longer.

A season for the Lord can be a relatively long period of time, particularly if it is leading up to the pouring out of His wrath, for He does not wish for any to perish but for all to come to repentance (2 Peter 3:9). The prophet Nahum put it this way: "The Lord is slow to anger and great in power, but the Lord will by no means leave the guilty unpunished" (Nahum 1:3).

Recognizing the Season

As we approach the Second Coming, we are nearing a time when God will pour out His wrath in an unprecedented manner (Isaiah 2:10-19). Jesus is returning to judge and make war against the enemies of God (Revelation 19:11). He is coming to pour out the wrath of God upon those who have rejected the love, grace, and mercy of God (Revelation 19:15).

Since God never pours out His wrath without warning, He is orchestrating the Second Coming patiently, taking the time to alert people to the need for repentance. He is raising up prophetic voices to call their nations to repentance, and He is placing judgments upon the nations to prod them toward repentance. He is also providing many signs of His Son's soon return through the fulfillment of ancient prophecies — like the regathering of the Jewish people and the re-establishment of their nation (Isaiah 11:10-12).

God is not interested in catching anyone by surprise with the return of His Son. That's why He has given us so many signs to watch for. The sad thing is that most people will be caught by surprise, "like a thief in the night" (1 Thessalonians

5:2), because they will refuse to read and believe God's Word.

The signs God is providing are found in both the Old and New Testaments, and there are a great number of them. For example, one out of every twenty-five verses in the New Testament specifically relates to the Second Coming. But what is not so well known is the fact that there are over 500 prophecies in the Old Testament which also relate to the Second Coming of Christ.

A great variety of signs are revealed in these scriptures. There are signs of nature, spiritual signs, signs that relate to the nature of society, international political signs, signs of technology, and signs that concern the Jewish people.

An Area of Ignorance

Many if not most Christians have ignored the study of these signs because they believe that since "Jesus is coming like a thief in the night," it is a waste of time to try to interpret the signs to anticipate the time of His coming.

It is true that Jesus said He would come like a thief in the night (Matthew 24:42-43). But Paul later explained that Jesus meant this statement for non-believers, and not for Christians.

Paul's Revelation

Paul makes this point in his first letter to the Thessalonians. In chapter five he says that although Jesus is coming back like a thief in the night, there is no reason for His return to surprise any Christian (1 Thessalonians 5:4). Why? Because, as Paul puts it, "You are not in darkness, brethren, for that day to surprise you like a thief. For you are all sons of light and sons of the day" (1 Thessalonians 5:4-5).

What does Paul mean by this seemingly enigmatic statement? I think he was referring to the fact the when we accept Jesus as our Savior, we are given the indwelling presence of the Holy Spirit. Through the Spirit we receive the power to become spiritually enlightened. John says in I John 2:27 that the Holy Spirit can illuminate our minds to understand the Word of God.

In other words, Paul is saying in First Thessalonians 5 that we can know the season of the Lord's return because we have been given spiritual discernment through the gift of the Holy Spirit. For that reason, Paul says point blank: "You are not in darkness, brethren, for that day [the day of the Lord] to surprise you like a thief" (1 Thessalonians 5:4).

But the spiritual discernment Paul is talking about is not gained by praying for God to zap us with it. It comes through the guidance of the Holy Spirit as we study God's Word. And because the study of prophecy has been so sorely ignored, many, if not most, Christians are going to be surprised by the return of Jesus.

Jesus' Concept

In Matthew 24, Jesus compared the signs of His return to the signs of a pregnancy. Think of it this way — you may not know the date when a pregnant woman is to deliver, but sooner or later, as you watch the development of her pregnancy, you will think to yourself, "That baby is going to be born soon!" Why? You can tell by looking.

Jesus said the signs pointing to His return would be like "birth pangs" (Matthew 24:8). Any woman who has ever given birth knows what Jesus meant by this remark. He was referring to the fact that as the time nears for His return, the signs will increase in frequency and intensity.

This is a crucial point that is usually overlooked. Thus, people often scoff at the signs by saying, "There have always been wars and rumors of wars and earthquakes and famines." Yes, there have always been such calamities, but they are now increasing in frequency and intensity, just as Jesus prophesied.

Peter's View

Peter tells us that one of the signs of the end times will be an outbreak of scoffing at the idea of the return of Jesus (2 Peter 3:3-4). We live in such times. The tragedy is that so much of the scoffing comes from Christians who are ignorant of God's Prophetic Word.

Peter also tells us that "God does not wish that any should perish but that all should be brought to repentance" (2 Peter 3:9). That's why God has given us so many signs to watch for. As the prophet Amos put it: "Surely the Lord God does nothing without revealing his secret to His servants the prophets" (Amos 3:7).

Jesus' Warning

Jesus condemned the religious leaders of His time because they refused to heed the signs of the times. On one occasion they came to Him and asked Him to perform a miracle to prove He was the Messiah. Jesus rebuked them severely. "You know how to interpret the appearance of the sky," He said, "but you can not interpret the signs of the times" (Matthew 16:3).

Jesus was trying to point out that although these men could predict the weather by reading the signs of nature, they could not interpret His significance by reading the signs of God's Word. What did Jesus mean by the "signs of the times?" He was referring to the fact that the Hebrew Scriptures contain more than 300 prophecies about His First Coming.

As I have already pointed out, these same scriptures contain many more signs about the Second Coming of Jesus, and those signs point to this day and age as the season of our Lord's return.

Living in the Season

I personally believe we have been in the season of the Lord's return for almost 100 years — ever since the ending of World War I. My conclusion is based upon the fact that God worked through that war to begin the implementation of His end time program to regather the Jewish people and re-establish them in their land. World War I resulted in the land of Palestine (as the world called it) being transferred from the Turks to the British. The British immediately proclaimed it to be a homeland for the Jews. That proclamation was contained in the Balfour Declaration of November 1917.

But the Jews did not return in large numbers because they had become acculturated to the nations where they had been dispersed. God worked through the horror of the Holocaust of World War II to provide the motivation for the Jews to return to their land to create their own state.

The Old Testament prophets teach that the Messiah will come in triumph to reign over all the world at a time when the Jews have been re-established in their land and in their city of Jerusalem (Isaiah 11:10-12; Jeremiah 23:5-8; Ezekiel 37; and Zechariah 12).

The state of Israel was proclaimed to the world on May 14, 1948. The Jews reoccupied the city of Jerusalem on June 7, 1967.

Two Jewish Signs

Jesus emphasized the significance of these two signs in His teaching. He mentioned both of them in His "Olivet Discourse," delivered to His disciples during the last week of His life.

Regarding the re-establishment of the state of Israel, He told His disciples to watch "the fig tree," because when it blooms again, all the things prophesied about the end times will come to pass (Matthew 24:32-34). The fig tree is one of the symbols of Israel in the Hebrew Scriptures (Hosea 9:10, Jeremiah 24:1-10, and Joel 1:7).

The day before, while walking with His disciples, Jesus had spotted a fig tree with no fruit. He pointed to the tree and put a curse on it. The tree immediately withered (Matthew 21:19). This action was a symbolic prophecy pointing to the fact that the wrath of God would be poured out on Israel because the nation had rejected its Messiah.

The next day Jesus referred back to this fig tree and said to watch for it to rebloom one day. He then added that the generation that witnesses the re-blossoming of the fig tree "will not pass away until all these things take place" (Matthew 24:34).

The fig tree bloomed on May 14, 1948. We are the terminal generation.

In the same discourse Jesus said for His followers to watch Jerusalem. "The Jews will fall by the edge of the sword and be led captive among all the nations," He prophesied. Then, He added, "Jerusalem will be trampled under foot by the Gentiles until the times of the Gentiles are fulfilled" (Luke 21:24).

Forty years after He spoke these words, the first part of His prophecy was fulfilled as the Romans conquered Israel, destroyed Jerusalem, and scattered the Jews worldwide. Jerusalem passed from the Romans to the Byzantines, and from them to the Arabs, the Crusaders, the Mamelukes, the Turks, the British, and — finally — the Jordanians.

For 1,897 years Jerusalem was under Gentile control. The liberation came on June 7, 1967. It is one of the surest signs that our time is short.

Can We Know?

So, can we know when Jesus will return? The answer is, "Yes and No." No, we cannot know the date. Yes, we can know the season. Jesus is coming soon. All the signs point to it. He is at the very gates of Heaven, waiting for His Father's command to return (Matthew 24:33). And for all those who have studied God's Prophetic Word, He will return as their "Blessed Hope" (Titus 2:13) and not as "a thief in the night."

We are in the season. We are living on borrowed time. Therefore we are warned in Luke 12:35-37 —

> Be dressed in readiness and keep your lamps alight. And be like men who are waiting for their master when he returns from the wedding feast, so that they may immediately open the door to him when he comes and knocks. Blessed are those slaves whom the master shall find on the alert when he comes . . .

Other Signs of the Times

The two Jewish signs I have mentioned are not the only ones that point to the fact that we are living in the season of the Lord's return. They are certainly two of the most important, but there are many others. Let's take a look at them.

The Signs of the Return   4

Looking for indicators.

The Bible says we cannot know the time of the Lord's return (Matthew 25:13). But the Scriptures make it equally clear that we can know the season of the Lord's return. Consider, for example, this passage from First Thessalonians 5:2-6 —

> You yourselves know full well that the day of the Lord will come just like a thief in the night . . . But you brethren, are not in darkness, that the day should overtake you like a thief; for you are all sons of light and sons of day. We are not of night or darkness; so then let us not sleep as others do, but let us be alert and sober.

This passage asserts that Jesus is coming like "a thief in the night." But then it proceeds to make it clear that this will be true only for the pagan world and not for believers. His return should be no surprise to those who know Him and His Word, for they have the indwelling of the Holy Spirit to give them understanding of the nature of the times.

Furthermore, the Scriptures give us signs to watch for — signs that will signal that Jesus is ready to return. The writer of the Hebrew letter referred to these signs when he proclaimed that believers should encourage one another when they see the day of judgment drawing near (Hebrews 10:25-27). Jesus also referred to the end time signs in His Olivet Discourse, given during the last week of His life (Matthew 24 and Luke 21). Speaking of a whole series of signs which He had given to His disciples, He said, "When you see all these things, recognize that He [the Son of Man — that is, Jesus] is near, right at the door" (Matthew 24:33).

A Personal Experience

Every time I think of "Signs of the Times," I am reminded of a great man of God named Elbert Peak. I had the privilege of participating with him in a Bible prophecy conference held in Orlando, Florida in the early 1990s. Mr. Peak was about 80 years old at the time.

He had been assigned the topic, "The Signs of the Times." He began his presentation by observing, "Sixty years ago when I first started preaching, you had to scratch around like a chicken to find one sign of the Lord's soon return."

He paused for a moment, and then added, "But today there are so many signs I'm no longer looking for them. Instead, I'm listening for a sound — the sound of a trumpet!"

The First Sign

At the beginning of the 20th Century, there was not one single, tangible, measurable sign that indicated we were living in the season of the Lord's return. The first to appear was the Balfour Declaration which was issued by the British government on November 2, 1917.

This Declaration was prompted by the fact that during World War I the Turks sided with the Germans. Thus, when Germany lost the war, so did the Turks, and the victorious Allies decided to divide up both the German and Turkish empires.

The Turkish territories, called the Ottoman Empire, contained the ancient homeland of the Jewish people — an area the Romans had named Palestine after the last Jewish revolt in 132-135 AD.

In 1917 Palestine included all of modern day Israel and Jordan. In the scheme the Allies concocted for dividing up the German and Turkish territories, Britain was allotted Palestine, and this is what prompted the Balfour Declaration. In that document, Lord Balfour, the British Foreign Secretary, declared that it was the intention of the British government to establish in Palestine "a national home for the Jewish people."

An Evangelical Response to the First Sign

The leading Evangelical in England at the time was F. B. Meyer. He immediately recognized the prophetic significance of the Declaration, for he was well aware that the Scriptures prophesy that the Jewish people will be regathered to their homeland in unbelief right before the return of the Messiah (Isaiah 11:11-12).

Meyer sent out a letter to the Evangelical leaders of England asking them to gather in London in December to discuss the prophetic implications of the Balfour Declaration. In that letter, he stated, "The signs of the times point toward the close of the time of the Gentiles . . . and the return of Jesus can be expected any moment."

Before Meyer's meeting could be convened, another momentous event occurred on December 11, 1917. On that day, General Edmund Allenby liberated the city of Jerusalem from 400 years of Turkish rule.

There is no doubt that these events in 1917 marked the beginning of the end times because they led to the worldwide regathering of the Jewish people to their homeland and the re-establishment of their state.

Since 1917

Since the time of the Balfour Declaration, we have witnessed throughout the 20th Century, and continuing to this day, the appearance of sign after sign pointing to the Lord's soon return. There are so many of these signs today, in fact, that one would have to be either biblically illiterate or spiritually blind not to realize that we are living on borrowed time.

I have personally been searching the Bible for years in an effort to identify all the signs, and it has not been an easy task to get a hold on them. That's because there are so many of them, both in the Old and New Testaments.

I have found that the best way to deal with them is to put them in categories, and in doing that, I have come up with six categories of end time signs.

1 The Signs of Nature

> . . . *and there will be great earthquakes, and in various places plagues and famines; and there will be terrors and great signs from heaven.* (Luke 21: 11)

This category of signs has always been the least respected, even among believers. The mere mention of it usually evokes a sneer accompanied by the words, "Come on, what else is new? There have always been earthquakes and tornados and hurricanes." But those who have this attitude forget that Jesus said the signs would be like "birth pangs" (Matthew 24:8). That means they will increase in frequency and intensity the closer we get to the Lord's return. In other words, there will be more frequent natural disasters and more intense ones.

And that is exactly what has been happening. For example, between October of 1991 and November of 2004 — a period of 13 years — the United States experienced:[1]

9 of the 10 largest insurance natural disasters in history.
9 of the 10 greatest disasters as ranked by FEMA relief costs.
5 of its costliest hurricanes in history.

3 of its 4 largest tornado swarms in history.

And keep in mind that these statistics were compiled before the Hurricane Katrina disaster in August of 2005!

2 The Signs of Society

Realize this, that in the last days difficult times will come. For men will be lovers of self, lovers of money, boastful, arrogant, revilers, disobedient to parents, ungrateful, irreconcilable, malicious gossips, without self-control, brutal, haters of good, treacherous, reckless, conceited, lovers of pleasure rather than lovers of God . . . (2 Timothy 3:1-4)

This passage sounds like a typical evening newscast today! Notice the three things it says people will love in the end times: self, money, and pleasure.

The love of self is Humanism — the belief that Man can accomplish anything on his own. The love of money is Materialism. When Humanism is your religion, your god will always be money. The love of pleasure is the third love that is mentioned. This is Hedonism, the lifestyle that is always produced by Humanism and Materialism.

But God cannot be mocked (Galatians 6:7). He therefore sees to it that when people choose Humanism, Materialism, and Hedonism, the payoff is always Nihilism — which is a fancy philosophical word for despair.

Need I emphasize that our world is wallowing in despair today? We live in a society plagued by abortion, homosexuality, domestic violence, child molestation, blasphemy, pornography, alcoholism, drug abuse and gambling.

Like the days of the Judges in the Old Testament, people are doing what is right in their own eyes, and the result is that people are calling evil good and good evil (Isaiah 5:20).

3 The Spiritual Signs

There are more signs in this category than any other. Many are evil in nature, but there are also some very positive ones.

Negative Spiritual Signs

Concerning the negative signs, a typical passage is the following one found in 2 Timothy 4:3-4:

> *The time will come when they [professing Christians] will not endure sound doctrine, but wanting to have their ears tickled, they will accumulate for themselves teachers in accordance to their own desires; and will turn away their ears from the truth, and will turn aside to myths.*

Some of the negative spiritual signs that are specifically prophesied include the following: false christs, cultic groups, heresies, apostasy, skepticism, deception, occultism, and persecution.

The one that Jesus mentioned most frequently was false christs and their cultic groups (Matthew 24:5, 11, 24). And in fulfillment of these prophecies, we have experienced an explosion of cults since 1850.

The Positive Sign
of the Outpouring of the Spirit

But, praise God, we are told that there will be some very positive spiritual signs in the end times. The most important one that is prophesied in many places is a great outpouring of the Holy Spirit (Joel 2:28-29).

This outpouring began at the dawn of the 20th Century, and proved to be one of the greatest spiritual surprises — and blessings — of the century. You see, when that century began, the prevailing viewpoint among both Catholics and

Protestants regarding the Holy Spirit was Cessationism. This view held that the gifts of the Spirit ceased when the last Apostle died. In effect, it was a belief that the Holy Spirit had retired in the First Century.

The 20th Century had hardly gotten started when a Holy Spirit revival broke out at a small Bible college in Topeka, Kansas in 1901.[2] Three years later, a similar Holy Spirit revival swept Wales and began to spread worldwide.[3] Then, in 1906, the Spirit fell with great power on a humble Black preacher in Los Angeles named William J. Seymour.[4] The Azuza Street Revival, as it came to be called, continued for four years and gave birth to the Pentecostal Movement.[5]

The "early and latter rains"

The Bible prophesies two great outpourings of the Spirit and symbolically pictures them as the "early and latter rains" (Joel 2:23), based on the two rainy seasons of Israel. The early rain occurred at Pentecost in the First Century when the Church was established. The latter rain was prophesied to occur after the Jewish people had been re-established in their homeland (Joel 2:18-26).

The latter rain began with the Pentecostal Movement, just as God began to regather the Jews to their homeland under the visionary leadership of Theodore Herzl. But the rain did not become a downpour until after the re-establishment of the state of Israel in May of 1948, just as prophesied by Joel.

First came the anointing of Billy Graham's ministry in 1949, followed by the Charismatic Movement of the 1960s. Today, most of Christianity, whether Pentecostal, Charismatic, or Traditional, fully recognizes that the ministry of the Holy Spirit is alive and well in Spirit-led worship, the continuing validity of spiritual gifts, the reality of spiritual warfare, and the importance of a Spirit-filled life in winning that warfare.

Additional Positive Spiritual Signs

In addition to the rediscovery of the Holy Spirit, there are other positive spiritual prophecies being fulfilled today — like the preaching of the Gospel worldwide (Matthew 24:14), the revival of Davidic praise worship (Amos 9:11) and the emergence of Messianic Judaism (Romans 9:27).

Another remarkable positive sign is the understanding of Bible prophecy. You see, the Hebrew prophets often did not understand the end time prophecies that the Lord gave to them. A good example can be found in Daniel 12:8-9 where the prophet complains to the Lord that he does not understand the prophecies that have been entrusted to him. The Lord's response was, "Don't worry about it. Just write the prophecies. They have been sealed up until the end times."

In other words, the Bible teaches that many of the end time prophecies will not be understood until the time comes for them to be fulfilled. And that is exactly what has been happening in the past 100 years. Historical developments and scientific inventions are now making it possible for us to understand end time prophecies that have never been understood before.

Take Israel for example. All of end time prophecy revolves around the nation of Israel. But how could those prophecies be understood as long as Israel did not exist and there was no prospect that the nation would ever exist again?

This is the reason that Hal Lindsey's book, The Late Great Planet Earth, became such a phenomenal bestseller in the 1970s. For the first time it explained the events prophesied in the book of Revelation in natural terms that people could easily understand.

4 The Signs of World Politics

You will be hearing of wars and rumors of wars . . . for nation will rise against nation, and kingdom against kingdom . . . (Matthew 24:6-7)

I taught international politics for 20 years before I entered the ministry full time, so this is an area that is particularly fascinating to me.

The Bible prophesies a very specific end time configuration of world politics. Israel is pictured as being re-established (Ezekiel 37:21-22) and surrounded by hostile Arab neighbors intent on its destruction (Ezekiel 35:1 – 36:7). This, of course has been the situation in the Middle East since the Israeli Declaration of Independence in May of 1948.

Daniel prophesied that the Roman Empire would be revived (Daniel 2:36-41), something many men — like Charlemagne, Napoleon, and Hitler — tried to do through force. But the prophecy had to await God's timing for its fulfillment, and that came after World War II, with the formation of the European Common Market that has since morphed into the superpower called the European Union.

The Bible pictures a great power located in the land of Magog in the "remote parts of the north." This nation will menace Israel in the end times and will ultimately lead an invasion of Israel together with specified allies, all of which are modern day Muslim states (Ezekiel 38:1 – 39:16). Russia, with all its Muslim republics and its Muslim allies, fits this description precisely.

All the nations of the world are prophesied to come together against Israel in the end times over the issue of the control of Jerusalem (Zech. 12:2-3) — a prophecy being fulfilled today.

The magnitude of warfare in the 20th Century is another fulfillment of end time prophecy related to world politics. The 20th Century was one of unparalleled war. Like birth pangs, the frequency and intensity of war increased exponentially. It is now estimated that more people died in wars

during the 20th Century than in all the previous wars throughout all of recorded human history.

5 The Signs of Technology

*Men will faint from fear over the expectation of
the things which are coming upon the world; for
the powers of the heavens will be shaken* (Luke
21:26).

The development of nuclear weapons seems to be fore-
shadowed by this prophecy in Luke 21 that speaks of people
"fainting from fear" due to the "powers of the heavens being
shaken."

The incredible carnage of the Seal and Trumpet Judgments portrayed in chapters 6 and 8 in the book of Revelation
indicates that the Antichrist will conquer the world through
the use of nuclear weapons. We are told that one-third of the
earth will be burned and that one-half of humanity will be
killed. Further evidence that this is a nuclear holocaust is
found in Revelation 16 where we are told that at the end of
the Tribulation the survivors will be covered with sores that
will not heal (Revelation 16:11).

As I pointed out earlier, there are many end time prophecies that simply cannot be understood apart from modern
technological developments. Consider the prophecy in Revelation 11 about the two witnesses who will call the world to
repentance during the first half of the Tribulation. When they
are killed by the Antichrist, we are told that their bodies will
lie in the streets of Jerusalem for three and a half days, and
the whole world will look upon them (Revelation 11:9). How
could anyone understand such a prophecy before the development of satellite television in the 1960s?

Likewise, how could the Antichrist control all buying and
selling worldwide (Revelation 13) without the aid of computer technology? How could the False Prophet create the

illusion of giving life to a statue (Revelation 13) without the technology of holograms, virtual reality, and robotics? How could an army of 200 million come out of the Far East (Revelation 9) before the population explosion that was produced by modern medical technology? How could the Gospel be proclaimed to all the world (Matthew 24) before the invention of motion pictures, radio, television, and the Internet? The list goes on and on.

6 The Signs of Israel

And it shall come about in that day that I will make Jerusalem a heavy stone for all the peoples; all who lift it will be severely injured. And all the nations of the earth will be gathered against it. (Zechariah 12:3)

The signs that relate to Israel are the most important of all because the Jews are God's prophetic time clock. What I mean by this is that the Scriptures will often tie a prophesied future event with something that will happen to the Jews. We are told to watch the Jews, and when the prophesied event concerning them occurs, we can be sure that the other prophesied event will also occur.

An example can be found in Luke 21:24 where Jesus prophesied that the Jews would be dispersed from Jerusalem and be led captive among the nations. But then He added that one day they would return to re-occupy Jerusalem, and when this happens, the end time events will occur that will lead to His return.

There are many prophecies concerning the Jews in the end times, many of which began to be fulfilled in the 20th Century, but there are four key ones. The first is their worldwide regathering in unbelief (Isaiah 11:11-12). In 1900 there were only 40,000 Jews in Palestine. By the end of World War II that number had risen to 800,000. Today, there are more than 5.8 million who have come from all over the world.

Very soon there will be as many Jews in Israel as died in the Holocaust.

The prophet Jeremiah says twice that when history is completed, the Jewish people will look back and conclude that their worldwide regathering was a greater miracle than their deliverance from Egyptian captivity (Jeremiah 16:14-15 and 23:7-8). We are truly living in momentous times!

The second key prophecy concerning the Jews is a natural consequence of their regathering. It is the re-establishment of their state which occurred on May 14, 1948 (Isaiah 66:7-8).

The third key prophecy is the re-occupation of Jerusalem which occurred on June 7, 1967 during the miraculous Six Day War (Zechariah 8:4-8).

The fourth key prophecy is the one whose fulfillment we are witnessing today — the re-focusing of world politics upon the nation of Israel (Zechariah 12:2-3). All the nations of the world, including the United States, are coming against Israel over the issue of the control of the nation's capital — the city of Jerusalem. The Vatican wants the city put under its control. The United Nations wants it to be internationalized. The European Union and the United States are demanding it be divided between the Arabs and the Jews. The Arabs want all of it.

Summary

And so you have it — six different categories of signs, each category containing many prophecies concerning the end times, all of which are being fulfilled before our very eyes. Let me conclude by specifically listing 50 of those prophecies.

1) Increasing instability of nature. (Matthew 24:7 & Luke 21:11)

2) Increasing lawlessness and violence. (Matthew 24:12)

3) Increasing immorality. (Matthew 24:37)

4) Increasing materialism. (2 Timothy 3:2)

5) Increasing Hedonism. (2 Timothy 3:4)

6) Increasing influence of Humanism. (2 Timothy 3:2)

7) Depraved entertainment. (2 Timothy 3:4)

8) Calling evil good and good evil. (2 Timothy 3:3 & Isaiah 5:20)

9) Increasing use of drugs. (2 Timothy 3:3)

10) Increasing blasphemy. (2 Timothy 3:2)

11) Increasing paganism. (2 Timothy 3:1-4)

12) Increasing despair. (2 Timothy 3:1)

13) Signs in the heavens. (Luke 21:11, 25)

14) Increasing knowledge. (Daniel 12:4)

15) Increasing travel. (Daniel 12:4)

16) The explosion of cults. (Matthew 24:11)

17) The proliferation of false christs. (Matthew 24:5)

18) Increasing apostasy in the Church. (2 Timothy 4:3-5)

19) Increasing attacks on Jesus. (Romans 1:18-19)

20) Increasing attacks on the Bible. (Romans 1:18-19)

21) Increasing persecution of Christians. (Matthew 24:9)

22) Increasing occultism. (1 Timothy 4:1)

23) Wars and rumors of wars. (Matthew 24:6)

24) Weapons of mass destruction. (Luke 21:26)

25) Increasing famine. (Luke 21:11)

26) Increasing pestilence. (Luke 21:11)

27) Computer technology. (Revelation 13:7)

28) Television. (Revelation 11:8-9)

29) Satellite technology. (Revelation 11:8-9)

30) Virtual reality. (Revelation 13:14-15)

31) Unification of Europe. (Daniel 2 and 7)

32) Far Eastern military powers. (Revelation 9:16 & 16:12)

33) Movement toward world government. (Daniel 7:23-26)

34) Regathering of the Jews. (Isaiah 11:10-12)

35) Re-establishment of Israel. (Isaiah 66:7-8)

36) Reclamation of the land of Israel. (Ezekiel 36:34-35)

37) Revival of Biblical Hebrew. (Zephaniah 3:6)

38) Re-occupation of Jerusalem. (Luke 21:24)

39) Resurgence of the Israeli military. (Zechariah 12:6)

40) Re-focusing of world politics on Israel. (Zechariah 12:3)

41) Russian threat to Israel. (Ezekiel 38 and 39)

42) Arab threat to Israel. (Ezekiel 35 and 36)

43) Denial of the Second Coming. (2 Peter 3:3-4)

44) Denial of creation by God. (Romans 1:18-22)

45) Outpouring of the Holy Spirit. (Joel 2:28-29)

46) Translation of the Bible into many languages. (Matthew 24:14)

47) Preaching of the Gospel worldwide. (Matthew 24:14)

48) The revival of Messianic Judaism. (Romans 9:27)

49) The revival of Davidic praise worship. (Amos 9:11)

50) The understanding of Bible prophecy. (Daniel 12:8-9)

This list could be greatly expanded, but the 50 examples above should be sufficient to show that we are living in the season of the Lord's return.

I want to emphasize once again that the Bible clearly teaches that God never pours out His wrath without warning, for He is a just and loving God who does not wish that any should perish (2 Peter 3:9). That's why He has provided so many signs to alert us to the fact that we are living on the threshold of the Tribulation.

And Yet . . .

An amazing thing to me is that despite the fulfillment of all these prophecies before our very eyes today, there are Bible prophecy scholars who insist that no end time prophecies are truly being fulfilled! They argue instead that what we are witnessing is merely "stage-setting." Let's consider that argument in detail.

Living in the end of the end times.

I am constantly running across articles in which the argument is presented that in order to be a "consistent futurist," you cannot contend that prophecies are being fulfilled today. Instead, it is argued that all end time prophecy relates to Israel in the Tribulation and Millennium. Therefore, all we are seeing today is "stage setting," but not the fulfillment of prophecy.

I strongly disagree with this viewpoint. First of all, there are four end time prophecies concerning Israel that were fulfilled even before the 20th Century began. They are:

1) The dispersion of the Jews worldwide — Deuteronomy 28:64.
2) The worldwide persecution of the Jews — Deuteronomy 28:65-67.
3) The desolation of the Jewish homeland — Deuteronomy 29:22-28.
4) The preservation of the Jewish people — Jeremiah 30:7 and Jeremiah 31:36-37.

Some might respond by saying these are not end time prophecies, but they are. The end times or the "last days" began at the Cross. The writer of the Hebrew letter referred to his day and time (the First Century) as the "last days." The Apostle Peter also called the time in which he was living the "last times" (1 Peter 1:5 & 20). And in the same letter he stated that "the end of all things is at hand" (1 Peter 4:7). The "end times" began 2,000 years ago. We are currently in the end of the end times, and we know this because God's Word gives us signs to watch for that will mark the end of the age.

The fulfillment of the prophecies listed above makes it clear that all future prophecies in the Scriptures regarding Israel do not relate to just the Tribulation and the Millennium. Additionally, there are other futuristic prophecies in the Scriptures regarding Israel that were either fulfilled in part or in whole during the 20th Century, and they are prophecies that point to the soon return of Jesus.

Current Fulfillment of Prophecies Related to Israel

Consider, to begin with, the most prolific futuristic prophecy in the Hebrew Scriptures — namely, that in the end times the Jewish people will be regathered in unbelief from the four corners of the earth.

This regathering began in the late 19th Century when Theodore Herzl wrote his book, *The Jewish State*, in which he advocated that the time had come for the Jews to return to their homeland.[1] In 1900 there were only 40,000 Jews in Israel. By the end of World War II this number had risen to 800,000. Today, it stands at nearly 6 million. The Jews continue to come, but there is no doubt this is a prophecy that is being fulfilled before our very eyes.

Or, consider the re-establishment of the state of Israel on May 14, 1948. This was a clear and definite fulfillment of Bible prophecy (Isaiah 66:7-8 and Matthew 24:32-35). It is an accomplished fact, and it is a miracle of God. It is not mere "stage-setting," it is a play that has already been performed in full.

Another accomplished fact is the revival of the Hebrew language from the dead. When the Jews were scattered from their homeland in the First and Second Centuries, they stopped speaking Hebrew. The Jews in Europe mixed Hebrew with German and created a new language called Yiddish. The

Jews in the Mediterranean Basin mixed Hebrew with Spanish and created a language called Ladino. But the Bible prophesied that the Hebrew language would be revived in the end times (Zephaniah 3:9), and that is exactly what happened in the late 19th and early 20th Centuries through the efforts of one man — Eliezar Ben Yehuda. Today, the people of Israel speak biblical Hebrew.[2]

Equally certifiable is the reclamation of the Jewish homeland. As pointed out earlier, the Bible prophesied that it would become a desolation after the Jewish people were expelled from it. But the Bible also prophesied that when the Jews returned to the land, it would once again become a land of milk and honey:

> The desolate land will be cultivated instead of being a desolation in the sight of everyone who passed by. And they will say, "This desolate land has become like the garden of Eden; and the waste, desolate, and ruined cities are fortified and inhabited." (Ezekiel 36:34-35)

When the Jews started returning to their homeland in the late 19th Century, it was a total wasteland. Nearly all the trees had been cut down and the soil was badly eroded. The land resembled a desert. Most of the valleys had become malaria-infested swamp lands. The Jewish pioneers began planting trees, reclaiming the soil, and draining the swamps. Today, Israel is the bread basket of the Middle East.

Another prophecy that has definitely been fulfilled in our times is the resurgence of the Israeli military. Zechariah 12:6 says that in the end times, God "will make the clans of Judah like a firepot among pieces of wood and a flaming torch among sheaves, so they will consume on the right hand and on the left all the surrounding peoples . . ." Further, it is prophesied that in the end times Israel will be like David against Goliath, and the Lord will "destroy all the nations that come against Jerusalem" (Zechariah 12:8-9).

The fulfillment of this prophecy can be seen today in the incredible military power of Israel. It is one of the world's smallest nations, yet it is ranked by all experts as one of the top 15 military powers in the world.[3]

Finally, with regard to Israel before the Tribulation begins, the Bible prophesies that Jerusalem will be re-occupied by the Jews (Zechariah 8:1-5) and that it will become the focal point of world politics (Zechariah 12:3). The Jews returned to the city when it was captured in the Six Day War in 1967, and today, all the nations of the world are coming against Israel over the issue of who will control Jerusalem in the future.

Current Fulfillment of Non-Jewish Prophecies

But end time prophecies regarding Israel are not the only ones we see being fulfilled in whole or in part before our very eyes. Daniel prophesied that in the end times the old Roman Empire would be revived (Daniel 2:31-45), and we can see that being accomplished today in the creation and expansion of the European Union.

The Bible prophesies repeatedly that in the end times there will be a great apostasy in the Church (1 Timothy 4:1, 2 Timothy 3:1,5 and 2 Timothy 4:3-4). We are up to our ears in that apostasy today as major Christian denominations ordain homosexuals, approve same-sex marriage, deny the deity of Jesus, and mock the inerrancy of the Scriptures.

In like manner, the Bible prophesies that "in the last days" society will disintegrate into a cesspool of immorality and violence (2 Timothy 3:1-5). Can there be any doubt that those days have arrived?

Daniel was told that the end time prophecies would not be completely understood until the end time — that is, until the time comes for their fulfillment (Daniel 12:8-9). That time must be upon us for we are living in the time when ancient prophecies are being understood for the first time ever, due to historical developments and technological advances.

Taking the Signs of the Times Seriously

I could go on and on, but I think I have made my point. *The future has arrived!* End time prophecies are being fulfilled today. What we are witnessing is much more than "stage-setting." God is clearly fulfilling promises He made thousands of years ago to the Jewish people. And God is orchestrating the fulfillment of end time prophecies that are not related to the Jewish people.

It is exciting to see these prophecies fulfilled, and I am tired of seeing people attempt to depreciate their importance by dismissing them in a cavalier way as nothing more than mere "stage-setting."

Jesus is coming soon. The signs of the times attest to that fact. God expects us to take those signs seriously because He is about to pour out His wrath upon this world in the Great Tribulation, and He does not desire that any should perish. The fulfillment of prophecy all around us today is God's way of waking us up to the fact that the Church Age is coming to an end. We need to respond to the sign of fulfilled end time prophecy by using the remaining time to commit ourselves to holiness and evangelism.

The Message

The bottom line message of the signs is that we are *living on borrowed time*. And the crucial question for every human being is "Are you ready?" Are you ready for the return of Jesus? Will He come as your Blessed Hope or your Holy Terror?

It will be one or the other, for God is determined to deal with sin, and He does so with either grace or wrath (John

3:36). If you have put your faith in Jesus as your Lord and Savior, then you are under God's grace. Your sins have been forgiven and forgotten, and you can look forward with confidence to that glorious day when Jesus will appear in the heavens.

But if you have never received Jesus as your Lord and Savior, you are under the wrath of God, and you have nothing to look forward to except the terror of His wrath.

The choice is yours. I personally cannot understand why anyone would turn their back on God's free gift of grace through faith in His Son. I have placed my faith in Jesus, and I therefore am able to look forward to His soon return with great anticipation and expectation. All that is within me cries out, "Maranatha! Come quickly Lord Jesus" (1 Corinthians 16:22).

Living on Borrowed Time

Part 2
A Prophetic Forum

Questions Concerning the Signs   6
Discussing key issues.

To provide you with a better feel for the signs of the times that surround us today, I submitted a series of 11 questions to 22 Bible prophecy experts concerning the signs of the times.

I deeply appreciate these people taking the time from their busy schedules to respond to my questions. I know their responses will supply you with some rich insights.

Before we consider the questions and their answers, let me introduce you to the persons who participated in the forum.

The Participants

Daymond Duck — Humorous author of many basic guides to understanding Bible prophecy, including *Revelation for the Biblically-Inept, Daniel for the Biblically-Inept*, and *Revelation for Teens*. Known for his capacity for in-depth biblical analysis. He is a native of Tennessee. His ministry is called Prophecy Plus.

Gary Fisher — Established Lion of Judah Ministries in 1994 after a career as an electronic technician. Conducts meetings and conferences and hosts tours to the Holy Land. Publishes a newsletter about how current events relate to Bible prophecy. His ministry is based in Franklin, Tennessee.

Jim Fletcher — Director of a ministry called Prophecy Matters which focuses on the prophetic implications of the modern rebirth of the nation of Israel. He is a former chief editor for a publishing company. He writes journalistic articles for a wide variety of publications.

Ray Gano — Founder and director of an Internet Bible prophecy magazine called *Prophezine*. In addition to in-depth articles about Bible prophecy, the Prophezine website provides daily updates on prophecy in the news and provides Internet radio shows. His ministry is located in Costa Rica.

Al Gist — A former petroleum engineer who became a Baptist pastor and served in that capacity for several years before forming a Bible prophecy ministry in 2000 called Maranatha Evangelistic Ministries. He holds meetings at churches and conducts tours of Israel. His ministry is located near DeRidder, Louisiana.

Phillip Goodman — Vice president of Thy Kingdom Come Ministries for many years before forming his own prophetic ministry in 2011 called Bible Prophecy As Written. He is a frequent speaker at Bible prophecy conferences, and he hosts a large conference each year. He is the author of several books about Bible prophecy. His ministry is based in Tulsa, Oklahoma.

J. R. Hall — Founder and director of Berean Watch Ministries, located in Saskatoon, Saskatchewan, Canada. Jeremy is a consulting engineer by trade, but he also serves as a speaker and writer about Bible prophecy. He also active in the field of Apologetics, writing in defense of the Christian faith.

Mark Hitchcock — Pastor of Faith Bible Church in Edmond, Oklahoma. He has a law degree from Oklahoma City University and a doctorate from Dallas Theological Seminary. He is a prolific writer who has produced more than 20 books related to Bible prophecy. His writings are non-speculative and are solidly Bible-based.

David Hocking — Founder and director of Hope for Today Ministries, founded in 1995 and based in Tustin, California. He has an earned doctorate from Grace Theological Seminary. He has been teaching the Bible for over 50 years and has been active in radio ministry ever since 1970. He is the author of more than 30 books, and is considered an expert on Israel in Bible prophecy.

Ken Humphries — Serves as the evangelist for Treasured Truth Today Ministries, located in Northern Ireland. He holds meetings and conferences that focus on the teaching and preaching of Bible prophecy and the message of the Lord's soon return. He is also heavily engaged in mission work in Eastern Europe.

Terry James — A public relations and marketing executive for 25 years before he lost his eyesight in 1992. Since that time he has devoted himself to the study and teaching of Bible prophecy and has become a well known editor of books about Bible prophecy. He is the co-host of the Rapture Ready website, considered to be the most influential of all Bible prophecy sites on the Internet. He makes his home in Benton, Arkansas.

Nathan Jones — Web Minister for Lamb & Lion Ministries. Graduate of the Philadelphia Biblical University, with graduate work at Southern Theological Seminary. Monitors Bible prophecy in the news and edits an electronic newsletter. He also maintains a blog where people from all over the world share their views about Bible prophecy.

Jack Kinsella — Spent many years doing research and writing for Hal Lindsey's TV program before he founded The Omega Letter website blog in 2001. Through that website he provided an online daily Christian intelligence digest analyzing current events in light of Bible Prophecy. His ministry was based in Ontario, Canada. He died in March of 2013.

Tim LaHaye — Probably the best known Bible prophecy expert in the world today. Author of the best-selling *Left Behind* series of novels based on Bible prophecy. Founder of the Pre-Trib Research Center which is devoted to studying, teaching and defending the concept of the Pretribulational Rapture.

Jan Markell — Founder and director of Olive Tree Ministries, based in Minnesota. She is a Messianic Jew who publishes a newsletter, hosts conferences on current issues, and produces a weekly live, call-in radio program that is broadcast nationwide.

Caryl Matrisciana — A well-known expert on ancient and modern world religions, contemporary cults, paganism and the occult. Best-selling author, journalist, researcher and commercial artist. Caryl has co-produced or contributed research and expertise to more than 55 documentaries in the past 30 years. Her ministry is based in Menifee, California.

Don McGee — Vietnam War veteran, former Louisiana State Trooper, and former pastor. Established Crown & Sickle Ministries in 2002. The ministry is dedicated to the proclamation of the soon return of Jesus. Holds church meetings, speaks at conferences and edits an electronic newsletter. The ministry is based in Amite, Louisiana.

Dennis Pollock — Associate Evangelist with Lamb & Lion Ministries for 11 years before establishing a ministry called Spirit of Grace which focuses on holding evangelistic and healing crusades in Africa as well as other Third World countries. Author and gifted speaker. His ministry is based in McKinney, Texas.

Ron Rhodes — Founder and director of Reasoning from the Scriptures Ministries located in Frisco, Texas. Specialist in Bible prophecy and Christian apologetics. Author of more than 50 books. Doctorate from Dallas Theological Seminary. Adjunct professor at several seminaries. He is a frequent conference speaker.

August Rosado — Dynamic preacher and teacher of Bible prophecy, with a photographic memory of Scripture. Holds meetings and conferences all across America and leads pilgrimages to Israel. His ministry, called Today in Bible Prophecy is based in Massachusetts.

Bill Salus — Bible prophecy researcher and writer based in La Quinta, California. Conducts an active blog at ProphecyDepot.com. Host of a weekly radio program called "Prophecy Update." Best known for his insightful book about the prophetic implications of Psalm 83, called *Isralestine*. He is also a frequent conference speaker.

Brian Thomas — Heads up a ministry in Knightdale, North Carolina called Blessings to Israel. Publishes a newsletter, conducts Bible prophecy conferences and hosts a radio podcast called, God 1st. Writes articles about Bible prophecy and a variety of other biblical topics.

1) Do you believe we are living in the season of the Lord's return, and if so, why?

All 22 of our Bible prophecy experts answered yes to this question, and most of them were passionate in their response.

Israel

As you might have guessed, 7 of them (Fisher, Fletcher, Gano, Gist, Hocking, McGee and Rosado) focused in on one sign as the cornerstone of their belief — the re-establishment of the state of Israel.

Gary Fisher was particularly eloquent on this point:

> We have license from Jesus to believe we are living in the season of His return as He stated in Matthew 24:32. He said that the generation that sees the fig tree "putting forth its leaves," would know that "summer" (a season) "is near". Therefore, we can know the season of His return.
>
> Jesus was of course using the natural process of trees budding in the spring and subsequent summer being near, to illustrate that His return would follow a chronological order. The spring represents all the different signs of His coming, and the summer representing His actual return.
>
> A logical question however is why was the fig tree singled out by Jesus and used here as an indicator? Perhaps Hosea 9:10 has the best answer to this question. God is speaking and says, ". . . I saw your forefathers as the earliest fruit on the fig tree in its first season." God Himself used the fig tree here as a symbol for Israel. Jesus was using that same symbol in Matthew 24:32 as a sign of His coming. The

nation of Israel seemed finished and was scattered all over the earth for nineteen centuries. At the turn of the 1900s, Jewish people started returning to the land of Israel and today it is a vibrant nation of Jewish people once again.

The "fig tree" has put forth its leaves. Summer is near!

Convergence

A plurality of the forum members — a total of 9 — said their belief that we are living in the season of the Lord's return was based on the convergence of signs that are on the scene today (Duck, Goodman, Hall, Humphries, James, LaHaye, Pollock, Rhodes and Salus).

Ron Rhodes referred to what he called "the convergence factor." Here's how he defined what he and the others were talking about:

Do I believe we are living in the season of the Lord's return, and if so, why? Yes. I say this because of what I call the "convergence factor." Not only has Israel come together as a nation again, as prophesied (Ezekiel 26-27), but a number of ancient prophecies of the end times seem to be converging in our day.

It has been said that biblical prophecies cast their shadows before them. Prophecies that relate specifically to the tribulation are presently casting their shadows before them, in our present day. For example, the prophecy of the Ezekiel [Gog & Magog] invasion that will take place as early as three-and-a-half years prior to the Tribulation period, or perhaps at the very beginning of the Tribulation period, seems to be drawing near. There are already alliances — political and military — developing between the invading nations (Russia, Iran, Turkey, Sudan, Libya, among others). The Muslim nations involved are strongly motivated to see Israel "wiped off the face of the earth."

Another example is how the temple will be built sometime in the first part of the tribulation period. Even today, money has been raised for the building of the temple, and temple artifacts and clothing have already been prefabricated. These and many other prophecies seem to be converging in our time.

Illustrating the convergence of signs, Daymond Duck and Jeremy Hall presented long lists of signs that have come together today, similar to the list I provided on pages 56 to 59. Both of them mentioned an important sign that was not in my list — the preparations for the rebuilding of the Third Temple. This is the temple that will exist during the Tribulation. Bill Salus also mentioned this sign.

It is true that the preparations for the Third Temple have advanced considerably in recent years. The Temple Institute in Jerusalem has been preparing the musical and sacrificial instruments, together with the clothing of the priests. Another group in Jerusalem is working on the architectural plans, and a third group is training young men to be priests.

Two members of the forum provided succinct summaries of the convergent factor:

> Dennis Pollock: "The spiritual and moral decay of society, the restoration of the nation of Israel, the development of weapons of mass destruction, a tremendous increase in evangelism in the last century, and a restoration of

the church from the time of Luther until today
all point to the soon return of Jesus."

Bill Salus: "Increased natural disasters,
heightened rumors of Middle East wars, and
collapsing global economies are all paving the
way for the rise of the Antichrist, and ultimately the return of the Lord to end the
Antichrist's tyrannical rule. In fact, presently,
every weapon is fashioned, technology developed, empire revived, and confederate
alliance formed, enabling all end time prophecies to be fulfilled.

Ken Humphries of North Ireland also stressed the importance of the convergence of signs. And he concluded his
observations by saying, "The signs indicate that we are to
look up and pack up, because we are going sooner than we
think!"

Israel and Convergence

Five of our forum members mentioned both Israel and the
convergence factor in their responses (Hitchcock, Jones,
Kinsella, Matrisciana and Thomas).

Jack Kinsella emphasized Jesus' fig tree parable in Matthew 24 and stated that he believed the generation referred to
in that parable is those born since 1948 when the nation of
Israel was re-established. He went on to speak of many other
signs converging, and then he concluded with these words:

Jesus said, "When these things begin to come
to pass, then look up and lift up your heads,
for your redemption draweth nigh."

Here lately, I've been craning my neck until it
hurts! [Jack did not live too long after he
wrote these words.]

The Days of Noah

One of our Bible prophecy experts, Jan Markell, identified as her most convincing sign what she called "the days of Noah." She went on to explain that Jesus prophesied that society would become every bit as immoral and violent in the end times as it was in the days of Noah (Matthew 24:37). She wrote:

> Never have we seen such recklessness and lawlessness . . . Evil is coming in every shade and flavor . . . the earth is just reeling. It is reeling because everyone is doing what is right in their own eyes. And what is right to most people is reckless, lawless, violent, and wouldn't even be considered in our parents' generation.

Summary

I would heartily agree with the emphasis on the convergence factor. Many times in the past, Bible prophecy experts have proclaimed the imminent return of Jesus based on one or two or even a dozen signs, but there were always many other signs that were missing from the world scene, the most important being the re-establishment of the state of Israel.

Today, for the first time ever, we have the full complement of signs surrounding us, and they are literally shouting: "Jesus is coming soon!"

2) What do you consider to be the single most important sign of the times, and why?

All but three (Fletcher, Markell and Rosado) of our forum members responded resoundingly that the most important of all end time signs is the re-establishment of the state of Israel on May 14, 1948.

Ron Rhodes explained that he was putting his emphasis on Israel "because so many of the biblical prophecies of the end times relate in some way to Israel — hence Israel must exist in order for the other prophecies to come to pass." To illustrate his point, Rhodes added, ". . . many of these other prophecies do not have meaning *until* or *unless* Israel is already a nation. For example, the prophecy that the Temple will be rebuilt in Israel makes little sense until and unless Israel already exists as a nation."

Phillip Goodman made the same point with an enlightening illustration:

> Every major prophetic passage in the Bible presupposes Israel at the center of the end-time map, and the centerpiece of the Last Days (Ezekiel 38:8; Matthew 24:15-21, etc.). Israel is the hub. All of the other signs are the spokes. The end time is the rim. The end time (the "rim") cannot happen without the signs (the "spokes"). Yet the signs have no prophetic significance as signs apart from the existence of Israel (the "hub").

Jeremy Hall, a Canadian, provided another symbolic illustration:

> On a long forgotten shelf, alone stood a clock. The clock was not forgotten because of lack of greatness, for the clock was a marvelously crafted clock, but for many, many years the clock lay silent. In years before it fell silent, it ran and chimed, and it ticked and it tocked, but for many years it lay dormant. Frozen in time, the clock sat quietly until it happened — On May 14, 1948 God's prophetic clock started ticking again — LOUDLY.

Tim LaHaye emphasized the miraculous nature of the re-establishment of Israel. "Just think," he wrote, "Israel was brought back into the Holy Land after 1,900 years, as God promised myriads of times." He continued, "No nation in the history of the world has been able to maintain its national identity after being uprooted from is home of origin more than 300 to at best 500 years, except Israel." He then added that their regathering from the four corners of the earth is "in itself a miracle, and that miracle has happened in our life-time!"

Gary Fisher emphasized the same point. He wrote: "We are the first generation in 19 centuries that has seen Israel back in her homeland, and this is a prerequisite for Jesus to return to earth. Israel in her place tells us that Jesus is about to return and take His place in Jerusalem as King of kings and Lord of lords."

Dennis Pollock summarized his emphasis on the prophetic importance of Israel in this way:

> To take the Bible literally and seriously forces one to say, "Jesus could never return to rule on the earth without a nation of Israel present and fully functional." For nearly two thousand years this was not the case. Today it is, and this surely points to the soon return of Jesus.

Upheaval in the Middle East

Two of our forum members, Jim Fletcher and Jan Markell, pointed to "Mid-East Turmoil" as the single most important indicator that we are living in the season of the Lord's return. Of course, this relates to the re-establishment of Israel, but their emphasis on the resulting turmoil is significant because the Bible prophesies that all the nations of the world will come together against Israel in the end times over the issue of the control of Jerusalem.

Jim Fletcher summed up his point with this observation:

> The world generally accepted the establish-
> ment of Israel in 1948, but that tenuous sup-
> port evaporated after the Six Day War. Begin-
> ning with Oslo, we began to see the left pub-
> licly calling for a divided Jerusalem. In a
> sense, Arafat's "no" to Israel's Ehud Barak at
> Camp David in 2000—when the Israeli pre-
> mier was prepared to give him the Temple
> Mount—set the stage for the final assault on
> Jerusalem, as prophesied in Zechariah. Every-
> one present at Camp David knew who torpe-
> doed the talks, yet Israel was and is blamed.

> Israel's sovereignty in Jerusalem represents
> the most acute point of hatred from the inter-
> national community, which as Barack Obama
> declared, "is getting tired of the status quo."
> This is telling, and chilling.

The Decay of Society

One forum member, August Rosado, departed from the
identification of Israel as the most important end time sign.
He pointed instead to the breakdown of society. He stated:

> We live in a society today where homosexual-
> ity is embraced and same-sex marriage is
> being legalized . . . Pornography has inun-
> dated the Internet . . . and wickedness is inten-
> sifying . . . The Bible says that the generation
> that will see the Lord's return will be the
> generation that will be living in "perilous
> times" (2 Timothy 3:1-5).

Summary

I would agree with our forum members that the key sign
of the end times — the cornerstone sign — is the re-estab-

lishment of the nation of Israel. As Phillip Goodman so vividly explained it, Israel is the hub of end time prophecy. All the other signs are the spokes radiating out from the hub.

The Puritans in the 16th and 17th Centuries began to proclaim the re-establishment of Israel as the key end time prophecy. People laughed and scoffed at them, saying that there was no possibility whatsoever that the nation of Israel would ever exist again.

Later, in the 19th Century, the Dispensationalists endorsed the Puritan belief and began to proclaim eloquently and decisively that one day the Jewish people would be regathered and the state of Israel would be re-established, heralding the soon return of Jesus. People continued to scoff and ridicule, and some continued to do so right up to the very day that the state of Israel was re-established on May 14, 1948.

Even after the state came back into being, the scoffers proclaimed it would be short-lived — that the Arabs would destroy it in no time at all.

Those who believed the Bible's prophecies concerning Israel in the end times have been vindicated. God did what He promised He would do.

3) What do you consider to be the second most important sign of the end times, and why?

Unanimity dissipated rapidly in the responses to this question, replaced by a great variety of interesting viewpoints.

Spiritual Corruption in the Church

The most frequently mentioned sign was the increasing apostasy in the Church. Six people mentioned the importance of this sign (Fletcher, Goodman, Hocking, Markell, Matrisciana and Salus).

Phillip Goodman made the point that Jesus Himself raised this sign of apostasy to a high level since it was the only sign He mentioned more than once in His Olivet discourse in which He outlined to His disciples all the end time signs that would point to the season of His return. In fact, Jesus mentioned this sign in various ways a total of four times (Matthew 24:5,10-11,24).

Jim Fletcher pointed in horror to the apostasy in the Church today, particularly within the Evangelical community as it is being infiltrated by the Emergent Church Movement:

> In 2 Peter 3 . . . we have the apostle telling us that at the time of the end, men in the Church will first deny the creation accounts in Genesis, and will logically then reject Bible prophecy. We have men in the Church today literally doing this.
>
> In 2 Timothy 3:14,15 we are told to keep to the faith we learned as children. The Emergent Movement today is encouraging everyone to shed his or her "old" faith and embrace the "changing Christianity."
>
> First John 4:4-6 outlines perfectly the mindset of the Emergents, who thirst for world approval, from lavishing praise on the deceased Steve Jobs — a Buddhist and ruthless businessman — to structuring megachurches and conferences to reflect worldly values . . . I consider the infiltration of the American evangelical church by Emergent leaders to be perhaps the biggest prophetic story going at the moment, rivaling what we see unfolding in the Middle East. It is a huge, huge story.

Jan Markell and Bill Salus both referred to what they called "the rise of the lukewarm church of Laodicia." Markell wrote, "Churches that were once sound are caving in to churches that tickle the ears and stress church growth."

Bill Salus described the problem in these words:

> Christ warned in the letter to Laodicea in Revelation 3:14-22 that the last day's condition of the Church would be nauseating. In fact He said in Revelation 3:17 that it would be wretched, miserable, poor, blind, and naked. In this apostate condition the Church would treat Christ as a stranger rather than acknowledge Him as the Savior. He portrayed Himself standing outside the doors of the unrepentant Church knocking to get back in (Revelation 3:20).

> The professing Church has been on a downward slide for about a century, but the relatively recent emergence of the "Emergent Church," is the tombstone of the dead church. Merging Christianity with New Age mysticism, Islam, and ancient Eastern religions, the Emergent Church epitomizes the warnings issued to Laodicea.

I would agree that the apostasy in the Church today is mind-boggling, and what is worse is that it is increasing exponentially, both in speed and content. Biblical morality is being thrown out the window as churches endorse homosexuality, ordain homosexuals, and perform same-sex marriages. And then there is the increasing tendency to embrace the concept of "many roads lead to God," making Jesus' death on the cross inconsequential and rendering Him a liar when He said He is the only way to God (John 14:6).

Spiritual Darkness in the World

Ken Humphries of Northern Ireland identified a sign simi-

lar to that of spiritual apostasy in the Church. He emphasized
the increasing spiritual darkness that characterizes society in
general.

I would certainly endorse this observation. The chatter on
the Internet these days concerning Christianity is becoming
increasingly vulgar and hostile. A shift in attitudes has occurred, from claiming that "Christianity is false" to "Christianity is evil." This diabolical trend is in itself a fulfillment
of end time prophecy as expressed in 2 Peter 3:3-4 where
Peter wrote: "Know this first of all, that in the last days
mockers will come with their mocking, following after their
own lusts . . ." This same prophecy is repeated in Jude 18.

European Consolidation

The second most frequently mentioned sign was the re-
emergence of the old Roman Empire in the form of the
modern day European Union. It was selected by 4 of the
forum members (Duck, Fisher, Gist and James).

Daymond Duck, in his usual thorough-going manner,
talked about how the European Union will provide the plat-
form for the emergence of the Antichrist who will ultimately
take over the whole world. Duck said he believed this will
take place in phases. The first phase has already occurred
with the creation of the United Nations. The second phase
will take place when the UN decides to divide the world into
ten administrative regions (in accordance with the prophecies
of Daniel). One of these will be the European Union, and out
of it, the Antichrist will rise.

Gary Fisher wrote that "Rome seemed hopelessly finished
until the 20th Century. But today, Rome is coming back
together. The kingdom of Jesus is close at hand."

I would agree that the emergence of the European Union
is a miraculous fulfillment of Bible prophecy. Many world
leaders have dreamed of reviving the Roman Empire, and

some, like Napoleon and Hitler, almost succeeded. But it was not God's timing. Then, when it was God's timing, the prophecy was fulfilled peacefully.

In the aftermath of World War II, when all of Europe lay in ruins, a visionary Frenchman named Jean Monet expressed the view that the only hope for revival was for the European nations to put aside their hatreds and form a transnational economic union to stimulate their moribund economies. That led to the creation of the European Economic Community which has since evolved into a political union that now includes 27 nations — and it continues to expand.

The Ezekiel Alignment
and Modern Technology

There was a tie for third place, with three people each mentioning two different signs — the Ezekiel alignment of nations (LaHaye, Rhodes and Rosado) and the explosion of technology (Jones, McGee and Pollock).

Tim LaHaye emphasized the fact that the alignment of nations mentioned in Ezekiel 38 and 39 — the Russian-led alignment that will invade Israel — is coming together before our very eyes. Russia is courting the Muslim nations of the Middle East and is signing mutual defense pacts with them.

Ron Rhodes summed up the situation as follows:

> More than a few students of the Bible have recognized that the very nations prophesied to join this alliance in the end times are, in fact, already making alliances with each other in our own day. The fact that these alliances are emerging after Israel became a nation again in 1948 — with Jews continuing to stream into their homeland ever since, so that today there are more Jews in Israel than anywhere else on earth — is highly significant. Prophetic Scrip-

ture speaks a great deal about end-time political alignments, and what we see today seems to be setting the stage.

Nathan Jones pointed in a different direction when he identified what he considers to be the second most important sign of the times:

> I may be partial, being a "Web guy" by profession, but I believe the second most important sign pointing to the return of Jesus Christ is the massive acceleration of technological development. I keep a pulse on the advancement of technology. And I have to tell you, the rapid advancements in technology continue to blow my mind. As a matter-of-fact, Daniel 12 teaches that this very acceleration of technology is a sign of the end of this age and the soon return of Jesus Christ.

Don McGee endorsed this observation and so did Dennis Pollock, who zeroed in on one particular development of modern technology — namely, atomic weapons:

> I would say that nuclear weapons are the second most important sign. For most of the history of the Church, readers of the book of Revelation had only two options: 1) to believe that the events John described must surely be symbolic, or 2) to believe that God was going to supernaturally bring these things about by His own sovereign power, without any help from man.
>
> Since the creation of nuclear weapons we now see that the mass destruction prophesied by John could easily take place by man's own hand. There will be no need of some supernatural zap by God. He may well simply take His

restraining hand off His rebellious creation and allow us to destroy ourselves. The dying out of vegetation, the poisoning of the oceans, the loss of visibility, the tremendous loss of life, with at least half of the population dying — all of these are possible by the hand of man, and to some degree likely at some point in human history.

Jerusalem

Two of our respondents — Jack Kinsella and Brian Thomas — picked the Jewish re-occupation of the city of Jerusalem on June 7, 1967 as their second most important sign.

Kinsella emphasized the historical fact that Jerusalem had been under Gentile control since Nebuchadnezzar sacked the city in 686 BC. He also pointed to the fact that Jesus Himself emphasized the importance of Jerusalem as an end time sign when He told His disciples: "Jerusalem will be trampled under foot by the Gentiles until the times of the Gentiles be fulfilled" (Luke 21:24).

Brian Thomas said that in his opinion, the Six Day War in 1967 that resulted in the re-occupation of Jerusalem was more important than the Declaration of Independence in 1948. For one reason, the re-occupation of Jerusalem is pro-voking all the nations of the world to come against Israel, as prophesied in Zechariah 12:1-3, and that is one the last prophecies mentioned about Israel before the beginning of the Tribulation.

Other Signs

Three other signs were selected as the second most im-portant, each by one person.

Jeremy Hall named the decay of society. In doing so, he emphasized that all aspects of the Apostle Paul's prophecy in

2 Timothy 3:1-5 are being fulfilled today. Paul said the end times would be "perilous times" when men would be "lovers of themselves," "lovers of money" and "lovers of pleasure rather than lovers of God."

Mark Hitchcock selected "Globalism" as his second most important sign of the times. He stated that every aspect of modern life — political, economic, social and religious — is "moving the world back to Babel."

Finally, Ray Gano pointed to the signs of nature because, as he put it, "even the heathen can see these things come to pass." To illustrate his point, he underlined how natural calamities are increasing in frequency and intensity like birth pangs, just as Jesus prophesied they would (Matthew 24:7-8 and Luke 21:11,25).

4) How do you interpret Matthew 24:32-35?

This passage of Scripture reads as follows:

> Now learn the parable from the fig tree: when its branch has already become tender and puts forth its leaves, you know that summer is near; so, you too, when you see all these things, recognize that He is near, right at the door. "Truly I say to you, this generation will not pass away until all these things take place. Heaven and earth will pass away, but My words will not pass away."

These words were spoken by Jesus during His Olivet Discourse which he delivered to his disciples on the Mount of Olives in Jerusalem during the last week of His life.

What does this enigmatic parable mean? What does the "fig tree" symbolize, and what "generation" was He talking about? The meaning of this parable has been hotly debated over the years, even among Bible prophecy experts.

With regard to our panel, let's begin with their interpretations of the meaning of the fig tree, and then we will take a look at their ideas as to the meaning of a generation as used in the context of this passage.

The Rebirth of the State of Israel

The majority viewpoint among our forum members was that the fig tree is a symbol of Israel, and in speaking of its putting forth leaves, Jesus was prophesying that the state of Israel would be re-established in the end times.

Of the 20 members of our forum who responded to this question, a total of 10 took this position (Duck, Fisher, Gano, Gist, Humphries, Kinsella, McGee, Pollock, Rosado and Thomas). In doing so, most of them referenced Hosea 9:10 where Israel is pictured as a fig tree.

Gary Fisher explained his reasoning in this way:

> Note here that Jesus did not choose just any tree as a sign. He chose the fig tree. He could have chosen flowers, grass, or even other trees, but He chose the fig tree. Why? I believe it is because the fig tree is a national symbol for Israel as is revealed in Hosea 9:10.

> Just as a tree grows dormant in the winter and displays no signs of life, Jesus knew that Israel would be scattered all over the earth and seemingly finished as a distinct nation, but would be regathered as a nation . . . The people who would see Israel display these new signs of life would know that Jesus' return is near.

The Convergence of Signs

Five of our respondents (Hall, Hitchcock, LaHaye, Matrisciana and Rhodes) took the position that the fig tree has no

particular significance apart from merely providing an illustration from nature about the signs of the times. Thus, just as
the blossoming of the fig tree points to the coming of summer, so also the fulfillment of the many end time signs Jesus
had given before He told the parable will point to His soon
return.

In dismissing the idea that Jesus was using the fig tree as
a symbol of Israel, Jeremy Hall pointed to the parallel passage in Luke 21:29-32 where Jesus is recorded as saying,
"Look at the fig tree, and all the trees; as soon as they put
forth leaves, you see it and know for yourselves that summer
is now near." The inclusion of the phrase, "and all the trees,"
makes Hall conclude "that we cannot read too much into the
mentioning of the fig tree in Matthew 24.

Hall went on to conclude that the passage is simply talking about how we can draw conclusions from the observation
of nature:

> When I see that the days are getting longer,
> the snow begins to melt (for us Canadians),
> the trees bud, and the grass begins to green, I
> know that summer is near. Likewise, all these
> signs we are witnessing (right now and in this
> generation) are simply the signs that summer
> is coming.

Mark Hitchcock expressed a similar feeling. He wrote:

> In the context of Matthew 24, I don't believe
> the fig tree here has anything to do with the
> rebirth of Israel. Jesus is probably simply
> using a natural illustration that anyone could
> understand. He is simply saying that just as
> one can tell summer is near by the blossoming
> of the fig tree, so those alive in the Tribulation
> will be able to see that His coming is near
> when the signs predicted in Matthew 24 begin

to happen.

The most surprising response came from Tim LaHaye:

> Perhaps the greatest mistake I have made in interpreting prophecy through the years was to follow my friend Hal Lindsey in assuming the generation that saw Israel back in the land as they were recognized by the UN in 1948, would not pass until the Rapture, or in that a generation was "40 years," meaning 1988. Obviously that has not happened.

This is a reference to the fact that Hal Lindsey, in his book, *The Late Great Planet Earth* (1970), took the position that the re-blossoming of the fig tree was fulfilled in the re-establishment of Israel and that the generation that witnessed that event would live to see the Lord's return. In all fairness, I think I should point out that Hal Lindsey never set a date for the Lord's return. What he said in his book was this: "A generation in the Bible is something like forty years. If this is a correct deduction, then within forty years or so of 1948, all these things could take place" (page 54 of the 1970 edition). Notice, he said they "could" take place, not that they would.

LaHaye proceeded to explain that he thinks the parable refers to those who "see world gospel preaching, the desecration of the Temple by the Antichrist during the Tribulation and many other events so mentioned for that seven year period . . ."

Both Israel and a Convergence of Signs

Another 5 of our Bible prophecy experts said they felt like the parable of the fig tree referred to both the re-establishment of Israel and the convergence of signs (Fletcher, Goodman, James, Jones and Salus).

Phillip Goodman went into considerable detail to explain why he feels the parable has both meanings. "It is not an either-or proposition," he wrote. "It is a double reference prophecy." He then explained that prophecies in the Bible often have more than one meaning. As an example, he cited the last two verses in the Old Testament which prophesy the future return of Elijah (Malachi 4:5-6). Jesus applied this prophecy to John the Baptist (Matthew 11:13-14) who came in the spirit of Elijah, but He also said it referred to the actual appearance of Elijah in the last days (Matthew 17:10-13).

In the same vein, Goodman pointed out that the prophecy instructing the Jews to flee Jerusalem has a double reference. It refers to the time of the Abomination of Desolation in the middle of the Tribulation (Matthew 24:15-21), but it also refers to the destruction of Jerusalem in 70 AD as recorded in Luke 21:20-24.

Concluding his argument, Goodman wrote, "In like manner, Matthew 24:32 refers to both Israel and the last day signs. Since Israel is the center of these signs, it is a perfect picture of the metaphorical fig tree with its budding leaves depicting all of the other signs."

The Meaning of a Generation

Let's shift our attention now to the second issue in the fig tree parable — namely, the meaning of the term, generation.

Five of our experts did not comment on this important point, leaving a total of 17 who did render their opinions. Seven of them (Duck, Fisher, Humphries, Jones, Kinsella, Pollock and Thomas) took the position that Jesus was referring to the generation in existence when the state of Israel is re-established. The remaining 10 all argued that Jesus was referring to the generation that would witness the fulfillment of all the signs — the generation living during the Tribulation.

Four of our experts attempted to provide a biblical definition of a generation. Duck quoted Psalm 90:10 which reads, "As for the days of our life, they contain seventy years, or if due to strength, eighty years."

Hall and Kinsella added Genesis 6:3 which speaks of a generation as lasting 120 years. Kinsella also mentioned the 40 years that the children of Israel wandered in the wilderness until the rebellious generation had died off. He then concluded with this observation: "So, a biblical generation is 20, 40, 70, 80 or 120 years. Somewhere within that time frame [measuring from the re-establishment of the state of Israel], I believe the Lord will return for His Church."

Terry James added off-handedly that in his opinion, a generation could consist of a time period of more than 100 years.

None of our respondents expressed a belief in another common definition of the generation referred to in this passage. I have in mind the interpretation that when Jesus said, "this generation will not pass away," He meant the Jewish people would not cease to exist before His Second Coming. Gary Fisher addressed this definition with the following observation:

> Much debate has taken place concerning the meaning of the word "generation" as it is used here. Some think it is declaring that the Jewish people will not cease to exist, but this statement would be unnecessary because of all the other Scriptures at our disposal that declare that the Jewish people will not cease. Passages like Isaiah 41:8-11 and Jeremiah 31:35-37 would be good examples.
>
> It better serves the context to believe that Jesus is saying that the people (generation) who witness the rebirth of the nation of Israel

will see all things mentioned in Matthew 24 take place, including the return of Jesus.

To summarize, the majority viewpoint among the members of our forum was that the term generation refers to those living at the time that all the end time signs are fulfilled, including the re-establishment of the state of Israel.

Bill Salus expressed the majority viewpoint in the following way:

> Certainly the main thing Christ alluded to was the nation of Israel as the parable of the fig tree, but the Lord didn't say "When you see that sole thing, the final generation exists." Christ alluded to everything that He had predicted throughout Matthew 24:2-29, 32.

> The point I believe the Lord was making, is that some generation will be able to say, "Yes, everything that Jesus Christ predicted in the Olivet Discourse has found fulfillment with 100% accuracy." That generation will be the Tribulation Generation . . .

An Ignored Issue

Only one person, Jeremy Hall, mentioned another crucial issue concerning the fig tree parable. He put it this way:

> Even if we could come up with a firm resolution for the meaning of a generation, we are still left with the question of when does the countdown begin? With the rebirth of Israel as a nation in 1948? Or maybe with the retaking of Jerusalem in 1967? I'm very cautious not to put my finger on a date or even a specific time . . . I do know, however, that we are commanded to "watch."

Some who believe a generation is 120 years have even selected November 2, 1917 as the starting point of the count down since that was when the British government issued the Balfour Declaration proclaiming its intention to make Palestine a homeland for the Jewish people.

Concluding Thoughts

I personally believe that the fig tree parable refers to the re-establishment of the state of Israel. Yes, the next verse refers to the generation that will "see all these things," referring to all of the end time prophecies Jesus had given in the Olivet Discourse. But I believe the lynchpin for all the rest of the prophecies is the rebirth of Israel.

One of the reasons I believe this so strongly is because of something mentioned by both Nathan Jones and Dennis Pollock. That is the fact that a few days before Jesus spoke the fig tree parable, He put a curse on a fig tree as His disciples watched, and the tree withered immediately. Jesus then said, "No longer will there be any fruit from you" (Matthew 18-19).

I believe this was a symbolic prophecy indicating that because Israel (the fig tree) was going to reject Him as their Messiah, God would pour out His wrath upon them and set them aside for a period of time (the Church Age). Then, a couple of days later, Jesus reminds his disciples of the fig tree and tells them to watch for it to blossom once again, marking the season of His return.

As for the meaning of the term, generation, it is true that a generation is defined in many different ways in the Bible, depending on the context. In addition to 20, 40, 70, 80 and 120 years, it is defined as 100 years (Genesis 15:13-16) and 51.4 years (Matthew 1:17 — 42 generations in 2,160 years).

But the term is also used generically in both the Bible and our daily speech. Thus, we refer to the "Nixon generation" or the "Beat generation." I believe that is the way the term is used in the Matthew 24 passage. I think it is just referring to the people who will be alive when the nation of Israel is re-established. I believe some of the people who were alive at that time will live to the time when the Rapture of the Church will take place. I could be wrong, but that is not only my belief, it is my fervent hope.

5) How do you interpret Daniel 12:4?

This passage of Scripture reads as follows:

> But as for you, Daniel, conceal these words and seal up the book until the end of time; many will go back and forth, and knowledge will increase.

Over the years, this passage has been interpreted in different ways by Bible prophecy scholars. What probably could be classified as the traditional interpretation during the past century until now is that this is a prophecy that transportation and knowledge will increase greatly in the end times.

The most common alternative interpretation is that the prophecy refers to the fact that in the end times people will be able to better understand the prophecies of Daniel.

Regarding the responses of our forum members to this question, they divided almost equally between the two viewpoints. Nine endorsed the traditional view (Duck, Fisher, Gist, Hall, James, Jones, Kinsella, McGee and Rosado). Eight embraced the alternative view (Fletcher, Gano, Goodman, Hitchcock, Humphries, Matrisciana, Rhodes and Salus).

Three said they thought both views were correct (LaHaye, Pollock and Thomas). Two did not express an opinion (Markell and Hocking).

The Traditional Interpretation

The traditional interpretation of this passage is reflected in the *Living Bible Paraphrase* (1971):

> But Daniel, keep this prophecy a secret; seal it up so that it will not be understood until the end times, when travel and education shall be vastly increased!

The best and most thorough expression of the traditional viewpoint came from Daymond Duck. It was so well written and so carefully reasoned, I decided to present it to you in full:

> Daniel 12:4 reads, "But thou, O Daniel, shut up the words, and seal the book, even to the time of the end: many shall run to and fro, and knowledge shall be increased."
>
> 1) I believe "shut up the words, and seal the book" means that from the time of Daniel until some point in the last 100 years or so, the Book of Daniel was a closed or sealed book. This means that there are things in the Book of Daniel that mankind could not understand or interpret for many years.
>
> 2) I believe "even to the time of the end" means the Book of Daniel would last at least until the end of the age. It is divinely protected and not one jot or tittle of it will pass away before the time of the end arrives.
>
> 3) I believe the "end" refers to the last days of the Church Age and the times of the Gentiles. I believe the Church Age will end with the Rapture and the times of the Gentiles will end with the Second Coming of Jesus.

4) I believe "even to the time of the end" implies that the Book of Daniel will be understood when the time of the end arrives. Therefore, when mankind can understand the prophecies in the Book of Daniel it is a sign that the time of the end has arrived.

5) I believe "run to and fro" refers to accelerated and constant travel. This is often interpreted to mean traveling at great speeds and traveling unceasingly in every direction to do whatever one wants to do.

6) I believe "and knowledge shall be increased" refers to a dramatic increase in knowledge of all kinds, including the Book of Daniel and all other Bible prophecy. Many see computers, the Internet and such as tools that are bringing about the fulfillment of this prophecy.

The bottom line is that the Book of Daniel and current events are clearly lining up and this is one more indication that the time of the end is at hand.

The Alternative Interpretation

Phillip Goodman made an excellent presentation of the alternative view that the passage refers strictly to the fact that in the end times, people will be able to better understand the prophecies of Daniel due to increased knowledge and more intense study. Goodman wrote, "Knowledge of the meaning of end time prophecies will skyrocket as true Bible believers "run to and fro" sifting and sorting the prophecies of Daniel and Revelation and all other prophetic passages, making sense of them as the Holy Spirit unseals their deeper truths."

Goodman explained that his interpretation of "run to and fro" is based on the use of the phrase in Amos 8:12 and

Zechariah 4:10 where it "depicts a busy searching back and forth," particularly a "searching through the Word of the Lord." Goodman concluded by observing, "Daniel, then, portrays exactly what is going on today among Bible believers — there is a Holy Spirit driven zeal to carefully and meticulously sift and sort, correlate and clarify Bible prophecy in light of today's unique prophetic events . . ."

Mark Hitchcock made a similar point in his response. He said he thinks the passage is "talking about men running to and fro during the last days studying the book of Daniel to find answers about what in the world is going on." He added, "As we approach the end of all things, the book of Daniel is being unsealed, and we are to 'rush here and there' searching its pages diligently to gain greater knowledge of God's prophetic program."

Bill Salus supplied an "Amen!" to these observations by Goodman and Hitchcock. He wrote: "What was important for Daniel to know was not that people would be able to scoot around all over the world, or be able to get information at the touch of a button, but that his prophecies would be understood and applied at the necessary time."

Ron Rhodes, who also endorsed the alternative interpretation, added a fascinating speculation. He suggested that during the Tribulation, when people will have a desperate need to understand what is going on amidst all the horrors, the book of Daniel will be very important to their understanding. "It is entirely feasible," he wrote, "that Daniel 12 may be one among other sermon topics of the Two Witnesses in Revelation 11, as well as the 144,000 Jewish evangelists of Revelation 7 and 14."

A Combination of Both Interpretations

Tim LaHaye took the position that the full meaning of the Daniel 12:4 passage can be found in a combination of both interpretations. He said that the increase in the speed of travel during the 20th Century from 18 miles per hour on a horse to over 17,000 miles per hour in a space craft is phenomenal, and he observed: "That the prophet, 2,600 years ago linked the capability of speed and travel to an 'increase in knowledge,' without which we could not generate the speeds we enjoy today, is a miracle in itself."

But LaHaye went on to also endorse the alternative interpretation that the prophecy refers to an increased intensity of study of Bible prophecies in the end times. He concluded with these words: "Either way you take it, the passage means this present time sets the stage for the Rapture, the Tribulation, the Glorious Appearing and the setting up of the kingdom of Christ . . ."

Conclusion

I would agree that the prophecy has a double application — that it refers both to an increase in knowledge and travel in the end times and it also refers to more intense study and fuller understanding of Daniel's prophecies.

Both interpretations are being fulfilled before our eyes today, indicating clearly that we are living in the end of the end times.

6) How do you interpret Daniel 12:8-9?

The passage reads as follows:

> As for me, I heard but could not understand; so I said, "My Lord, what will be the outcome of these events?" And he said, "Go your way, Daniel, for these words are concealed and sealed up until the end time."

All of those who responded to this question agreed that these two verses mean that the prophecies given to Daniel would not be fully understood until the time for them to be fulfilled — in "the end time." And all agreed that since we are now understanding them fully for the first time, that fact is a clear sign of the time that we are living in the season of the Lord's return.

As Ron Rhodes pointed out in his response, the Bible is progressive in its revelation about the end times. "Daniel wanted more revelation about the end times . . . than God was ready to reveal at that time."

The books of Daniel and Revelation fit together like a hand in a glove. Neither can be fully understood apart from the other. Revelation was written about 650 years after Daniel, and several of our respondents pointed out that the book of Revelation ends with the opposite admonition that was given to Daniel: "Do not seal up the words of the prophecy of this book, for the time is near" (Revelation 22:10).

Once the book of Revelation was completed, the book of Daniel was much more understandable, but unfortunately about 300 years later in 400 AD, the Church officially adopted the Amillennial view of prophecy which spiritualized end time prophecies and rendered them incapable of being understood for their real meaning.

Thus, the prophecies of Daniel and Revelation continued to be sealed up until about 200 years after the Reformation — until students of the Scriptures started interpreting them for their plain sense meaning.

Jack Kinsella concluded his observations regarding this question with the following summary:

> Daniel was once reputed to be one of the most difficult books of Scripture. Today, Daniel is perfectly understandable because many of the events he prophesied are playing out on our evening news cycles. Why? Because this IS the "time of the end."

7) Do you believe God is speaking today through signs of nature?

The reason this question was asked is because many Christians take the position that although God worked through signs of nature in the past, He no longer does so today. This is part of what is known as the Cessationist viewpoint — the idea that God working supernaturally in the world ceased at the end of the First Century, with the death of the last Apostle. Thus, to this group, all natural calamities are just that — nothing more than the natural outcome of forces of nature. They therefore refuse to believe that an increase in natural disasters could be a sign of any fulfillment of Bible prophecy.

All of our Bible prophecy experts, without exception, agreed that God definitely speaks today through signs of nature. Some pointed out that to say otherwise would violate the biblical statements that God does not change (Malachi 3:6) and that He is the same yesterday, today and forever (Hebrews 13:8).

Daymond Duck responded with an extensive listing of the many times that God has used natural disasters as remedial judgments, to call people to repentance or to punish them for not repenting. He mentioned the Noahic Flood, the ten plagues on Egypt, and the severe drought that was placed upon the land of Judah when they failed to rebuild the Temple (Haggai 1:1-11) after their return from Babylonian captivity. He also mentioned 2 Chronicles 7:13 where God specifically states that He is the one who sends drought, locusts and pestilence as punishments. He concluded his survey by saying, "There is more, but the bottom line is that people have to reject what the Bible says to not believe that God has and will send natural disasters."

Gary Fisher and Brian Thomas both emphasized the connection today between our nation's treatment of Israel and natural calamities that we have experienced. As an example, Fisher mentioned the "Perfect Storm" of 1991:

> God has used hurricanes several times now to signal to the United States specifically to stay out of the politics of forcing Israel to give up her land and divide it with the Palestinians. In 1991, the Madrid Peace Conference was to take place on October 30, the first such meeting designed to force Israel to surrender land. On the same day, the hurricane called the "Perfect Storm," slammed into the East Coast of the United States. Waves of up to 30 feet were recorded from Canada to Florida. Over 100 homes in Maine were destroyed and Massachusetts suffered considerable damage including the vacation home of George H. W. Bush, President of the U.S. at the time and the one who had ordered Israel to make necessary compromises at the Madrid Peace Conference.

Another example that both Fisher and Thomas referred to was Hurricane Katrina. Thomas explained it this way:

> On August 15, 2005, 9,000 Jewish settlers were ordered to leave their homes in the Gaza Strip. This act, to force residents of 35 years to leave Gaza within 48 hours or be forcefully removed, was backed by our government . . .

> While this removal was taking place, Hurricane Katrina began forming in the Gulf of Mexico on August 23. It immediately grew into a major storm . . . Katrina slammed into New Orleans on August 29th. This was one of the worst natural disasters in U.S. history as nearly 2000 perished.

I think God was letting us know that He will
judge for decisions that oppose His Word.

I would agree wholeheartedly with Thomas' conclusion,
for Joel 3:2 says that God will place judgment upon any
nation in the end times that is involved in dividing up the land
of Israel.

Tim LaHaye, Mark Hitchcock and Ron Rhodes submitted
words of caution. They expressed concern that too much
importance could be given to natural calamities as end time
signs of nature. Hitchcock expressed it this way:

> I think we can safely say that God uses disas-
> ters to wake people up, show us His power,
> show us our own helplessness and that noth-
> ing here is permanent. He can also use natural
> disasters as judgment on people or nations, as
> He will do in the Tribulation. But today,
> without some specific revelation from God,
> we must proceed with caution in this area.
> Natural disasters mostly happen because we
> live in a fallen world that is groaning as it
> awaits redemption.

Without denying that God does still speak through natural
disasters, Tim LaHaye stated, "The jury is still out in my
mind as to how much significance to place on the seeming
increasing weather phenomena . . ."

Conclusion

God has always worked through signs of nature, and the
Bible says He will continue to do so in the future. The
prophecies concerning the end times strongly warn of natural
disasters increasing like birth pangs — that is, increasing in
frequency and intensity (Matthew 24:8).

That, of course, does not mean that every natural disaster
is a remedial judgment of God. Some are the result of natural

forces of nature. Those that are remedial in nature can be identified by their intensity or their timing or both.

8) What do you consider to be the most important technological development from an end time prophetic viewpoint, and why?

The responses to this question were absolutely fascinating. Six people named the Internet and five the computer, the former being dependent upon the development of the latter. And most of the other developments mentioned, such as satellites and mass communications, were tied in some way to computer technology. So, overall, the computer came through as the most significant development, either directly or indirectly.

In their explanations of their selections, nearly all pointed to the need for modern technology in order for the end time prophecies about the Antichrist to be fulfilled. How else would he be able to keep track of all buying and selling and mark those who give their allegiance to him?

The Specific Selections

Let's take a look at the specific selection of each individual:

Daymond Duck — "The ability to track all buying and selling," which, in turn, required a number of technological developments such as electricity, computers, bar codes and their readers, satellites and the rockets to put them in orbit, and the Internet, to name only a few.

Gary Fisher — The computer, which, together with the Internet has become "an almost limitless research library in the hands of the common man."

Jim Fletcher — "A horse-race between nuclear power and the Internet," but coming down on the side of the Internet. "The Internet has made possible a metastasized and diabolical connection between global change agents in the areas of government, society and religion . . . thus helping usher in a one-world religion."

Ray Gano — The Internet. "My own ministry, Prophezine, was born on the Internet . . . It is amazing that I can sit in Costa Rica and boldly share the gospel and the blessed hope of our Lord's soon return to people I do not even know. But more than that, I can do it in real time and to people all over the world without ever leaving my desk."

Al Gist — The computer, resulting in "great networking systems . . . and planetary communications."

Phillip Goodman — Digital-electronic systems. "This technology is the basis of instant satellite-Internet global communications systems predicted in Revelation 11:8-2. It is the basis of the delivery and trigger mechanisms for nuclear-chemical weapons inferred in Ezekiel 39:6, Matthew 24:22, Revelation 6:3-4 and 11:18. And it is already sophisticated enough to serve as the basis for the universal pin number inscribed on the hand or forehead of the followers of the Antichrist in Revelation 13:16-18."

Jeremy Hall — "Satellite communications and the Internet together because these make possible the fulfillment of prophecies in the book of Revelation — like all the world being able to look upon the bodies of the Two Witnesses lying in the streets of Jerusalem" (Revelation 11:9-12).

Mark Hitchcock — "The technology that gives the ability to know where people are and track their whereabouts."

David Hocking — "The computer because it makes possible the fulfillment of many end time prophecies such as the vast increase in knowledge."

Ken Humphries — The Internet, "the greatest man-made machine ever built," making it possible for the Bible and the gospel to be distributed world wide.

Terry James — The computer and "all the peripheral technologies that go with it which will allow the Antichrist to enslave much of planet Earth."

Nathan Jones — "The proliferation of mass communications" because this development makes it possible to "unite mankind into one global body informationally and culturally."

Jack Kinsella — "The transistor chip because it is the invention that has made possible the technological revolution in computer technology and communications."

Tim LaHaye — The computer which has made possible "all means of electronic wizardry." He added, "I must admit that I am still trying to get into the 20th Century and thus can use only 10% of my computer's capability."

Jan Markell — "The computer because it has made it possible for human tracking."

Caryl Matrisciana — The Internet and global communications because "it has the unique capability of spreading Holy Scripture globally, contributing to the prophecy in Daniel that knowledge would increase in the end times (Daniel 12:4) and that the gospel would be preached to all the world (Matthew 24:14)."

Don McGee — Mass communications because "super population monitoring and control are impossible without quantum communication capabilities," which the Antichrist will need to track humanity.

Dennis Pollock — Nuclear weapons because "these weapons give man the ability to bring about the dire predictions of the disasters which are detailed in the book of Revelation. The loss of vegetation, the slaughter of half the world's population, the poisoning of the water supply, sores breaking out upon people" — all point to the use of atomic weapons. "Before the nuclear age, there was nothing we knew that could bring this about, and so people who believed Revelation in a literal sense concluded that God would simply cause it to happen supernaturally. Today we can easily see that this may not be God's direct work, but a result of God taking His restraining hand off our sin-crazed world and allowing us to do to one another what we would have done long ago apart from His mercy."

Ron Rhodes — "I can't narrow it down to just one technological development." He proceeded to mention a number of inventions necessary for the fulfillment of end time prophecies, such as the computer, satellites, the Internet, global media, rapid transportation, biometric identification, RFID chips and smart card technology.

August Rosado — Satellite technology which "allows us to see events going on around the entire globe."

Bill Salus — The Internet for many reasons, but "most importantly because it enables the Word of God and Christian commentaries to be transmitted exponentially throughout the world to interested parties . . ."

Brian Thomas — The Internet because "it has allowed the world to be connected in real time. This development has led to the spreading of the gospel to the far corners of the earth. That's the positive side of it. But just as a butcher's knife in the hand of a chef can be used to prepare a gourmet meal but can be used for serial killing in the hand of a mad man, the Internet has a negative side. For one, it is full of filth like pornography. I also think it is likely that the Antichrist will somehow use the Internet for his system."

Conclusion

I must agree with Ron Rhodes that it is extremely difficult to select the one most important technological development relating to end time Bible prophecy.

Basics would include such things as electricity, the split-ting of the atom, and the transistor. Overall, I would probably have to select the computer and the ability it gives me through the Internet to communicate with all the world from my desk at home or the office. More important, the computer is what is going to make it possible for the Antichrist to control his worldwide kingdom.

9) Do you believe the development of the European Union is a fulfillment of end time prophecy?

As background to this question, I should point out that the traditional Premillennial interpretation of Nebuchadnezzar's dream, as recorded in Daniel 2:31-45, is that it prophesies a revival of the old Roman Empire in the end times from which the Antichrist will arise.

Twenty-one of our forum members responded to this question, and 14 of them responded with a resounding, "Yes!" Six said "Perhaps so, but not yet." There was one who said no.

The Muslim Empire Theory

The person who answered no was Ray Gano who has bought into the new idea that the empire to be revived is the Muslim Caliphate out of which will arise a Muslim Anti-christ. He referred to the revival of the Roman Empire as a misguided assumption of a "western mindset."

One of many problems with Gano's position is that it does not fit the imagery of Nebuchadnezzar's dream. In that dream, Nebuchadnezzar saw the statue of a man with a head of gold, a chest of silver, thighs of bronze, two legs of iron, and feet of iron mixed with clay.

In the interpretation given to him by God, Daniel told the king that the head represented his Babylonian Empire which would be overthrown by the Medo-Persian Empire repre-sented by the chest of silver. In turn, that empire would be overthrown by the Greek Empire symbolized by the thighs of bronze. The empire represented by the legs of iron was not identified, but we know from history that it was the Roman Empire which followed the Medo-Persian and which ultimately split into two parts, represented by the two legs. The feet of iron mixed with clay represented the end time revival of the empire of iron (the Roman) in the form of a loose confederation of nations. That would be the empire out of which the Antichrist would arise, and it would be the last Gentile world empire before the return of the Messiah.

As you can see, there is no place in this imagery for the Ottoman Empire that overthrew the Eastern wing of the Roman Empire in 1453. The parts of the image end with the Roman Empire. There is no part of the image that represents the Ottoman Empire, so how could the image refer to a revival of the Ottoman Empire in the form of a new Muslim Caliphate?

The Roman Empire Viewpoint

All the rest of our Bible prophecy experts said they believe Nebuchadnezzar's dream points toward a revival of the Roman Empire. This was the belief of even those who took the position that the European Union is not that fulfillment — at least not yet.

Daymond Duck argued that the revival of the Roman Empire must occur, not only because of the imagery of Nebuchadnezzar's dream, but also because Daniel 9:26 says that the Antichrist will arise out of the people who would destroy the Jewish Temple, and that proved to be the Romans in 70 AD.

Nathan Jones, in arguing that the European Union is a fulfillment of the Daniel prophecy, stated, "Like the miracle of the nation of Israel reforming nearly 1,900 years after it was destroyed as a political entity, so too the squabbling, bickering nations of Europe, with their long centuries of genocide, coming together as an economic and then political superpower is truly a marvel to behold." He then pointed out that he thought it was particularly significant that the treaty that forms the basis of the European Union is called "The Treaty of Rome."

Several of our forum members, while endorsing the idea that the European Union is in the process of fulfilling the prophecy of reviving the old Roman Empire, issued statements of caution. For example, Jim Fletcher wrote:

> Yes, I do believe that the European Union is a fulfillment of end time prophecy because such an alliance is clearly described in Revelation. However, I think we should let it unfold rather than paint ourselves into a corner over such things as the identity of the member states. I believe this because geopolitics can change so rapidly.

Prophetic Problems with the European Union

Another commonly expressed concern related to the fact that in Nebuchadnezzar's dream the ten toes of the iron and clay empire are stressed, indicating that the empire will be divided into ten parts. This is underlined later in the book of Daniel when the prophet is given a vision of the same succession of empires in the form of ravenous beasts (Daniel 7:1-7). In this vision, the last empire is pictured as a beast with ten horns (Daniel 7:7). And then, in Daniel 7:24 we are told that this final kingdom will produce ten kings, three of which will be overthrown when the Antichrist takes over (Daniel 7:8).

The usual interpretation of this imagery has been that the revised Roman Empire would be divided into ten parts, with a king or chief executive responsible for each part. And thus the problem: no such division of authority yet exists in the European Union. Therefore, several of our experts, like Mark

Hitchcock took the position that the European Union might be a partial fulfillment of the prophecy, but it would not be a fulfillment until "the Group of Ten rises to lead it. "Five others (Hocking, James, Kinsella, Rhodes and Salus) agreed with this observation.

Jack Kinsella summed up this concern with these words: "The European Union is not the final form of revived Rome because revived Rome is pictured in the prophecies of Daniel as consisting of ten kingdoms . . . but its ongoing development is, I believe, a fulfillment-in-progress of Daniel's prophesied final world government." Terry James expressed an identical sentiment when he wrote, "The EU is not the final form of the reviving Roman Empire, but, certainly it is at the heart of stage-setting for that coming super-power which will eventuate in the ten kings and kingdoms."

A different concern was expressed by Phillip Goodman. He believes the European Union will not fulfill the prophecies of Daniel until it expands to incorporate all the Mid-East territories that were included in the Eastern wing of the old Roman Empire. He stated that it is unthinkable that such diverse nations could come together in one such expanded empire, but as he put it, "the unthinkable with man is thinkable with God."

Conclusion

I personally have no doubt that the European Union is a modern day revival of the Roman Empire. As such, I am not at all convinced that it must ultimately incorporate all the territories of the ancient empire.

I do believe it must be divided into ten administrative units, and I think that will happen. Already, there is a great emphasis within the EU for people to think of themselves as Europeans rather than as Germans, Frenchmen, Spaniards, etc. And already, representatives in the EU Parliament are not allowed to be seated by nations, but rather by political philosophy.

I believe this strong emphasis on trans-nationalism will ultimately result in the EU being divided into ten administrative units that will cross national lines. Others, like Bill Salus, believe the United Nations will divide the world into ten areas, one of which will be the European Union.

10) Do you believe there are signs of the times that are unique to our day?

The importance of this question is related to the fact that people often respond to sermons about the signs of the times by saying: "Come on now, let's get real. There have always been earthquakes and apostasy and persecution and wars and rumors of wars. What else is new? Show me something unique to our day and age."

All but one of our respondents agreed that there are signs unique to our day and age in the sense that some of the signs prophesied in the Bible are showing up on the world scene for the first time ever.

Phillip Goodman began his discussion of this question with this insightful observation:

> My great grandmother, and all of the genera-
> tions before her, did not witness the rebirth of
> Israel, the umbrella of Internet linkage over
> our planet, the global threat of universal
> atomic destruction, the unification of the old
> Roman states, etc. She read about these things
> in the Bible as dimly-lit prophecies, but we
> are seeing them appear in newsprint in flam-
> ing reality.

Thirteen of our forum members pointed to the re-establishment of the state of Israel. Nine mentioned technological developments like satellite television and the Internet. Six focused on political alignments coming into existence in accordance with the prophecies of Psalm 83 and those of Ezekiel 38 and 39. Seven stressed the rapidly growing apostasy in the Church. Three pointed to nuclear weapons.

Other unique aspects of our day that were mentioned included the European Union, the exponential increase in population, the rapid decay of society, the increasing frequency and intensity of natural calamities, and the preparations being made for the reconstruction of the Jewish Temple.

The Unique "No" Answer

Only one of our respondents, Ray Gano, took the position that there are no unique signs on the scene today. In justifying his surprising conclusion, he quoted Ecclesiastes 1:9 which says, "there is nothing new under the sun."

That observation may apply to human behavior, but it certainly does not apply to modern technology. We have many technological developments on the scene today that have never existed before.

Gano took this position because he wanted to take the opportunity to give a mini-sermon regarding his favorite topic — what he claims will be the central role of the Muslims in the fulfillment of end time prophecy. Thus, he wrote a long statement about why the concept of Muslim hegemony in the end times is nothing "new." Rather, according to him, it was postulated by Martin Luther, John Calvin and Jonathan Edwards.

Conclusion

There is no doubt that we are seeing signs prophesied in ancient times becoming a reality on the world scene today. Prophecies that were never understood before are now perfectly understandable because of either historical developments, like the re-establishment of Israel, or technological innovations like television.

Both the convergence of signs and the understanding of them is evidence that we are truly living in the season of the Lord's return.

11) The Bible speaks of spiritual signs in the end times, both positive and negative in nature. Which do you consider to be the most important, and why?

Nineteen of our forum members responded to this question (the other three misinterpreted it). Of the 19, a total of 13 selected apostasy in the Church as the most significant spiritual sign of the times. Most expressed their feeling in very strong terms. Here are some examples:

> **Hitchcock:** "Surging apostasy"
> **Hocking:** "Overwhelming apostasy"
> **Jones:** "Rampant apostasy"
> **Rhodes:** "Massive apostasy"

Gary Fisher provided a good overview of this very negative spiritual sign of the times:

> Paul gives us some very indicting insights into the Church in the last days in 1 Timothy 4:1. He says that "some will fall away from the faith, paying attention to deceitful spirits and doctrines of demons."
>
> Seducing spirits are very much alive in the Church today! This is why much of the Church today has concluded that there are many ways to God, or that Jehovah and Allah are the same, or that the nation of Israel today is not important, or that God smiles on same-sex marriage, or that God is simply a God of love and grace and not of justice also.
>
> In his second letter to Timothy, Paul gives further insight into the end-time Church. In 2 Timothy 4:3-4, Paul saw a day when the

Church would not endure sound doctrine but
would rather accumulate for herself teachers
"in accordance to their own desires" and "will
turn away their ears from the truth." This is
very much the Church of today and much of it
is on open display on television.

Ron Rhodes expressed a similar sentiment, and he got
very specific about some of the apostasies that have infiltrated the Church of today. In particular, he mentioned a
denial of Christ (1 John 2:18), a denial of Christ's return (2
Peter 3:3-4), a denial of the faith (1 Timothy 4:1-2), a denial
of sound doctrine (2 Timothy 4:3-4), a denial of morals (2
Timothy 3:1-8), and a denial of authority (2 Timothy 3:4). He
concluded by observing that "we are truly living in days of
deception!"

Nathan Jones expressed his dismay over the impact of the
"seeker-friendly" movement that has swept throughout
American Christianity.

The Church has become so seeker-sensitive
that we have filled our churches with unbelievers and now are putting unbelievers into
church pulpits. These new church leaders are
rarely even saved. They have no fruits of the
Spirit. They have no signs in their lives that
show that they are saved . . . They teach their
own flavor of universalism with its belief that
everybody will get to Heaven and that all
paths lead to God.

The Laodicean Example

Gary Fisher continued in his analysis to talk about his
conviction that the church in Laodicea in the book of Revelation is a prophetic symbol of what the Church will be like in
the end times (Revelation 3:14-22). Several others made this
same point (Hall, James and Thomas).

The Laodicean church is described in Revelation as a lukewarm church. Accordingly, Al Gist pointed to the fact that the Church of today has lapsed into a "cooling off" period where "stringent adherence to the absolutes of God's infallible and inerrant Word has been replaced with the doctrine of tolerance, accepting all beliefs as equally valid."

Speaking of the lukewarm church at Laodicea, which is described in Revelation 3:16-17 as "wretched and miserable and poor and blind and naked," Jeremy Hall wrote:

> False converts and tares are growing up among the wheat within our churches, and we need to do something about it. We need to preach the gospel of Jesus Christ which is the only way by which man can be saved. We need to stop entertaining the goats and get back to feeding the sheep. Old-fashioned, Spirit-filled, Christ-honoring, sin-hating, soul-winning, Bible-preaching is the hope of the Church. It is the hope of the nation. It is the hope of the world. And yet like an endangered species, it is seldom seen or found. And this is why our times are spiritually "perilous."

Additional Negative Spiritual Signs

Other negative spiritual signs that were mentioned by respondents were as follows:

Duck: The acceptance of homosexuality.
Fletcher: The disintegration of civility in society.
James: People without natural affection.
Kinsella: The overall decay of society.
McGee: Growing secularism worldwide.

Positive Spiritual Signs

Although our respondents focused on the negative spiritual sign of apostasy, several also mentioned a positive spiritual sign, and the one most frequently cited was the Bible's promise of a great outpouring of the Holy Spirit in the end times (Joel 2:28-29).

Several manifestations were mentioned as evidence that this prophecy is being fulfilled today. Duck, Goodman, Jones, LaHaye, Pollock and Thomas pointed to the worldwide spread of the gospel, as prophesied in Matthew 24:14. In addition to traditional missionary and Bible translation activities, some also cited supernatural activity on the part of the Holy Spirit. For example, Brian Thomas wrote:

> As for the most important positive spiritual sign, that would be the outpouring of God's Spirit. The prophet Joel said that in the last days people shall prophesy, see visions, and dream dreams. I constantly hear account after account of Muslims in the Arab world coming to faith by seeing visions of Jesus Christ. Their stories are almost identical in which they state how Jesus Christ appeared to them and they immediately accepted Him as Lord and Savior. This is yet another of the many signs that let us know we are in the last days. And I believe this sign will increase to its ultimate fulfillment during the Tribulation.

Tim LaHaye also mentioned the same sign, describing it in these words:

> Joel 2:28-32 has long been an exciting study of end time spiritual signs that have a physical affect, some of which I am beginning to think are already happening. As God is pouring out His Spirit on "all flesh" and our missionaries are meeting people who have seen Jesus in dreams and visions and prayed to receive Christ even before the missionaries get there,

> just as He predicted, particularly in mid-east-
> ern countries where it almost seems that God
> is preparing a supernatural harvest in coun-
> tries that humanly speaking have no other way
> of getting the Gospel.

Jim Fletcher cited another manifestation of the outpouring of the Holy Spirit in these end times. As a person who keeps his hand on the pulse of Israel, he related how he is amazed at the spiritual awakening that is occurring today throughout that nation:

> There is a spiritual awakening taking place in
> Israeli society. This was clearly prophesied
> throughout the Old Testament, and we are
> seeing it unfold today. Ezekiel's vision saw
> the Jew's being spiritually awakened after
> their physical restoration to the land (Ezekiel
> 37:1-14). This is happening in a very signifi-
> cant way right now in Israel. My wife and I
> recently saw this in secular, racy Tel Aviv, on
> Yom Kippur, when the city literally came to a
> standstill for 24 hours. There are also mezu-
> zahs on the doorposts of hotel rooms, posters
> in Jerusalem heralding the soon-coming of the
> Messiah, and there is an awakening to Christ
> among both Jews and Arabs. This is a huge
> prophetic sign.

Conclusion

I believe our respondents were right on target when they identified the two most important spiritual signs of the end times to be apostasy in the Church and the preaching of the Gospel all over the world. The irony is that the two signs appear on the surface to be contradictory. If the worst negative sign is apostasy in the Church, then how could the best positive sign be the preaching of the Gospel all over the world? To put it another way, why would an apostate Church be interested in proclaiming the Gospel?

The answer, of course, is that the apostate Church has no such interest, particularly since it believes "all roads lead to God." But there are still plenty of faithful churches and ministries that have an intense desire to reach the lost with the good news of Jesus, and they are utilizing every possible technological method to do so — things like short wave radio, satellite television, computer generated Bible translations and the Internet.

One of the most amazing forms of worldwide outreach is the Jesus Film Project developed in 1971 by Campus Crusade for Christ. This project distributes the film "JESUS," a two-hour docudrama about the life of Christ based on the Gospel of Luke. The film has been translated into 1,200 languages and has been seen in every country of the world. To date, it has been shown over 6 billion times and has resulted in more than 200 million people accepting Jesus as their Lord and Savior. There are 449 JESUS Film teams working in 123 countries worldwide showing the film daily, some in very remote areas using an old 16mm movie projector connected to a car battery.

Another stunning development is the increasing pace of Bible translations, making the Bible available to all the major language groups in the world, and to hundreds of language sub-groups. Most of those without a translation today are tribal groups consisting of less than 100,000 persons. And through the Internet, people can download the Bible in whole or in part without having to purchase one. This is particularly important in areas of the world where the importation of Bibles is prohibited.

Jesus said, "This gospel of the kingdom shall be preached in the whole world for a witness to all the nations, and then the end shall come" (Matthew 24:14). This prophecy, which applies to the Second Coming and not the Rapture, is in the process of being fulfilled before our very eyes today. Its complete fulfillment will not occur until the end of the Tribulation. At that time, right before the final outpouring of God's wrath in the form of the Bowls of Wrath Judgments (Revelation 16), God will send forth an angel who will circumnavigate the earth, proclaiming the Gospel to every living person (Revelation 14:6-7).

Living on Borrowed Time

Part 3
The Key Signs

The Re-establishment of Israel   7
Witnessing the cornerstone miracle.

At the beginning of the 20th Century there was not one definite, tangible, objective sign that we were living in the season of the Lord's return. Today, the signs are everywhere. A person would have to be spiritually blind to be unaware of them. There are so many, and they are so intense, that they are like a neon sign flashing in the sky proclaiming, "Jesus is coming soon!"

The First Sign

The very first sign of the time pointing to the soon return of Jesus appeared on the world scene on November 2, 1917. On that day the British government issued the Balfour Declaration, which took the form of a letter addressed to Lord Rothschild, President of the British Zionist Federation. The letter was from Arthur Balfour, the Foreign Minister in the government of Lloyd George. It read as follows:

> I have much pleasure in conveying to you, on behalf of His Majesty's Government, the following declaration of sympathy with Jewish Zionist aspirations which has been submitted to, and approved by, the Cabinet.
>
> His Majesty's Government views with favour the establishment in Palestine of a national home for the Jewish people, and will use their best endeavours to facilitate the achievement of this object, it being clearly

understood that nothing shall be done which
may prejudice the civil and religious rights of
existing non-Jewish communities in Palestine.

Arthur Koestler, in his book, *Promise and Fulfillment*,
characterized this letter as "unorthodox, unpolitic, and
freakish."[1] His analysis was right on target, for the British
government was promising the Jews a land that belonged at
the time to the Ottoman Empire!

Why would the British be so audacious? What most
Americans do not remember is that the Turks sided with the
Germans in World War I, and thus the Allies intended to
divide up the Ottoman Empire after they defeated the Ger-
man-Turkish Alliance. Even so, the Balfour Declaration was
issued a year before the war officially ended on November
11, 1918.

So, the Declaration was a bold expression of British im-
perialism. Later, it was learned that the Declaration was based
on a secret pact between the British and the French that had
been signed in January 1916. It was called the Sykes-Picot
Agreement. It provided for all the Middle East to be divided
between France and Britain.

A Key Personality

The Declaration had been urged upon the British government by Dr. Chaim Weizmann, a Russian Jew who was later
to serve as the first president of Israel.

At the outbreak of World War I, Weizmann was 40 years
old and living in England where he was serving as a chem-
istry professor at the University of Manchester. He was also
the leader of a committee of Zionists who were seeking a
homeland for the Jews.

Because of his political interests, Weizmann made con-
tacts with all the key British political leaders, many of whom,
including Lloyd George and Arthur Balfour, were Evangeli-

cal Christians. These men knew Bible prophecy and were sympathetic to Jewish desires to return to their homeland which was then called Palestine — a land which had been under Turkish control for 400 years.

Weizmann endeared himself to the British leaders when he solved a critical shortage of acetone, an ingredient necessary for the production of the naval explosive cordite. After two years of research, Weizmann invented a method of producing synthetic acetone.

The Origin of the Declaration

According to Howard Sachar in his book, *A History of Israel*, this background of Anglo-Zionist cordiality gave impetus to Weizmann's promptings for a "British protectorate over a Jewish homeland."[2] The appeal struck an increasingly responsive chord among British government officials.

Even so, there was fierce debate within the British Cabinet over the wording of the Declaration. The Zionist draft, which served as the basis of the Declaration, proposed recognition of "Palestine as the National Home of the Jewish people." The final draft called instead for "the establishment in Palestine of a National Home for the Jewish people." It was a subtle but important change in wording. As William Hull put it in his book, *The Fall and Rise of Israel*, "Palestine as a Home was vastly different from a Home in Palestine."[3]

There has been much speculation over the years as to the motives of the British War Cabinet for issuing the Declaration. Undoubtedly the motives were mixed in nature. But regardless of the motives, God fulfilled the promise He had made.

A Fulfillment of Prophecy

What I want to emphasize is that the Declaration started a series of events that were to lead to the re-establishment of the state of Israel, in fulfillment of Bible prophecy.

Many people are not aware of the fact that the most prolific prophecy in the Old Testament — mentioned more times
than any other one — is that the Jews will be regathered in
the end times in unbelief to their homeland. Over and over,
the Hebrew Scriptures state that the Jews will once again
occupy the land given to them by God.

Consider, for example, this remarkable passage from
Isaiah 11:11-12 —

> Then it will happen on that day that the Lord
> Will again recover the second time with His hand
> The remnant of His people, who will remain,
> From Assyria, Egypt, Pathros, Cush, Elam, Shinar,
>   Hamath,
> And from the islands of the sea.
>
> And He will lift up a standard for the nations
> And assemble the banished ones of Israel,
> And will gather the dispersed of Judah
> From the four corners of the earth.

Notice that the prophet says this will happen "on the day."
This phrase and a similar one, "in that day" are used throughout the book of Isaiah to refer to the end times. Next, he says
that this will be a "second" regathering of the Jewish people.
The first was from Babylon. Then he specifies that the people
will be regathered "from the islands of the sea," which is a
Jewish colloquialism for the whole world, as he makes plain
in the next verse when he says they will come "from the four
corners of the earth." And finally, he states that this will be a
regathering of all the Jewish people, both those of Israel and
Judah.

The prophet Ezekiel was given a vision that communi-
cated the same prophecy. In chapter 37 of his writings, he
states that while "the hand of the Lord was upon him," he was
placed in a valley full of dry bones. Ezekiel was ordered to
preach to the bones, and when he asked what he should

preach, the Lord said tell them that "I am going to cause breath to enter them and they will come to life."

Ezekiel proceeded to preach the message, and to his astonishment the bones began to move and come back together and stand up. At that point, the Lord explained to Ezekiel the meaning of the vision he was experiencing Ezekiel 37:11-13):

> Then He said to me, "Son of man, these bones are the whole house of Israel; behold, they say, 'Our bones are dried up and our hope has perished. We are completely cut off.'
>
> Therefore prophesy and say to them, 'Thus says the Lord God, 'Behold, I will open your graves and cause you to come up out of your graves, My people; and I will bring you into the land of Israel.
>
> Then you will know that I am the LORD, when I have opened your graves and caused you to come up out of your graves, My people.'"

This prophecy plainly says that God will one day bring the Jewish people back alive as a nation by gathering them back to their homeland. They will be brought back from their "graves" — the nations to which they had been scattered all over the world.

And notice, it says they would be brought back to the land of Israel and not the land of Canaan or the land of Judah or the land of Palestine. Thus, when the regathered Jews decided to select a name for their new state in 1948, there were many suggestions, like Zion, but they decided on the name, Israel, in fulfillment of this prophecy.

Other Prophetic Fulfillments

The regathering prophecy is not the only one relating to the Jewish people that has been fulfilled in modern times.

God also promised that He would preserve the Jewish people during their dispersion throughout the earth, making it possible for them to be regathered in the end times. Isaiah emphasized this point when he quoted God as saying that He could no more forget Israel than a mother could forget her nursing child. He also quoted God as saying, "Behold, I have inscribed you [Israel] on the palms of my hands" (Isaiah 49:14-16). In Jeremiah 30:11 the Lord is quoted as saying to the Jewish people, "I am with you . . . to save you; for I will destroy completely all the nations where I have scattered you, only I will not destroy you completely."

No other nation in all of history has been scattered world wide and been able to keep its identity. The preservation of the Jewish people is a fulfillment of prophecy and is one of the greatest miracles of history.

In fact, the preservation and regathering of the Jews is so miraculous that two times in the book of Jeremiah the prophet says that when history is completed, the Jewish people will no longer swear by the God who delivered them from Egyptian captivity, but by the God "who brought up the sons of Israel from the land of the north and from all the countries where He had banished them" (Jeremiah 16:14-15 and 23:7-8). Both Gods spoken of in these verses are the same one. The point is that the Jewish people will consider their regathering in the end times to be a greater miracle than their deliverance from Egyptian captivity! And you and I are blessed to be living in the time when that prophecy is being fulfilled.

And then, of course, the establishment of the state of Israel after the regathering of the Jewish people is another fulfillment of specific prophecies. One of my favorite prophecies regarding this subject is a symbolic one found in

Isaiah 66:7-8, which reads as follows:

Before she travailed, she brought forth;
Before her pain came, she gave birth to a boy.

Who has heard such a thing? Who has seen
    such things?
Can a land be born in one day?
Can a nation be brought forth all at once?

Here we have a prophecy that a nation would be born in one day, and its birth would take place before the birth pains began. Birth pains after the birth? Who has heard of such a strange thing?

Yet, that is exactly what happened! The rebirth of the Jewish state took place on May 14, 1948, and the birth pains began the next day when 5 Arab states attacked the new nation, determined to annihilate it. And the birth pains have continued to this day with war after war.

Another prophecy fulfilled during all these wars is the preservation of the Jewish state. The book of Zechariah prophesied that the renewed nation would be able to withstand all its enemies. The prophet said that Israel would be like a "flaming torch among sheaves," consuming "on the right hand and on the left all the surrounding peoples." Further, he stated that "in that day, the Lord will defend the inhabitants of Jerusalem" and the most feeble among the Jews will be like David against Goliath (Zechariah 12:6,8).

Another end time prophecy concerning the Jews that has been partially fulfilled is the promise that they would once again occupy their beloved capital city of Jerusalem. Zechariah, in his prophecies, speaks repeatedly of the time when the Jewish people will once again live in the city of Jerusalem. Here is one of the promises that God gave through him (Zechariah 8:8-9):

Thus says the LORD of hosts, "Behold, I am
going to save My people from the land of the
east and from the land of the west; and I will
bring them back and they will live in the
midst of Jerusalem . . .

The promise is repeated in Zechariah 12:1-9 where it is
stated that the Jewish people will be living in Jerusalem in the
end times, and that God will protect them from their enemies.

Jesus referred to these prophecies in His Olivet Discourse
when He stated that the Jews would be scattered from Jerusalem and the city would be trampled down by the Gentiles
until the "times of the Gentiles be fulfilled" (Luke 21:24). We
know from other prophecies that the times of the Gentiles will
not be fulfilled until the end of the Tribulation and the
destruction of the final Gentile empire of the Antichrist.
That's why I said that what we are witnessing today in the
return of the Jews to Jerusalem on June 7, 1967 is a partial
fulfillment. Interestingly, it is a necessary event for the Jews
to rebuild their Temple — the Tribulation Temple — something that is clearly prophesied in many scriptures, both in the
Old Testament and the New.

The Balfour Declaration's Impact

British Evangelicals in the 19th Century were well aware
of all these prophecies. They believed in them and looked
forward to their fulfillment. That's what prompted them to
build the first Protestant church in the city of Jerusalem. It
was called Christ Church. It was constructed near the Jaffa
Gate and dedicated in 1849. The church was built in anticipation of the worldwide regathering of the Jews prophesied in
the Hebrew Scriptures. It was even designed to look like a
synagogue.

With such expectations long established, it is no wonder
that the Balfour Declaration electrified the British Evangelical community. The person who seemed to be impacted

by it the most was Dr. F. B. Meyer, one of the best known and most highly respected evangelical leaders of the time. He quickly huddled with other English Evangelicals and issued a manifesto to the press on the 8th of November (just six days after the issuance of the Declaration). Entitled "The Significance of the Hour," it included the following points:[4]

1) That the signs of the times point toward the close of the times of the Gentiles.

2) That the return of our Lord may be expected at any moment when He will be manifested as evidently as to His disciples on the evening of His resurrection.

3) That the completed Church will be translated to meet the Lord in the air, and to be forever with the Lord.

4) That Israel will be restored to their own land in unbelief, and be afterwards converted by the manifestation of Christ as their Messiah.

5) That all human schemes of world reconstruction must be subsidiary to the Lord when all nations will be subject to His rule.

6) That under the reign of Christ there will be a further effusion of the Holy Spirit upon all flesh.

Meyer's group also called for an all-day meeting to be held on December 13 at Queens Hall in London. The purpose of the meeting was to provide an opportunity to emphasize that "the times of the Gentiles" (Luke 21:24) were clearly drawing to a close and that consequently the return of Jesus for His Church might be expected imminently.

The Liberation of Jerusalem

Before the meeting could be held, General Edmund Allenby, the commander of the Allied forces in the Middle East, liberated the city of Jerusalem from 400 years of Turkish rule. Allenby was a devout Christian, and on the day he entered the city — December 11, 1917 — he refused to ride his horse. He walked in because the Scriptures say that the Messiah is the one who will enter Jerusalem on a white horse at the time of His Second Coming (Revelation 19:11).

The Arab world initially looked upon Allenby's capture of Jerusalem as a matter of divine intervention. This was due to the mistaken impression that the name, Allenby, was a combination of Allah (God) and Neby (prophet), and that he was, therefore, a prophet of God.

Evangelicals in England also considered the liberation of Jerusalem to be a divine act, as did Bible-believing Christians worldwide. As one minister put it, "Christianity the world over put on her garments of praise. Songs were sung, poetry was recited, prayers offered, and sermons preached."[5]

Birth of a Ministry

By the time Dr. Meyer and his colleagues gathered at Queens Hall on December 13, the atmosphere was electric. There was an overwhelming consensus that God had begun the implementation of His end time program for regathering the Jews to their homeland. A dozen preachers spoke that day to a packed house. Included among them was Dr. G. Campbell Morgan who asserted: "We all feel that never in the history of the church have the signs seemed so definite to point to the fulfilling of Gentile times as they do today. Our loins should be girt about, and our lamps should be burning. We should be occupying until He comes."[6]

The meeting resulted in the formation of an organization called The Advent Testimony Movement. Dr. Meyer was appointed the president. The organization immediately launched a series of Bible prophecy conferences which were held throughout England.

The conferences rapidly spread to the Continent, to Australia and South Africa, and to the United States. In America, the meetings were so large that it was impossible to find buildings big enough to accommodate the crowds. When a conference was held in Philadelphia, it filled the largest hall in the city and four other churches at the same time!

The ministry founded by Dr. Meyer in 1917 continues to this day under the name, The Prophetic Witness Movement International.[7] It is still headquarted in England.

British Duplicity

At the end of World War I, Palestine was assigned to the British as a League of Nations Mandate, meaning that the English were responsible for tutoring the people within the area toward self-rule. Palestine at that time included all of present day Jordan. The Jews looked forward eagerly to the day when this territory would become their home.

But they were severely disappointed in 1922 when the British government suddenly issued a White Paper in which it announced that two-thirds of Palestine would be set aside for an Arab state to be known as Trans-Jordan. This decision was prompted by a desire to placate the Arabs in the area who opposed the Balfour Declaration. And, in turn, the desire to curry favor with the Arabs was related to the British desire to gain access to the oil that was being discovered throughout the Arab world.

This is the reason that to this very day Israeli leaders point out that a Palestinian state already exists — the state of Jordan, as it is known today. In fact, over 70% of its population is made up of Palestinians.

The Jews continued to look forward to the day when they would be able to establish their own state in the small sliver of land that was left — an area smaller than the state of New Jersey. But they were destined to experience some more disappointments. In 1936 an Arab revolt broke out aimed at uprooting the Jews and forcing the British to allow the establishment of another Palestinian state under Arab control. The British responded by sending a Royal Commission of Inquiry led by Lord Peel.

British Appeasement

The Peel Report, issued in July 1937, recommended seriously restricting Jewish immigration (at a time when the Holocaust was getting started in Germany). It also recommended limiting land sales to Jews. Finally, it proposed that Palestine be partitioned again, creating Jewish and Arab states. The Arabs flatly rejected the report, and the proposals were shelved.

Then, in May of 1939, the government of the great appeaser, Neville Chamberlain, caved in to Arab violence and issued another White Paper which, in effect, constituted a repudiation of the Balfour Declaration.

The White Paper announced the goal of establishing a state of Palestine within ten years. But it stacked the cards in favor of the Arabs by imposing a severe limitation on Jewish immigration, limiting it to 10,000 per year. The coup de grace was prohibition of further land sales to Jews in 95% of Palestine!

William Hull, in his landmark book, *The Fall and Rise of Israel*, states that British policy between 1917 and 1939 toward the establishment of a Jewish Home in Palestine could be summed up in one word: ***whittling***.[8] When the Jews were first promised a national home, the area included Trans-Jordan — a total of 45,000 square miles. In 1922 when Trans-Jordan was given to the Arabs, only 10,000 square miles were left for the Jewish home. The partition plan of the Peel Commission in 1937 would have given the Jews only 2,000 square miles. The new regulations under the 1939 White Paper cut the area to 260 square miles!

Jewish Aid and Opposition

Despite the double-dealing of the British, Jews worldwide rallied to the British cause during World War II, doing everything they could to help the Allies defeat the Nazis. In contrast, the Arabs sat on the sidelines, and the Grand Mufti of Jerusalem actually collaborated with Hitler, encouraging his policy of Jewish genocide.

When the war ended, the Jews expected to be rewarded by the British with a lifting of the restrictions of the 1939 White Paper. This failed to happen, despite the fact that hundreds of thousands of Holocaust survivors were clamoring to get into Palestine. The result was the birth of the Jewish Revolt headed up by Menachen Begin.

Begin's revolt proved effective. Besieged by both sides, the British decided the time had come to terminate the Mandate. A United Nations committee recommended a Solomonic solution: "Cut the baby in half." The committee recommended that the remaining sliver of Palestine be divided between the Jews and Arabs, creating two patch-work states intermingled with each other.

The UN General Assembly agreed with the plan, and on November 29, 1947, the United Nations voted by a two-thirds majority to partition Palestine. Again, the Jews were disappointed with another division of their land, but they agreed to the partition. The Arabs denounced the resolution and prepared for war.

The True Arab Intent

And war it has been ever since, simply because the Arab desire is not for the creation of an Arab state within Palestine, but rather, the incorporation of all Palestine into an Arab state. Or, to put it another way, the true aim of the Arabs is to annihilate the state of Israel and drive the Jews into the sea.

Again, we come across an end time fulfillment of Bible prophecy, for the Bible says that the Arabs will lust for the land of Israel in the end times and will try to take it for their own. One of those prophecies is found in Ezekiel 35 and 36 where we are told that in the time of the end (35:5) the Arabs will desire to possess the land of the Jews (35:10) and that God will deal harshly with the Arabs, making a desolation of their lands (35:15 and 36:1-7).

Recognizing the Season

Noah preached for 120 years that his generation was living in the season of the pouring out of God's wrath. In like manner, I believe we have been in the season of the Lord's return since November 2, 1917.

The Bible says the generation that witnesses the rebirth of Israel is the one that will witness the return of the Lord (Matthew 24:32-35).

The Bible also says that in the end times, right before the return of the Lord, the Jews will be back in their land and their city, and the whole world will come against them over the issue of the control of Jerusalem (Zechariah 12:1-4).

That's exactly where we are today on the prophetic time line. And that means we are living on borrowed time. The crucial question for every person is this one: "Are you ready for the Lord's return?"

The Revival of the Roman Empire 8
Experiencing the fulfillment of Daniel's prophecy.

The most important prophetic development of the 20th Century was the regathering of the Jewish people to their historic homeland in the Middle East, resulting in the creation of the state of Israel on May 14, 1948. The second most important development was the formation of a European confederation which today is known as The European Union. Both of these momentous historical events point to the fact that we are living in the end times, right on the threshold of the Tribulation and the Lord's return.

Writing about Europe in Bible prophecy, Kenneth Humphries, a Bible prophecy teacher and preacher based in Northern Ireland, had this to say:

> An often asked question these days as I travel from place to place preaching the prophetic message is, "Does Europe really have a role in biblical prophecy?" The answer to this question is an emphatic, "Yes!" In fact, the role of a unified Europe in end time prophecy is much clearer in the Bible than the role of the world's only current super power — the United States. The book of Daniel establishes with certainty that a unified Europe will rise in the end times out of the ashes of the old Roman Empire.[1]

Throughout the centuries since Rome fell, many political leaders have dreamed of resurrecting the Roman Empire, and a number of them, like Napoleon Bonaparte and Adolf Hitler, have tried to accomplish that goal through the use of military force. All shared the vision of a United States of Europe. But that vision had to await God's timing for its fulfillment. That timing came at the end of World War II.

The Historical Origins of European Unity

Most of Europe was completely devastated by the war. That devastation prompted various nations in Western Europe to put aside their age-old hatreds and jealousies in order to reach out to each other for mutual support and aid. The result was a series of economic unions which helped to spur the European economy.

In 1950 two Frenchmen, Jean Monet (a businessman) and Robert Schuman (the French Foreign Minister), got the ball rolling toward European cooperation and unity with a proposal for an integration of the coal and steel industries of Western Europe. The next year, six nations (Belgium, France, West Germany, Italy, Luxembourg and the Netherlands) signed the Treaty of Paris which created the European Coal and Steel Community. This effort proved so successful that within a few years the decision was made to integrate other sectors of the countries' economies. This resulted in the Treaty of Rome, signed in 1957. It created the European Economic Community and the European Atomic Energy Community.

In 1992 the Treaty of Maastricht transformed the European Economic Community from a strictly economic union to one that was both economic and political, creating the European Union.

The collapse of Communism throughout Eastern Europe in the late 1980s and the early 1990s removed the biggest remaining barrier to European union. Germany was reunited and all of Eastern Europe was liberated to seek its own destiny. That destiny has proved to be an expanding European union. From a total of 15 member states in 1995, the EU has expanded to a membership of 27 today, with several applicant states waiting for approval. The combined population of the member states now exceeds 500 million people.

Recent Developments

The EU is based upon a series of very complex treaties. To clarify these treaties and to provide a more substantial political structure for the EU, a European Constitution was drafted and signed by all the member nations in Rome in October of 2004. Its full implementation was dependent upon its ratification by all the member states, several of whom decided to submit it to national referendums.

The Constitution was intended to provide the EU for the first time with a "legal personality." This meant it would be able to represent itself as a single body under international law, thus being able, for example, to sign treaties for all the member states. It was also designed to streamline the structure, increase the power of its Parliament, and create some important new leadership positions.

A Shocking Setback

But to the astonishment of the EU leadership, two key nations refused to approve the Constitution in public referendums. They were France and the Netherlands. Since the Constitution required unanimous approval, it was placed on hold for what was called "a period of reflection."

In March of 2007 the three key leaders of the EU — the presiding officers of the Parliament, the Council and the Commission — ended this period with the signing of a document called the Berlin Declaration. This document was intended to provide renewed impetus toward the breaking of the ratification deadlock. It called for a solution to the problem to be reached before the European Parliament elections scheduled for June of 2009.

The Treaty of Lisbon

In December of 2007 the European Council agreed to drop the proposed Constitution, but to retain most of its changes in the form of another treaty called the Treaty of Lisbon. This treaty increased the power of the European Parliament in the legislative process (which had been dominated by the European Council); created a High Representative for Foreign Affairs; and made the EU Human Rights Charter legally binding on all the member states.

Perhaps the most important change from a biblical viewpoint was the fact that the treaty created a new kind of president of the Council, the EU's most powerful body. In the past this position had been held by the head of government of the state chairing the Council, with rotation every six months. The Treaty of Lisbon created a president elected by the heads of state to serve for a term of 2½ years. This prestigious new position is being referred to in European newspapers as "The President of Europe." It is this position that the future Antichrist is most likely to hold.

Another Setback

Although the Treaty of Lisbon basically constituted the defeated constitution, since it was in the form of a treaty, all the member states decided to ratify it by parliamentary votes rather than public referendums. All, that is, except Ireland. The Irish decided they were compelled by a 1987 decision of their Supreme Court to submit the treaty to a public referendum. The election was held in June of 2008, and the Irish people rejected the treaty. Since the implementation of the treaty depended on unanimous ratification, it had to be placed in suspension.

The EU leaders refused to renegotiate the treaty. They talked the Irish into conducting another election on the condition that they would provide some legal guarantees that certain EU rules concerning "family issues" would not be imposed upon Ireland. These included abortion, euthanasia and gay marriage. They also agreed to allow the Irish to retain their traditional state neutrality.

With these conditions, the Irish agreed to hold another election, and the treaty was approved in October 2009. The Lisbon Treaty went into force on December 1, 2009.

The Future

The bottom line is that the leaders of the EU are determined to pursue ever greater economic and political union, regardless of the will of their people. Thus when their proposed constitution failed to gain the necessary approval in public referendums, they simply converted it into a treaty that would have to be ratified only by the parliaments of each member state.

Even with the new constitution, the EU will remain a loose confederation of states for the time being. This is in conformity with end time Bible prophecy which portrays the revived Roman Empire as a mixture of iron and clay (Daniel 2:41-43). It will not become a unified political superpower until the Antichrist takes it over and consolidates it into his power base from which he will conquer the world (Revelation 13:7).

The development we should watch for is the division of the EU into ten administrative units which will cut across national boundaries, with a president heading up each of the areas. The book of Daniel says the Antichrist will rise to power within the revived Roman Empire by subduing three of these leaders and then taking over the entire organization (Daniel 7:24-25).

Emergence of a Super-State

As you can see, the movement for European unity which was launched in 1950 by Robert Schuman and Jean Monet has gradually evolved into a super-state.

The Union now manifests several of the most important characteristics of a state. It has a unified economic system, an integrated political structure, and a shared vision for the future. Even more important, due to the approval of the Treaty of Lisbon, the EU now has a legal personality, enabling it to be represented in international organizations like the United Nations. It also has a designated leader and foreign minister.

What the Union officially lacks is a military force. But it is in the making. A military staff has been assembled, with a commander-in-chief, and it currently has at its disposal about 60,000 front line troops on standby, with 400 assault aircraft and up to 80 warships.[2] The British government refers to it as a "Rapid Reaction Force." That is nothing but a euphemism for an army. It has been dubbed "Eurocorps" by the rest of Europe. The British are downplaying this military arm of the Union because they want to continue their partnership with the United States in NATO. The French would like to see the Eurocorps replace NATO, as it probably will.

Surrender of Sovereignty

What most people do not realize is the degree to which the member states of the European Union have surrendered their national sovereignty.

Consider, for example, the power of the European Court of Justice, headquarted in Luxembourg. Judgments of the Court in the field of EU law are binding on all member states, their national courts, their companies, and their private citizens.

This means the decisions of the EU Court override those of the supreme national court of each member nation. Thus, if a British citizen loses his case before the Supreme Court of England, then he can appeal it to the European Court of Justice, and that court can overrule the British decision.

In like manner, the chief legislative bodies of the EU have the power to overrule national laws of member states.

Another significant surrender of sovereignty has to do with currency. The EU attempted to create a common currency with the establishment of the "Euro-zone" in 1999. The hope was that all the member states would surrender their national currencies and adopt a common currency called the Euro. A majority of 16 agreed to do so, but to date a total of 11 have kept their national currencies, including England. Nonetheless, there is tremendous pressure for all the member nations to adopt the Euro as their national currency.

The European Attitude

The significance of this new political union in the European mind is well stated in an official publication of the European Union, published in 1997:[3]

> The building of a united Europe is undoubtedly one of the greatest historical undertakings of the 20th Century. It is a process grounded in the positive values with which our civilization identifies — the preservation of peace, economic and social progress, respect for the person, and the predominance of right over might . . .

> The 20th Century bears tragic scars left by the rise and then the collapse of the totalitarian ideologies. As the third millennium dawns, the movement towards a voluntary union among Europe's peoples is . . . clearly

the only credible answer to the hazards and opportunities posed by the increasing globalization of the world economy.

In the minds of many Europeans, the foremost symbol of this new European confederation is the Euro, the new currency that went into effect in most of the member nations in 2002. The announcement of an agreement on the Euro was greeted in some quarters with an enthusiasm that bordered on blasphemy. Portuguese Prime Minister Antonio Guterres raved: "As Peter was the rock on which the church was built, so the Euro is the rock on which the European Union will be built."[4]

The Biblical Significance

The biblical significance of these momentous developments in Europe has been widely recognized by students of Bible prophecy. For example, commenting on the signs of the times that point to the Lord's soon return, Dr. S. Franklin Logsdon wrote the following words in 1973, long before the European Economic Community had evolved into the much stronger and more significant European Union:[5]

> The present statehood of Israel is a powerful indication of the ending of the age. The Ecumenical Movement is another. Perhaps equal to either of these is the European Common Market with its many implications . . . it is an economic community, a breaking down of national barriers, a getting together on certain common bases.

> The whole idea is to re-shape the face of Europe. This was attempted by Caesar, by Napoleon, and by Hitler, but their means to this end were not subtle or as workable as those proposed by the Common Market. *They used ammunition; today's promoters use*

> *bread.* And let it be said that the re-shaping of
> the face of Europe approximates the kingdom
> to arise out of the old Roman Empire — the
> last Gentile power. (Italics added.)

The question is, can we find this newly emerging power bloc in Scripture? There is no doubt. In chapters 2 and 7 of Daniel we find the European sign revealed. We are specifically told that the prophecies given to Daniel in these chapters relate to "the latter days" (2:28), "to what would take place in the future" (2:29).

Daniel's prophecies are based upon a dream which God gave to Nebuchadnezzar (2:31-35). Interpreting that dream, Daniel concluded that it revealed a succession of Gentile empires, beginning with the Babylonian Empire, followed by Medo-Persia, Greece and Rome (2:36-40).

The last Gentile world empire will be a confederation of nations (2:41-43) that will arise out of the old Roman Empire (7:7-8). And out of that confederation, the Antichrist will arise, using the revived Roman Empire as his base to conquer the world (7:8, 23-25). But this final Gentile empire will be short-lived, for it will be suddenly crushed by the return of the Messiah who will "set up a kingdom which will never be destroyed" (2:44).

Religious Aspects of the European Union

Perhaps the most surprising thing about the EU is that it has adopted a myriad of religious symbols to express its overall purpose of uniting all of Europe into a super-power that can dominate the world. These symbols are so evident and so powerful, that Alan Franklin, a Christian newspaper editor from London, England has characterized the EU as a new version of the old Holy Roman Empire:[7]

> What is emerging in Europe is a new Holy
> European Empire, an attempt to resurrect the

old Holy Roman Empire that existed under the Pope. This is becoming increasingly blatant. The Vatican is playing a major role in the creation of the new European Empire, and Catholic social values — so-called "Christian Socialism" — are at its heart. The present Pope [John Paul II] has repeatedly called for religious unity in Europe. This means a united, Catholic Europe, which was consecrated to Mary by the Vatican in 1309.

One of the most prominent religious symbols appears on the EU flag. It is a circle of 12 stars on a background of blue. Leon Marchal, a former official of the EU, affirmed in some public remarks that the stars represent "the woman of the Apocalypse."[8] This is a reference to the woman portrayed in Revelation 12 who has a crown of 12 stars on her head. In the context of that chapter, she represents Israel, but the Roman Catholic Church has always claimed that she is a symbol of the virgin Mary.

In his explanation of the ring of stars, Marchal proclaimed, "It's wonderful that we have gotten back to the Introit of the new Mass of the Assumption. It's the *corona stellarum duodecim* (the crown of the twelve stars) of the woman of the Apocalypse."[9]

The EU, which now has 27 member countries, has confirmed that the number of stars will always stay at 12, which indicates that the stars do not represent countries.[10]

The EU has also adopted an anthem that has religious undertones. The tune is "Ode to Joy," which, of course, is the last movement of Beethoven's ninth symphony. EU documents refer to this anthem as an "ode to freedom," celebrating the decision of European nations to unite in peace.

But, as Alan Franklin has noted, the "Ode to Joy" is "not quite that innocent." He points out that the lyrics, by a man named Friedrich von Schiller, "concern the entering of the shrine of a pagan goddess and the uniting of all men in brotherhood, by the power of magic."[11]

An amazing poster has been published by the EU that touts its work toward the unification of Europe. It shows the Tower of Babel and carries the slogan: "Many tongues, one voice." In the background a crane is pictured rebuilding the tower. Above the Tower of Babel, the eurostars from the EU flag are pictured, but they are inverted, as in witchcraft.

Commenting on this poster, Alan Franklin writes:[12]

> The story of the rise and fall of Babylon told in Genesis chapter eleven should have been a warning to all men for all time. Nimrod and his followers tried to build a tower to reach the heavens, but it was the counterfeit building of a counterfeit religion. Mystical Babylon is now being rebuilt in Europe . . .

This same Satanic imagery has been incorporated into the architecture of the Parliament building in Strasbourg, France. Its entrance is shaped in the form of an enormous replica of the unfinished tower of Babel. It's as if Satan is going out of his way to proclaim that the European Union belongs to him.

In that regard, Alan Franklin reports that on the opening day of the Parliament building, one of the EU representatives from the United Kingdom observed: "We realize we are not merely entering a building, but being allowed access to the temple of a bold new empire."[13] Even the secular press could not miss the connection between the old and new towers of Babel. They labeled the new Parliament building as "The Tower of Eurobabel."[14]

But as bad as the Tower of Babel imagery may be, there is another EU image that is even more diabolical in nature, and it has become one of the most prolific symbols used by the EU. It is the symbol right out of Revelation 17 that pictures a woman riding a beast! In the context of Revelation this image represents the corrupt church of the Antichrist.

This symbol can be seen everywhere among the buildings of the EU. It appears as a mural on walls and as a tile decoration on floors. Large statues of the image can be seen on the grounds of EU buildings, and in some of these depictions, the beast is pictured as riding on waves, just as in Revelation 17. The image has also appeared on EU coins and stamps, and it has been pictured prominently in non-EU publications, such as the covers of European news magazines.

Europeans seem oblivious to the demonic nature of this image. They view it as a representation of an ancient Greek myth about a woman named Europa who was captured and raped by the god Zeus who disguised himself as a bull. But even so, why would anyone want to use such a pagan, repulsive story as the symbol of a new super state?

But regardless of the origin of the symbol, it is used today to symbolize the belief that the European Union will be successful in taming the beast of nationalism. In short, it is an expression of the pride of Man, just as was the Tower of Babel.

Scripture is being fulfilled before our eyes, for those with eyes to see.

It's interesting that even secular writers have been able to discern that something very special is happening in Europe. Consider the following comments taken from the CIA Factbook regarding the European Union:[15]

> The evolution of what is today the European Union (EU) from a regional economic agreement among six neighboring states in 1951 to today's hybrid intergovernmental and supranational organization of 27 countries across

the European continent stands as an unprecedented phenomenon in the annals of history. For such a large number of nation-states to cede some of their sovereignty to an overarching entity is unique.

Conclusion

The stage is set for the rise of the Antichrist out of the resurrected old Roman Empire. And Europeans are ready for him to appear. Sixty years ago as the foundation of the European Union was being laid, Paul Henri Spaak, the Prime Minister of Belgium, spoke these chilling words:[16]

> We do not want another committee. We have too many already. What we want is a man of sufficient stature to hold the allegiance of all people, and to lift us out of the economic morass in which we are sinking. Send us such a man and, be he God or the devil, we will receive him.

The Bible paints a picture of an end time configuration of world politics. That configuration has formed:

- Israel has been re-established as a state.

- The Roman Empire has been revived.

- The Arab states are seeking to destroy Israel.

- Russia is menacing Israel from the north.

- The whole world is coming against Israel over the control of Jerusalem.

We are living on borrowed time.

Recognizing false Christs.

Jesus warned repeatedly that in the end times the world would witness many false Christs and false prophets. In His Olivet Discourse, when He listed the signs of the times that would point to His soon return, the very first sign He mentioned was an epidemic of false Christs. "Many will come in My name, saying, 'I am the Christ,' and will mislead many" (Matthew 24:5).

This is the only sign that He repeated in that memorable speech — and He repeated it twice. In verse 11 He focused on false prophets: "And many false prophets will arise, and will mislead many." And, again, in verse 24, He mentioned both groups: "For false Christs and false prophets will arise and will show great signs and wonders, so as to mislead, if possible, even the elect."

This latter statement is particularly chilling since it indicates that the cult leaders of the end times will have supernatural powers and will therefore be able to deceive many people through the performance of miracles.

Apostolic Warnings

The warnings of Jesus are not the only ones in the Bible concerning cults. His apostles warned repeatedly about the danger of false and deceptive teachers.

John warned that Christians are to be on guard against "antichrists" — whom he defined as those who deny that Jesus is the Christ (1 John 2:18,22). He also challenged believers to "test the spirits to see whether they are from God; because many false prophets have gone out into the world" (1 John 4:1). The test He prescribed was to ask the person in question to confess that "Jesus Christ has come in the flesh" (1 John 4:2).

Nearly all of John's second epistle is devoted to a warning against false teachers. As John puts it: "Many deceivers have gone out into the world" (2 John 7). He then states that "anyone who goes too far and does not abide in the teaching of Christ, does not have God," and he admonishes believers in the strongest of terms to avoid association with such people: "If anyone comes to you and does not bring this teaching [the teaching of Christ], do not receive him into your house, and do not give him a greeting; for the one who gives him a greeting participates in his evil deeds" (2 John 9-11).

Likewise, Paul speaks out strongly against false and deceptive teachers. Paul says that if an angel of God were to come with a gospel different from the one revealed in the Scriptures, we should reject his message and "let him be accursed" (Galatians 1:8-9). In his first letter to Timothy, Paul warned about deception in the end times: "The Spirit explicitly says that in later times some will fall away from the faith, paying attention to deceitful spirits and doctrines of demons" (1 Timothy 4:1).

Peter contributed to this chorus of warnings when he wrote that there will be false teachers "who will secretly introduce destructive heresies, even denying the Master who bought them" (2 Peter 2:1). He says some will be motivated by sensuality and others by greed (2 Peter 2:2-3).

Early Cults

All these apostolic warnings were much needed, for the early Church was assaulted by false teachers and cultic groups from the beginning.

The first to arrive on the scene were the Judaizers who responded to the inclusion of Gentiles in the Church by demanding that they be circumcised in order to be saved (Acts 15:1). They also demanded that the Gentile converts observe the Law of Moses (Acts 15:5).

These demands caused such a crisis that a convention of church leaders was called in Jerusalem to discuss and decide the matter. The convention reaffirmed that salvation comes "through the grace of the Lord Jesus," and not through obedience to the Law (Acts 15:11).

The Judaizers were severely rebuffed by this decision, but they continued to plague the early Church. At one point, Paul had to publicly rebuke Peter for playing politics to please what he called "the party of the circumcision" (Galatians 2:11-14). Paul also devoted much of his Galatian letter to denouncing the teachings of the Judaizers.

The Gnostics were the second major cultic group that afflicted the early Church.[1] They refused to accept the truth of the incarnation because they did not believe you could mix the holiness of God with flesh. They took this position because they considered all material things to be inherently evil. They therefore taught that Jesus was a spirit being — an angel who was neither fully God or man. In doing this they denied both the physical death of Jesus and His bodily resurrection. This is the reason that John told the early Church to test all teachers by asking them to confess "that Jesus Christ has come in the flesh" (1 John 4:2).

Modern Cults

False Christs, false prophets, and their cultic groups have continued to afflict the Church throughout its history from time to time. But the acute danger of the cults that Jesus warned would characterize the end times did not begin to manifest itself until the early part of the 19th Century when an American by the name of Joseph Smith founded a religious movement that was destined to become the world's largest cult — the Church of Jesus Christ of Latter Day Saints, better known as the Mormons. Today the Mormons number more than 14 million worldwide.[2]

Before the end of the 19th Century several more cultic organizations had been founded, including the Jehovah's Witnesses and several spiritist groups like the Church of Christ Scientists.

The 20th Century proved to be the age of the cults. They multiplied with great rapidity to the point that some cult-watching organizations now list more than 500 cultic groups operating in America.

The Dangers of the Cults

These cults present a clear and present danger to the true Church. That danger takes two forms. First, the cults are converting many professing Christians. One expert on the cults who grew up in a cultic group once expressed this problem to me in these terms: "Christians convert pagans. Cults convert Christians."

The statement is very true. The average cult member is thoroughly indoctrinated. He knows what he believes and why he believes it. The average Christian, by contrast, usually has little biblical knowledge. He's not sure what he believes and cannot defend his faith. The result — as cult expert Walter Martin once put it — is that "the average Jehovah's Witness can turn the average Christian into a theological pretzel in two minutes flat."

Tens of thousands of professing Christians are being de-ceived each year by the cults. They are being sucked into spiritual darkness by clever and deceptive peddlers of false messiahs, and the result is the damnation of their souls. The Church needs to face up to this problem and start responding to it by grounding its members in the fundamentals of the faith so that they will know what they believe and why.

Doctrinal Influence

The second danger of the cults is their penetration of the Church with their heretical doctrines. Their "doctrines of demons" (1 Timothy 4:1) are creeping into the mainline Church in many forms. It is not at all unusual anymore to hear liberal denominational leaders deny the divinity of Jesus or His bodily resurrection or His Second Coming. Likewise, many mainline Christian leaders are now denying the reality of Hell — either denying it exists or claiming it is a temporary place of cleansing before the salvation of all people.

One of the favorite liberal themes today is the teaching that there are many different roads to God — that God has revealed Himself in Buddha, Confucius, Abraham, Jesus, Mohammed, and many other persons. The natural conclusion of such thought is that it is improper for Christians to seek to convert people of other religions to Jesus.

Even Evangelical churches have gotten caught up in cultic doctrines. A popular fad is the teaching that the power of prayer is not to be found in faith but in the imagination, or visualization. This is a heresy straight out of Eastern mystical religion. It is a practice of Shamanism that is being embraced by many Christian groups today.

Another cultic doctrine that has invaded the Church is the incredible teaching that our salvation was not won on the Cross by the shedding of the blood of Jesus, but was won instead at the hands of Satan as he tortured Jesus in Hell for the three days between His death and His resurrection. This nonsense ignores the fact that Jesus declared on the Cross, "It is finished!" (John 19:30). It denies the clear teaching of the Scriptures that we are saved by the blood of Jesus (1 John 1:7). And it ignores the fact that there is no mention in the Bible of any visit to Hell by Jesus or any suffering on His part after His death.

Equally incredible is the cultic doctrine that is being taught on Christian television today which holds that those who are born again are "little gods." This is the lie that Satan told to Eve in the Garden of Eden, and it is the same lie that is taught by many cultic groups like the Mormons.

Christian Involvement

Additional evidence of cultic influence on the Church is to be found in the growing acceptance of the cults by some church leaders.

Several very well known Evangelical leaders have recently reached out to Mormons, and some have even indicated that the time has come to accept them as brothers in Christ![3] Another endorsement of a cultic group occurred when one of Christendom's leading televangelists served as the featured speaker at the dedication of the new international headquarters of the Unity Church, a classic cult that teaches reincarnation! He even conducted a seminar for them on church growth.[4]

Definition

What is a cult? The typical dictionary definition is so vague and general that the term could be applied to any religious group. For example, The American College Dictionary defines a cult as "a particular system of religious worship." In practice the term is used in many different ways and is usually used in a very indiscriminate manner.

Some use the word in a very broad sense to refer to any religious group that is non-Christian in nature. Thus, they will lump together pseudo-Christian groups (like Armstrongism and Mormonism) with completely non-Christian groups (like Muslims and Hindus).

I prefer to give the term a more technical meaning. Within Christianity, I consider a group to be a cult if it masquerades as being Christian, but is not. It employs Christian terms, quotes the Bible, and uses Christian symbols. But it is not a true expression of the Christian faith.

There are two fundamental things that set a cult apart from orthodox Christianity. One is their emphasis on works salvation. They always have a plan of salvation that depends on works, usually in the form of being obedient to their rules.

But their most distinguishing characteristic is their concept of Jesus. That concept is always distorted and perverted. In short, cults present a false Jesus. Consider the examples below:

Christadelphianism: A created being with a sin nature.

Christian Science: A man in tune with the Divine Consciousness, but not the Christ.

Jehovah's Witnesses: Michael the Archangel, a created being.

Mormons: One of thousands of gods created by the super god.

Moonies: A man who failed in his mission.

Unity Church: A great healer, miracle worker, and mystic.

New Age Groups: A man who achieved the Christ consciousness that all of us are capable of achieving.

The teaching of a false Jesus is a very serious matter because our salvation depends upon our relationship with Jesus — the true Jesus from Nazareth who revealed Himself to the world as God in the flesh (John 14:9-11). There is salvation in no other person (Acts 4:10-12). There is salvation in no other way (John 14:6). Jesus Himself put it this way, while speaking to His Father in prayer: "And this is eternal life, that they may know You, the only true God, and Jesus Christ whom You have sent" (John 17:3).

We can be wrong about many things, but if we are right about Jesus, we can be saved. Likewise, we can be right about many things, but if we are wrong about Jesus, we can be lost. To be saved, we must put our faith in Jesus — the Jesus revealed by the Word of God (John 17:3).

Other Characteristics

With respect to organization and operation, there are two types of cultic groups.

One type — the rarer form — operates openly and encourages freedom of thought. The Unitarian Church and the Mind Science Churches are examples of this type.

The more common type of cult are those that operate in some degree of secrecy and which exercise a large degree of thought control over their members. These groups share six characteristics:

1) **Leadership** — There is usually a dynamic, charismatic founder or leader who considers himself to be either the true Christ or the last prophet of God. Examples are Joseph Smith, the founder of the Mormons, and Sun Myung Moon, the leader of the Moonies.

2) **Writings** — There are always some extra-Biblical writings which are considered equal to or superior to the Bible. The Mormons have the *Book of Mormon* and the *Pearl of Great Price*. The Children of God look to the letters of their founder, Moses David (David Berg). The prophetic proclamations of Herbert W. Armstrong are revered as scripture by many Armstrongites. And the Jehovah's Witnesses have their own eccentric "translation" of the Scriptures. It is actually a version that simply rewords all the verses that conflict with their theology.

3) **Salvation** — There is always a perverted view of salvation. Cults emphasize salvation by works. Their faithful followers are therefore zealous about knocking on doors or

giving their time or money.

4) Doctrine — Cults always have some weird doctrines that are not biblically based. Many of the Mind Science groups teach reincarnation, and all of them deny the reality of evil, disease, and death. Nearly all the cults deny the existence of Hell. Many, like the Unitarians, advocate universalism — the ultimate salvation of all people. The Children of God practice sexual permissiveness. Mormons believe in baptism for the dead. The Armstrongites teach that the Anglo-Saxon peoples are the true Jews.

5) Attitude — The groups are always very exclusivistic because they view themselves as God's only true church and refuse to have anything to do with any other group. They are often very secretive in nature — as evidenced by the secret temple rites of the Mormons.

6) Government — The authoritarian groups are dictatorial, and some even totalitarian, in their governing structure. Someone at the top — either an individual or a collective leadership — calls all the shots.

Borderline Groups

There are a number of religious groups that manifest many of the characteristics listed above, but I do not consider them to be cults because they have an orthodox view of Jesus as God in the flesh.

These groups tend to be sectarian, legalistic, and exclusivistic to the point that each of them consider their particular group to be the one and only true church. Accordingly, they have almost nothing to do with other Christian groups.

I classify these groups as sects. They usually have a number of peculiar doctrines like Sabbath observance, water regeneration, and dietary laws — all of which they consider to be significant enough for lines of fellowship to be drawn concerning them.

I personally grew up in a church like this. We had a biblical view of Jesus, but we considered ourselves to be members of the one and only true church. We were so legalistic that we constantly fought among ourselves and divided over things that should have been matters of opinion — like the frequency of communion.

The rest of Christendom falls into the category of denominations like the Baptists, Methodists, and Assemblies of God. These are orthodox Christian groups who are non-sectarian and thus consider themselves to be a part of the body of Christ — but only a part. These groups view the true Church as being composed of all born again people, regardless of their denominational or sectarian label.

The World's Largest Cult

The cult with the largest membership in the world is one that very few Americans have ever heard of. It is called Igesia ni Cristo (Tagalog for Church of Christ).[5] It was founded in the Philippine Islands in 1914 by a man named Felix Y. Manalo, who is considered to be God's last prophet, sent by God to re-establish the original church of the New Testament. The church is usually referred to as INC. It claims a worldwide membership today of over 27 million people. (The Mormons claim 14 million; the Jehovah's Witnesses, 7.5 million.)

The INC denounces the Roman Catholic Church as apostate and argues that Protestant Christianity is not any better. The church denounces the Trinity as a heresy. It argues that Jesus was created by God the Father and is therefore not divine. The INC contends that its members are the "elect of God" and that there is no salvation outside of their church.

The cult puts a strong emphasis on unity, and therefore does not tolerate differing opinions on anything, including politics. The INC has a long tradition of decreeing whom its members are to vote for.

The INC has experienced explosive growth since the beginning of the 21st Century. They have sent out missionaries all over the world and are utilizing all aspects of modern technology to proclaim their message. Currently they are operating in 96 countries and 7 territories. They currently have 150 churches in the United States, scattered among 39 states. They are evidently getting ready to make a big push in the U.S. because in 2011 they purchased 59 parcels of land in South Dakota for approximately $700,000.

The Newest Cult

One of the newest cults on the scene today, and one that is growing rapidly, is Creciendo en Gracia (Spanish for Growing in Grace), which is based in Miami, Florida.[6]

The founder, José Luis de Jesús Miranda, was born in Puerto Rico in 1946 and grew up in extreme poverty. He burst on the religious scene in 1998 when he claimed he was the reincarnation of the Apostle Paul. In 2005 he announced that he was the Second Coming of Christ. He said that Jesus had "integrated with him" in 1973. Then, in 2007 he took his bizarre claims one step further into the Twilight Zone by proclaiming that he is the Antichrist!

You might wonder how anyone could give their allegiance to such a person. The answer lies in the doctrines he teaches, all of which appeal to the flesh. He argues that the devil has been destroyed and that sin and Hell do not exist. He says he has come to deliver people from their religious hangups and to help them understand that the grace of God covers everything.

He teaches that Peter, James and John conspired to silence Paul and to eventually kill him because he was preaching grace. They wanted to keep Christians in bondage to the Law of Moses. He says he is the Antichrist because he teaches that Christians should not follow "the Jewish teachings" of Jesus, but rather, the grace teachings of Paul.

An Attractive Facade

Cults are incredibly deceptive. They not only use Christian language and symbols, but many of them also display worthy attributes like zeal, dedication, and concern for the individual.

Another thing that makes some of them attractive is that they exhibit very fine moral qualities. Take the Mormons for example. They are a people committed to personal holiness, and they put great importance on the value of the family.

To put it another way, the cults are full of very sincere and religious people. But no one can be saved by sincerity or by being religious. No one can earn salvation. Again, salvation comes by grace through faith in a person (Ephesians 2:8-10), and that person is Jesus — the true Jesus revealed in the Bible.

Cults are a perfect example of what the Bible means when it says that "Satan disguises himself as an Angel of light. . . and his servants as servants of righteousness" (2 Corinthians 11:14-15). They are like the white washed tombs which Jesus said were full of dead men's bones — beautiful to behold, but full of spiritual death.

A Challenge

The Word of God challenges us to test everything because we are all subject to deception. We are told to "test the spirits to see whether they are from God; because many false prophets have gone out into the world" (1 John 4:1).

We are even exhorted to test ourselves. Here's how Paul puts it: "Test yourselves to see if you are in the faith; examine yourselves!" (2 Corinthians 13:5).

The test of all teaching and all doctrine is the Word itself. We are called to be like the Bereans who tested everything Paul taught by the Word of God (Acts 17:10-11).

Conclusion

We are in the midst of the explosion of false Christs, false prophets and cultic groups that Jesus warned would be one of the surest signs of the end times and His soon return. We need to be on our spiritual guard at all times, for these are days of deception.

Satan knows how to read the signs of the times. He knows his time is short, and he has shifted into overdrive in an attempt to deceive as many people as possible. He wants to take as many people as he can to Hell with him.

As the cults proliferate and the false Christs and prophets become more bold and extreme, we need to keep in mind that we are living on borrowed time.

The Convulsion of Nature   10
The message of natural disasters.

We have arrived at a very important category of end time signs — the Signs of Nature — and yet, it is the category that receives the least respect. There are two reasons for this, one that is conceptual, and another that is philosophical.

The conceptual problem resides in the fact that there have always been signs of nature. So, when confronted with the prophesied signs of nature, many people shrug their shoulders and ask, "What else is new? There have always been tornados, hurricanes, and earthquakes."

What they overlook is that Jesus said these signs would be like "birth pangs" (Matthew 24:8). That means they will increase in frequency and intensity the closer we get to the Lord's return. And that is exactly what appears to be happening today.

The philosophical problem many people have with the signs of nature is due to the fact that we have been brainwashed by Western scientific rationalism into believing that for something to exist, you must be able to see it, measure it, weigh it, and dissect it.

In contrast, the Bible teaches there is a whole realm of the supernatural that cannot normally be perceived by the senses. This realm includes angels, demons, and the operation of the Holy Spirit. It also includes God's intervention from time to time through natural disasters.

God and Signs of Nature

Sometimes God uses signs of nature to underline the importance of major events. Thus, at the birth of Jesus, God placed a special light in the heavens, probably a manifestation of His Shekinah glory. When Jesus was crucified, the earth experienced three hours of darkness and a major earthquake. And the Bible says that when Jesus returns, the world will experience the greatest earthquake in its history. Every island will be moved, valleys will be lifted, mountains will be lowered, and the city of Jerusalem will be lifted up like a jewel, possibly becoming the highest place on earth (Revelation 16:18-21 and Isaiah 40:3-5).

More often, God uses signs of nature as remedial judgments to call nations to repentance. Both the Bible and history attest to the fact that God has a pattern of dealing with nations. To begin with, He is the one who establishes nations, and He is the one who takes them down (Daniel 2:20-21). When a nation rebels against God, He responds first by raising up prophetic voices to call the nation to repentance. These are not people with supernatural knowledge of the future. They simply have the gift of discernment to see where a nation is missing God's mark. To put it another way, they know how to apply the Scriptures to contemporary events.

If a nation refuses to listen to the prophetic voices, God will then send remedial judgments. These can take many forms. Deuteronomy 28 mentions economic failure, rebellion of youth, an epidemic of divorce, confusion in government, foreign domination, and military defeat. The chapter also mentions natural disasters like drought, crop failure, and pestilence.

Finally, if a nation digs in against God and sets its jaw against His calls to repentance, a point of no return will be reached — often referred to as "when the wound becomes incurable" (Nahum 3:19, Jeremiah 30:12, and Micah 1:9). At this point, the Lord will deliver the nation from judgment to destruction. That destruction may occur quickly — as with Babylon and the Soviet Union — or it may occur gradually over a period of time, as with the Roman Empire.

Examples of Remedial Judgments

There are many examples of remedial judgments in the Bible that involve natural disasters. Take for example the plagues with which God afflicted Egypt in order to convince Pharaoh that he should release the children of Israel from captivity. The Lord sent plagues of frogs, gnats, flies, and locusts. In addition, He contaminated the nation's water, afflicted the livestock with pestilence, struck the people with sores and boils, engulfed the land in a thick darkness, and finally took the lives of the first born of both men and livestock.

When King Ahab led the Israelites into the worship of a pagan god, the Lord raised up the prophet Elijah to call the king and his people to repentance. When they ignored Elijah, the Lord then put a remedial judgment on the land in the form of a severe three and a half year drought (1 Kings 17 and 18).

The book of Joel tells about a locust invasion that afflicted Judah. This was one of the worst calamities that could befall an agricultural society. It appears that people began bemoaning their "bad luck," when God sent the prophet Joel to inform them that the disaster had nothing to do with luck. Joel boldly proclaimed that the locusts had been sent by God to call the people to repentance. He warned that if they did not repent, the Lord would send something even worse — an enemy army. The people ignored Joel and the prophets who followed him, and God ultimately sent the army, delivering them from judgment to destruction.

Seventy years later when the Babylonian captivity ended, the Jews who returned to Judah laid the foundation for a new temple and then quickly lost interest in the project. They turned their attention instead to the building of their personal homes. For 14 years the foundation of the temple stood vacant. Finally, God raised up an elderly, tough-talking prophet named Haggai. He confronted the people by asking them: "Have you noticed that when you plant your crops, they are destroyed by root rot? And when you replant them, they are destroyed again by hail? And when you replant, a wind storm comes? God is speaking to you! He is calling you to repent of your misplaced priorities and give attention to the rebuilding of His temple." For once, the people listened, obeyed, and were blessed.

The Nature of God

God has continued throughout history to use signs of nature to call nations to repentance. Some people say, "Oh no, God doesn't do that anymore because this is the 'Age of Grace.'"

Well, the first problem with that statement is that it implies there was a previous time of no grace. The fact of the matter is that there is only one way of salvation that has ever existed: namely, grace through faith (Joel 2:32).

Furthermore, the Bible says God is "the same yesterday, today and forever" (Hebrews 13:8). There is no such thing as the Old Testament God of wrath and the New Testament God of grace. God does not change (Malachi 3:6).

The Old Testament God of wrath is the one who showed grace toward the wicked city of Nineveh when its people repented in response to the message of Jonah. The New Testament God of grace is the one who warned the church at Thyatira that if it continued to tolerate a false prophetess, He would "cast her upon a bed of sickness and those who commit adultery with her into great tribulation." Further, He threatened to "kill her children with pestilence" (Revelation 2:22-23).

Our God is a God of grace, mercy, and love. But He is also a God of holiness, righteousness, and justice. The balanced view of God is presented by the prophet Nahum. Speaking of God's grace, he wrote: "The Lord is good, a stronghold in the day of trouble, and He knows those who take refuge in Him" (Nahum 1:7).

But Nahum warned that the same God is one who is righteous and holy and who will not tolerate sin (Nahum 1:2-3):

> A jealous and avenging God is the Lord;
> The Lord is avenging and wrathful.
> The Lord takes vengeance on His adversaries,
> And He reserves wrath for His enemies.
> The Lord is slow to anger and great in power,
> And the Lord will by no means leave the guilty
> unpunished.

The Role of Satan

Some counter by trying to argue that natural calamities come from Satan and not God. But the Bible teaches that God is sovereign. Satan is not free to do anything he pleases. When he wanted to torment Job, he had to ask God's permission, and when he was granted permission, God laid down rules about what he could and could not do (Job 1:6-12).

The Bible says God does not tempt us (James 1:13). Yet Jesus taught us to pray, "Lead us not into temptation" (Matthew 6:13). How can these statements be reconciled? The answer is that although Satan is the tempter, he cannot do so unless God allows it.

Again, God is sovereign, and nothing happens that He does not allow, either in His perfect will or His permissive will. That is the reason the Bible attributes all natural disasters to God.

Crucial Questions

Are all natural calamities a product of Man's sin? Yes, absolutely. The original creation was perfect. Natural calamities are a result of the curse that God placed on the creation in response to Man's sin. When Jesus returns, the curse will be lifted and natural calamities will cease.

Do all natural calamities represent remedial judgments of God? No — most are products of the natural processes of our weather systems.

How then can we determine when a natural calamity is a remedial judgment? One important factor is the timing of the event as it relates to the sins of the nation. Another factor is the magnitude of the event. Remedial judgments are designed to have great shock value in order to capture people's attention and force them to think with an eternal perspective. The most important factor is God's Spirit witnessing to the spirits of those to whom He has given the gift of prophecy. They will be motivated to speak forth with a united voice.

The Example of the United States

We can see all these principles operating in the history of our own nation. We were founded as a Christian nation, committed to Christian values, and God greatly blessed us. But in the 1960s we began to thumb our nose at God as a cultural revolution was launched. Our society quickly descended into a cesspool of sexual promiscuity, drug abuse, abortion on demand, legalized gambling, rampant blasphemy, and a flood of pornography. Our national slogan became, "If it feels good, do it!" We adopted a hedonistic lifestyle, calling evil good and good evil.

God responded by raising up prophetic voices to call the nation to repentance. One of those was Dave Wilkerson, pastor of Times Square Church in New York City. I call him "God's Jeremiah to America." In the 1970s he began writing a series of books in which he clearly outlined the sins of America and warned of judgments from God if we did not repent. Like Jeremiah, his popularity plummeted because people — even church people — did not want to hear his "doomsday message."

When the prophetic voices were ignored, God began to place remedial judgments on our nation — things like our defeat in the Vietnam War, the AIDS epidemic, the plague of sexually transmitted diseases, the scourge of homosexuality, and natural disasters in the form of monster earthquakes and killer tornados and hurricanes. We even experienced an unprecedented volcanic eruption of Mount St. Helens in 1980 — an eruption so severe that it blackened the sky from Seattle to New York City and as far south as Oklahoma.

The culmination of the remedial judgments seemed to come with the 9/11 terrorist assault in 2001 when two symbols of American pride were attacked: the Twin Towers in New York and the Pentagon in Washington, D.C. The towers stood as symbols of our wealth; the Pentagon symbolized our military power.

As I have stated before, I believe this event was a wake-up call from God for our nation to repent. Instead, like a drowsy man who doesn't want to wake-up, we merely rolled over and hit the snooze button on the alarm clock.

A New Factor

I don't think there is any doubt that our national sins have called down remedial judgments from God. But what I think we may have failed to realize is that since 1991, many of the judgments we have experienced have been directly related to our mistreatment of Israel.

The Bible says that God will bless those who bless Israel, and He will curse those who curse Israel (Genesis 12:3). The Bible also says that he who touches Israel touches "the apple of God's eye" (Zechariah 2:8).

History attests to the truth of these statements. Spain was at the height of its power as a world empire in the 15th Century when it launched the Inquisition and drove its Jewish population out of the country. Within a short time thereafter, the empire no longer existed. Hitler was well on his way to conquering all of Europe when he launched the Holocaust. His Third Reich soon ended up in ashes.

I believe that many of our blessings as a nation have been due to the fact that we have historically been a safe haven for the Jewish people. Also, we have been Israel's best friend ever since the nation came back into being in 1948.

But the Bible says that in the end times all the nations of the world will come together against Israel over the issue of Jerusalem (Zechariah 12:3). And in the early 1990s we began to turn against Israel in our determination to maintain access to Arab oil.

The Decisive Year

The turning point was in 1991 when the Soviet Union collapsed and Russian Jews began flooding into Israel at the rate of 2,000 to 3,000 a day for one year. The tiny nation of Israel was overwhelmed by the refugees. The Israeli government appealed to the World Bank for a $5 billion loan. The bank said it would grant the loan only if the U. S. guaranteed it. The Bush Administration agreed to underwrite the loan on one condition: the Israelis had to go to the bargaining table and start trading land for peace.

Yes, we were the ones who forced Israel into adopting the current suicidal policy of appeasement, and we have been twisting their arm ever since, pressuring them to divide up the land which God gave them as an everlasting possession. Keep in mind that we can apply enormous pressure because our veto in the United Nations Security Council is the only thing standing between Israel and economic sanctions that could easily and quickly destroy the Israeli economy.

A Prophetic Book

In 2006 a White House correspondent (one of 250 in the world) named William Koenig wrote a book entitled, *Eye to Eye*. It was subtitled, "Facing the Consequences of Dividing Israel."[1] The thesis of the book was that many of the natural calamities, economic setbacks, and political crises experienced by the United States since 1991 have been directly related to actions we have taken to force Israel to surrender territory to the Arabs.

Koenig is a devout Evangelical Christian who has the gift of prophecy. Accordingly, he has the discernment to see the supernatural relationship between world events and judgments of God.

His book had a very prophetic cover. It showed President Bush looking over his right shoulder at a hurricane, and in the eye of the hurricane was a Star of David, the symbol of Israel.

The title of the book, *Eye to Eye*, was suggested by Koenig's wife.[2] She took it from Matthew Henry's commentary on Isaiah 52:8 —

> They [the watchmen] shall see an exact agreement and correspondence between the prophecy and the events, the promise and the performance; they shall see how they look upon another *eye to eye*, and be satisfied that the same God spoke the one and did the other.[3]

In other words, in the end times there will be people who are prophetically gifted to recognize the correspondence between Bible prophecies and world events.

In his book, Koenig shows the amazing parallels between U.S. mistreatment of Israel and subsequent natural calamities, economic setbacks and political crises. Let me share just a few of the examples he gives.

The Madrid Conference — This conference, which we forced on Israel, marked the beginning of the "land for peace" process. The opening of the conference on October 30, 1991, coincided with the formation of "the Perfect Storm." This was the record breaking storm along our Atlantic seacoast which produced 100 foot high waves and heavily damaged President Bush's home at Kennebunkport, Maine. The headlines of *USA Today* on November 1, 1991, had the stories of the storm and the Madrid Conference side by side.[4]

Round Six of the Bilateral Peace Talks — In June of 1992 Yitzhak Rabin was elected the new Prime Minister of Israel. The U.S. government immediately insisted that he come to Washington, D.C. and meet with Yasser Arafat. The day that meeting began, August 24, 1992, Hurricane Andrew slammed into Florida with winds of 177 miles per hour. The damage done amounted to over $30 billion — the most costly hurricane in U.S. History to that point in time.[5]

Arafat at the United Nations — In September of 1998 Yasser Arafat was invited to speak to a special session of the United Nations that was held in New York. President Clinton arranged a meeting with him to put pressure on Israel. As the meeting took place, Hurricane Georges smashed into the Gulf Coast causing over $6 billion in damage.[6]

Arafat and a Palestinian State — With U.S. encouragement, Arafat announced that he was going to proclaim a Palestinian state on May 4, 1999. Even though President Clinton later persuaded Arafat to postpone the declaration to at least December, on the very day the proclamation was to have been made (May 3rd in the U.S.; May 4th in Israel), the most powerful tornado in U.S. history tore through Oklahoma City with wind speeds of 316 miles per hour, destroying over 2,000 homes.[7]

The Camp David Summit — From July 11 through July 24 in the summer of 2000, President Clinton hosted a summit conference between Israel and the Palestinian Authority. Clinton pressured Israeli Prime Minister Ehud Barak to surrender the heartland of Israel. During these precise dates, a major heat wave struck the South Central U.S. and fires broke out in our Western states. At one point, there were over 50 active fires that consumed over 500,000 acres before the end of the month.[8]

White House Ramadan Celebration — On Thursday evening, November 7, 2002, President Bush hosted a dinner at the White House to honor the Muslim religious holiday called Ramadan. In his speech that evening, the President said:[9]

> . . . this season commemorates the revelation of God's word in the holy Koran to the prophet Muhammad. Today this word inspires faithful Muslims to lead lives of honesty and integrity and compassion . . .
>
> We see in Islam a religion that traces its origins back to God's call on Abraham . . .

Two days later a total of 88 tornados hit Arkansas, Tennessee, Alabama, Mississippi, Georgia, Ohio, and Pennsylvania.

The Middle East Peace Plan — On April 30, 2003, U.S. Ambassador Daniel Kurtzer presented the "Road Map" peace plan to Israeli Prime Minister Ariel Sharon. It was a plan formulated by an ungodly coalition called "the Quartet." This group was made up of Russia, the European Union, the United Nations, and the United States. It called for Israel to surrender Gaza and its heartland of Judea and Samaria to the Palestinians. On May 3rd Secretary of State Colin Powell departed for the Middle East for talks to implement the plan.

On May 4th Secretary Powell met with terrorist leader Hafez Assad of Syria and made a commitment to him to include the surrender of the Golan Heights in the peace plan. That day a swarm of tornados began tearing apart the Central United States. Over the next 7 days, there was a total of 412 tornados — the largest cluster ever observed by NOAA since it began its record keeping in 1950. The previous record had been 177 in 1999.[10]

In summary, between October 1991 and November 2004, the United States experienced:[11]

- 9 of the 10 largest insurance events in U.S. history.

- 9 of the 10 greatest natural disasters as ranked by FEMA relief costs.

- 5 of the costliest hurricanes in U.S. history.

- 3 of the 4 largest tornado swarms in U.S. history.

All of which were linked to our attempts to pressure Israel into either dividing up its land or surrendering part of its capital city of Jerusalem.

The world would laugh and call these coincidences, but I don't believe in coincidence. I believe only in God-incidences. God is sovereign. He is in control.

The Gaza Withdrawal

One of the most recent chaotic events in Israel was the forced withdrawal of all Jews from Gaza in the summer of 2005. It began on August 7th and continued through the 22nd, as nearly 9,000 Israelis were uprooted from their land and homes.

Many had been in the area for as long as 35 years. Their withdrawal was made at the insistence of the U.S. government as part of the appeasement policy of "trading land for peace."

It was a heart-wrenching event to watch women and children manhandled, synagogues violated, torah scrolls desecrated, houses bulldozed, graves dug up, and farms destroyed. Entire Jewish communities were forcibly removed from land which God has given to the Jewish people as an everlasting possession (Psalm 105:8-11).

The economic impact on the Israeli economy was overwhelming. The farms in Gaza represented 70% of Israel's organic produce, 60% of the nation's exported herbs, 15% of its total agricultural exports, 60% of its exported cherry tomato crop, and $120 million of its flower exports.

And while this travesty was taking place, Secretary of State Condoleezza Rice began applying more pressure with the following statement: "Everyone empathizes with what the Israelis are facing . . . but it cannot be Gaza only."[12]

The Supernatural Response

The withdrawal from Gaza ended on August 22, 2005, and on the very next day, the government of Bermuda announced that a tropical depression had formed off its coast. Dubbed "Katrina," the storm quickly developed into the most powerful hurricane in modern history. It slammed into New Orleans and the Mississippi coast four days later on the 27th. The hurricane disrupted 25% of our crude oil production and destroyed our nation's largest port (the 5th largest in the world in terms of tonnage).

I think it is interesting to note that the hurricane hit just three days before New Orleans — which often refers to itself proudly as "Sin City USA" — was scheduled to host an ungodly event that had come to be called "The Gay Mardi Gras." The theme that year was to be "Jazz and Jezebels." The previous year the event drew 125,000 revelers who proudly flaunted their perversion publicly in a parade that featured the bizarre. Incredibly, this event is sponsored by a group that has named itself "Southern Decadence."

New Orleans is known for its occult practices, particularly voodoo. The city is also infamous for its high murder rate and its rampant political corruption.

Nonetheless, I did not believe the storm was meant primarily as a judgment upon the city of New Orleans. Rather, I saw it as a judgment on our entire nation for our mistreatment of Israel. The consequences of the storm were national in scope. It resulted in higher fuel prices which led to higher prices for all goods. It disrupted indefinitely the flow of goods into and out of our country. It resulted in a significant increase in our national debt. It shamed us before the world as we mishandled the aftermath. And it has deeply scarred the Bush Administration.

The Impact of Theology

Speaking of President Bush, many wondered at that time why such a committed Evangelical Christian would put such inordinate pressure on Israel. Many people asked, "Why doesn't President Bush see the prophetic significance of end time Israel?" I put that question to Bill Koenig when I interviewed him on television. His response was very illuminating.[13]

Koenig pointed out that President Bush was raised in the Episcopal Church and in recent years had attended the Methodist Church. Although there are pastors in both of these churches who recognize the prophetic significance of modern Israel, the vast majority of the spiritual leaders in both churches (and especially those on the national level) believe in Replacement Theology. This is the theology that says God washed His hands of the Jewish people in the First Century and replaced Israel with the Church. They therefore see no prophetic significance to the re-establishment of Israel.

Koenig stated that within the Bush Administration the President is not the only victim of this erroneous theology. He is surrounded by godly people who have also grown up spiritually in Replacement churches. So, even though these people may respect the Judaic roots of their faith, they have no appreciation for the prophetic significance of modern day Israel.

The Message of Katrina

I believe the message of Katrina and similar natural disasters is that God is on His throne. He is in control. He cannot be mocked. He will not tolerate the division of His Holy Land. Nor will He tolerate gross immorality that mocks everything that is moral and decent.

God loves our nation. He has blessed us more than any other nation. His Word says that to those to whom much is given, much is expected (Luke 12:47-48). His Word also says He disciplines those whom He loves (Hebrews 12:7).

Another thing His Word makes clear is that when He sends discipline, the fundamental purpose is never to punish. Instead, the purpose is to call us to repentance so that we might be saved. Here's how the prophet Isaiah expressed it: "When the earth experiences Your judgments, the inhabitants of the world learn righteousness" (Isaiah 26:9b).

A Personal Experience

I know the truth of this statement first-hand. In May of 1953 when I was 15 years old, an F5 tornado hit my home-town of Waco, Texas. To this day it is the most deadly tornado in Texas history. It killed 114 people and injured 597. It ripped through the center of the downtown area and leveled five story buildings with ease. When it was over, the city looked like it had been hit with an atomic bomb.

For three months thereafter, the churches of Waco were packed with standing room only crowds as people sought to cope with the tragedy. People were forced to think about eternity. But gradually the pain subsided, people returned to their old ways, and church attendance fell off.

Our God is truly a God of amazing grace. Even when He pours out His wrath, He does so hoping that it will provoke repentance so that people can be saved.

Attempts to Respond Spiritually

With regard to Hurricane Katrina, the Governor of Louisiana, Kathleen Blanco, called for a statewide day of prayer: "As we face the devastation wrought by Katrina, as we search for those in need, as we comfort those in pain, and as we begin the long task of rebuilding, we turn to God for strength, hope, and comfort."[14]

Noble words. But notice, there was no call to repentance.

In like manner, President Bush called for a national day of prayer. He asked the nation to pray for the victims and to reach out to them in compassion. Again, noble words, but no expression of repentance.[15]

New Orleans City Council President Oliver Thomas came the closest of all public officials in recognizing that Katrina had a spiritual message. Referring to Sodom and Gomorrah, he said, "Maybe God is cleansing us."[16]

But cleansing requires a response of repentance, something God is calling for from the whole nation, and not just the citizens of New Orleans.

The Proper Response

No public official in our nation has yet seen the spiritual implications of a disaster as clearly as did Abraham Lincoln when he evaluated the cause of the Civil War. In a proclamation dated March 30, 1863, the President called for "a national day of prayer and humiliation."

He began the proclamation by observing: "It is the duty of nations as well as men to own their dependence upon the overruling power of God, to confess their sins and transgressions, in humble sorrow, yet with assured hope that genuine repentance will lead to mercy and pardon."

The heart of the proclamation read as follows:[17]

> And, insomuch as we know that, by His divine law, nations like individuals are subjected to punishments and chastisements in this world, may we not justly fear that the awful calamity of civil war, which now desolates the land, may be but a punishment, inflicted upon us, for our presumptuous sins, to the needful end of our national reformation as a whole People?

> We have been the recipients of the choicest bounties of Heaven. We have been preserved, these many years, in peace and prosperity. We have grown in numbers, wealth, and power, as no other nation has ever grown. But we have forgotten God. We have forgotten the gracious hand which preserved us in peace, and multiplied and enriched and strengthened us; and we have vainly imagined, in the deceitfulness of our hearts, that all these blessings were produced by some superior wisdom and virtue of our own.

> Intoxicated with unbroken success, we have become too self-sufficient to feel the necessity of redeeming and preserving grace, too proud to pray to the God that made us!

> It behooves us then, to humble ourselves before the offended Power, to confess our national sins, and to pray for clemency and forgiveness.

How we need such a proclamation today! The sad thing is that we have become so secular and pagan that if our President were to issue such a statement, members of Congress would probably bring impeachment proceedings against him for "violation of the separation of church and state."

End Time Signs of Nature

In Jesus' Olivet Discourse, delivered to His disciples on the Mount of Olives during the last week of His life, He specifically spoke of signs of nature to watch for in the end times.

Matthew recorded Him saying, ". . . and in various places there will be famines and earthquakes . . ." (Matthew 24:7). Luke's account of the same speech is more detailed. He quotes Jesus as saying (Luke 21:11,25):

> . . . there will be great earthquakes, and in various places plagues and famines; and there will be terrors and great signs from heaven . . .

> There will be signs in sun and moon and stars, and on the earth dismay among nations, in perplexity at the roaring of the sea and the waves . . .

We are witnessing all these things today worldwide. All sorts of weather calamities appear to be happening more frequently and causing greater damage — hurricanes, tornados, earthquakes, floods and forest fires.

Famine continues to rage throughout Africa, and other Third World areas. Plagues like AIDS and SARS continue to challenge and perplex medical science. A new danger is the return of diseases thought to be under control due to the development of antibiotic resistant strains.

And for the first time ever, we are living in a time when we can see incredible sights in outer space due to the Hubble Space Telescope, satellite probes which we have sent to other planets, and the landing of men on the moon.

The Birth Pangs Effect

With regard to natural calamities, some simply dismiss them in a cavalier manner by asking, "What else is new?" But as I have already mentioned, Jesus said that the signs in the end times would be like "birth pangs" (Matthew 24:8), meaning they will increase in frequency and intensity. And that is what has been happening.

Take earthquakes for example. In the decade of the 1980s, there were a total of 1,085 earthquakes worldwide that measured 6.0 or greater in magnitude. In the 1990s there were 1,492. In the first ten years of this century, the number jumped to 1,591. With regard to monster quakes of 8.0 or greater, in the 1980s there were 4; in the 1990s, 6; and in the first decade of this century, 13.[18]

There's a better way to look at natural disasters than to consider them by category, such as the frequency and intensity of tornadoes, for the number and intensity will go up and down from year to year, although showing an overall increase over a period of time. The best way to view natural disasters is to consider all of them grouped together. When you do that the statistics show that they are rapidly increasing, from an average of 300 per year in the 1980s, to 490 per year in the 1990s, to almost 1,000 per year in the first ten years of this century.[19]

Oddly, one of the reasons for considering natural disasters overall rather than individually is because one type of natural disaster can restrain other types.

Let me illustrate what I mean: In 2012 our nation experienced one of its worst droughts in modern history — with over 61% of America affected. Now, one side effect of that drought is that we experienced the lowest number of tornados in 60 years — after all, you can't have tornados without thunder storms. The same was true of flooding.

Conclusion

We as a nation have set our jaw against God. We are tempting Him to move us from judgment to destruction. Our God is so merciful. He is patiently sending us one wake-up call after another because He never pours out His wrath without warning.

Pray that our eyes will be opened and our hearts melted. Pray for a great national revival. Pray too for the hearts of our leaders to be opened to the significance of the natural disasters that are relentlessly afflicting our nation.

Pray that people around the world will be awakened to the reality that God is proclaiming from the heavens that His Son is about to return and that we are living on borrowed time.

The Growth of Apostasy 11
Watching the Church abandon the Faith.

The Bible clearly prophesies that the Church of the end times will be characterized by apostasy, meaning that people will depart from the fundamentals of the Christian faith. Jesus prophesied that "many will fall away" and "most people's love will grow cold" (Matthew 24:10, 12).

In like manner, the Apostle Paul forecast that in the end times there will be those who "fall away from the faith" because they will pay attention to "deceitful spirits and doctrines of demons" (1 Timothy 4:1). The Apostle Peter joined the chorus in 2 Peter 3:3-4 where he warned that in "the last days mockers will come with their mocking" of the promise that Jesus will return.

In the book of Revelation, chapters 2 and 3, the Apostle John records seven letters of Jesus to seven churches in the area of modern day Turkey. Among other things, these letters present a panoramic prophetic survey of the Church in history.

The last of the churches mentioned, the one that represents the Church of the end times, is the church at Laodicea. It is pictured as a church that is neither hot (healing) nor cold (refreshing), but rather is lukewarm or tepid (Revelation 3:15-16). In short, it is a church that is apathetic.

Jesus also pictures it as a worldly church enamored with its wealth (Revelation 3:17). The Lord is so dissatisfied with this church that He declares, "Because you are lukewarm, and

neither cold nor hot, I will vomit you out of My mouth"
(Revelation 3:16).

Clues from the Apostle Paul

Paul supplies us with some strong clues as to why the end
times Church will be weak, vacillating, and full of apostasy.
One of those clues can be found in 2 Timothy 4:3-4 which
says that "the time will come when they [Christians] will not
endure sound doctrine; but wanting to have their ears tickled,
they will accumulate for themselves teachers in accordance
to their own desires; and will turn away their ears from the
truth, and will turn aside to myths."

Another clue is located in Paul's famous prophecy about
end time society, the one in 2 Timothy 3. After describing in
graphic detail how society will fall apart in the end times,
Paul adds that the basic reason will be due to people "having
a form of godliness but denying its power" (2 Timothy 3:5).
There will be no lack of religion, says Paul, but people will
deny the true power that is able to transform society for the
good, producing peace, righteousness and justice.

What is that power? First and foremost it is the power of
the blood of Jesus — the very power that was blasphemed by
the regional minister who confronted me, claiming that
salvation can be achieved apart from Jesus. It is also the
power that comes from accepting the Bible as the infallible
Word of God. It is the power of believing in a Creator God
with whom all things are possible. And certainly it includes
a belief in the power of the Holy Spirit.

Today, these essential beliefs, which constitute the power
of Christianity, are being subjected to an unparalleled assault
from within the Church itself. The Bible says that in the end
times people will mock the promise of the Lord's return (2
Peter 3:3-4). What is so shocking is that a lot of the mockery
is coming from within the Church!

The Root of Apostasy

How have we reached this crisis point in the Church? It is rooted in what is called the German School of Higher Criticism which invaded this country big-time in the 1920s. According to the "scientific approach" of this school of skeptics, the Bible is not the revealed Word of God. Rather, it is Man's search for God, and therefore it is filled with myth, legend and superstition. They therefore approach the study of the Bible in the same manner as if it were the works of Shakespeare, not to find God's truth for Mankind, but for the purpose of analyzing it critically.

Today this viewpoint dominates the seminaries of America. The Bible is studied not to be believed and obeyed but to be analyzed, dissected, and criticized. The result is that the Scriptures have lost their authority.

Accordingly, so what difference does it make if the Scriptures condemn homosexuality? The critics argue that the relevant verses were written thousands of years ago by men who knew nothing about modern physiology or psychology, and who certainly did not understand that homosexuality is "natural" or genetically determined. They view Paul as simply a victim of his own prejudices, and they suspect that he was probably a homosexual himself who was simply engaged in self-loathing. Absurd? Yes, but not from the viewpoint of those Christian leaders who have rejected the authority of the Scriptures.

Early Apostate Leaders

One of the trail blazers of apostasy in the United States was Harry Emerson Fosdick (1878-1969).[1] He started out as a Baptist minister in 1903 after graduating from Union Theological Seminary. He quickly gravitated to the preaching of liberal theology based on a rejection of the Bible as the inerrant Word of God. He became pastor of the prestigious interdenominational Riverside Church in New York City, a church financed by John D. Rockefeller, Jr.

In the 1920s Fosdick began publicly attacking what he called "Fundamentalism." In the process, he repudiated the core beliefs of the Christian faith. He declared that belief in the virgin birth of Jesus was unnecessary. He argued that the inerrancy of the Scriptures was untenable. And He denounced the doctrine of the Second Coming of Jesus as "absurd." [2]

Fosdick's mantle was inherited by Norman Vincent Peale (1898-1993) who became the father of the positive-thinking, self-esteem gospel, which is a mixture of humanistic psychology, eastern religion, and Bible verses taken out of context. He taught that people — whether Christians or not — could tap into the power of God that he claimed resided within every person.[3]

In 1984 Peale appeared on the Phil Donahue program. Peale announced, "It's not necessary to be born-again. You have your way to God; I have mine. I found eternal peace in a Shinto shrine . . . I've been to Shinto shrines, and God is everywhere."

Phil Donahue was so shocked that he actually came to the defense of Christianity. "But you're a Christian minister," he retorted, "and you're suppose to tell me that Christ is the way and the truth and the life, aren't you?"

Peale replied, "Christ is one of the ways. God is everywhere."[4]

Look again at Peale's incredible statement: "It's not necessary to be born-again." What did Jesus say? "Truly, truly, I say to you, unless one is born-again, he cannot see the kingdom of God" (John 3:3). Who are we to believe?

Rick Miesel of Biblical Discernment Ministries points out that Peale was a thorough-going modern day exponent of the Fourth Century apostasy called Pelagianism — that is, he was "someone who believed that human nature is essentially good and that human beings are saved by developing their inner potential."[5]

Schuller's Apostate Gospel

Peale's leading disciple, Robert Schuller, has proceeded to outdo his teacher with the development of his "gospel of possibility thinking." In his book, *Self Esteem: The New Reformation,* Schuller states that the leaders of the Reformation Movement made a mistake in centering their theology around God instead of Man! [6]

Schuller teaches that the essence of Man's problem is low self-esteem.[7] The Bible teaches it is pride. Schuller says that when Jesus referred in John 7:38 to "rivers of living water" flowing out of believers, He was speaking of self-esteem.[8] The very next verse says He was speaking of the Holy Spirit. Schuller argues that sin is anything that robs us of our "divine dignity" (our "divine dignity"?).[9] The Bible says sin is rebellion against God.

Like Peale, Schuller redefines the meaning of being born-again. He says it means being "changed from a negative to a positive self-image — from inferiority to self-esteem, from fear to love, and from doubt to trust."[10] The Bible denies that being born-again is the result of changes in attitude. Rather, the Bible teaches that being born-again relates to coming alive spiritually through faith in Jesus as Lord and Savior. Being born-again is a spiritual phenomenon, not a psychological one. The experience will certainly result in changes in attitude, but it is not produced by them. Schuller confuses cause and effect.

In a long letter published in the October 5, 1984 issue of *Christianity Today,* Schuller made an incredible comment that has haunted him to this day:[11]

> I don't think anything has been done in the name of Christ and under the banner of Christianity that has proven more destructive to

human personality and, hence, counterproduc-
tive to the evangelism enterprise than the
often crude, uncouth, and unchristian strategy
of attempting to make people aware of their
lost and sinful condition.

As a writer for *Time* put it in an article in 1985, "For
Schuller, an acknowledgment of self-worth, more than a
confession of sinfulness, is the path to God."[12]

Further Evidence of Schuller's Apostasy

In an appearance on the Phil Donahue show in 1980,
Schuller tried, incredibly, to portray Jesus as an egotist!
Here's what he said:[13]

The Cross sanctifies the ego trip. That's very
significant. In other words, Jesus had an ego.
He said, "I, if I be lifted up, will draw all men
to me." Wow! What an ego trip He was on!

What blatant blasphemy — to accuse the One who was
the very essence of humility of being an egotist!

Schuller also seems to teach universalism — the apostate
idea that all men will ultimately be saved. In the summer
1986 issue of his magazine, *Possibilities,* Schuller declared,
"The Christ Spirit dwells in every human being whether the
person knows it or not."[14]

Schuller gave a speech at the headquarters of the Unity
Church in Lees Summit, Missouri and shared with their
pastors his church growth principles. This is a cult that denies
the deity of Jesus and which teaches reincarnation! He also
dedicated a new Unity Temple in Warren, Michigan, in spite
of warnings from a local Baptist pastor not to do so because
of the errors of this cult.[15]

In a speech honoring an Islamic spiritual leader named
Alfred Mohammed, Schuller said that if he were to come

back in 100 years and find his descendants to be Muslims, it wouldn't bother him! Dave Hunt responded to this statement by saying, "Apparently, Schuller is unconcerned that Islam denies that Jesus is God and that He died for our sins" and that Islam "offers a gospel of good works salvation, and death in jihad [holy war] as the only sure way to the Muslim 'heaven' where the faithful are rewarded with rivers of wine . . . and harems of beautiful women."[16]

Modern Day Apostate Leaders

In recent years, John Spong, former Episcopal Bishop of Newark, New Jersey, has become the poster boy of Christian apostasy. He has written books in which he denies the virgin birth, denies the miracles of Jesus, denies the resurrection, denies the Second Coming, and argues that Paul and Timothy were homosexual lovers. Bishop Spong has become so enamored with other religions that he has announced he will no longer witness to those caught up in the spiritual darkness of pagan faiths![17]

A similar spokesman for apostasy today is R. Kirby Godsey who served as President of Mercer University in Georgia for 27 years, from 1979 to 2006. During that time the school was affiliated with the Georgia Baptist Convention. Today, he continues with the school as Chancellor. He denies the inerrancy of the Bible, the unique power and authority of God, the validity of the gospel accounts of the life of Jesus, the efficacy of Jesus' atonement, and the uniqueness of Jesus as the only Savior.[18] In 2005 the Georgia Baptist Convention ended its affiliation with the school, but the school continues to claim to be Baptist in theology!

Another modern day apostate is the Reverend Bill Phipps who was elected moderator of the United Church of Canada in 1998. This is the largest Protestant group in that nation. At a press conference following his election, Phipps proceeded to deny all the fundamentals of the Christian faith, including the deity of Jesus. "I don't believe Jesus was God," he said. He added, "I don't believe Jesus is the only way to God. I don't believe He rose from the dead . . . I don't know whether these things happened. It's an irrelevant question."[19]

Note the gross apostasy in this man's statements. When he denies that Jesus is the only way to God, he makes Jesus out to be a liar, for Jesus said, "I am the way, the truth, and the life. No one comes to the Father except through Me" (John 14:6). When he states that the truth regarding the resurrection is "irrelevant," he makes a liar of the Apostle Paul who wrote, "If Christ is not risen, then our preaching is empty . . . And if Christ is not risen, your faith is futile . . ." (1 Corinthians 15:14, 17).

Of course, these men would probably respond to any quotation of Scripture with contempt, arguing that Scripture is unreliable. That's exactly what the so-called "scholars" of the highly-touted "Jesus Seminar" concluded.

An Apostate Seminar

The Jesus Seminar was formed in 1985 by Robert Funk, a New Testament scholar at the University of Montana. The avowed purpose of the Seminar was "to renew the quest for the historical Jesus."[20] The Seminar conducted this quest in a very unusual way. Meeting twice a year for six years, the group voted on each of the sayings of Jesus recorded in the Gospels. They voted by dropping colored beads in a box. A black bead meant Jesus definitely did not make the statement in question. A gray bead meant he did not say it, but it might have represented His thinking. A pink bead meant He probably said something like this, but not in the words recorded. A red bead meant He definitely made the statement.[21]

As you can see, the very approach expressed contempt for the veracity of the Gospel accounts. What a spectacle this must have been to the Lord as He watched these so-called scholars vote on passages from His Word. "Professing to be wise, they became fools" (Romans 1:22).

The Seminar began with 30 scholars. Over the following six years, more than 200 persons participated in the deliberation. But only 74 hung in to the end. Most of those who dropped out did so because of their disgust with the process and their discomfort with the fact that the radical fringe element of New Testament scholarship in America was disproportionately represented.[22]

The final product of the Seminar, published in 1993, was a blasphemy of God's Word. It was titled, *The Five Gospels.*[23] The title comes from the fact that the Seminar decided to grant the apocryphal Gospel of Thomas equal standing with the four traditional Gospels.

Only fifteen sayings of Jesus made it into *The Five Gospels* in red! In Matthew's account of the Lord's Prayer, the only words that made it in red were, "Our Father." Only one saying in the entire book of Mark was colored red. It is the statement of Jesus in Mark 12:17 where He told His disciples to "Render to Caesar the things that are Caesar's, and to God the things that are God's." Likewise, only one statement from the Gospel of John qualified for the red coloring: "A prophet has no honor in his own country" (John 4:44).

The chilling thing to keep in mind is that the men who produced this spiritual pornography are professors at seminaries across America. They are the ones who are training the current generation of pastors and teachers.

Recent Apostate Developments

- In 1988 the United Church of Canada became the first Christian denomination to authorize the ordination of Homosexuals.[24]

- In the 1990s the Methodist and Presbyterian hierarchies teamed up twice to sponsor what they called "Re-Imaging Conferences for Women." At both, women were called upon to repudiate the "male chauvinist God of the Scriptures" in favor of female goddesses like Sophia, Isis, Aphrodite, and the Irish goddess, Brigid.[25]

- In 1997 the Anglican Bishop of Jarrow in England — The Right Reverend Alan Smithson — announced that his sacrifice for the 40 days of Lent would be Bible reading! Instead, he said he was going to devote his time to reading the Koran in order to achieve "higher consciousness."[26]

- In 1999 the Archbishop of Canterbury, George Carey, publicly expressed doubt about the resurrection of Jesus: "I can tell you frankly that while we can be absolutely sure that Jesus lived and that He was certainly crucified on the Cross, we cannot with the same certainty say that we know he was raised by God from the dead."[27]

- In 2003 Gene Robinson became the first homosexual bishop of the Episcopal Church, after he had ditched his wife and family for his homosexual lover.[28]

- In 2005 The United Church of Christ became the first American Christian denomination to officially approve same-sex marriage.[29]

- In 2006 the Episcopal Church elected Katharine Jefferts Schori to a 9 year term as Presiding Bishop of the Church. When asked how she could reconcile her support of homosexuality with the Bible's condemnation of it she replied, "The Bible was written in a very different historical context by people asking different questions." In other words, the Bible is irrelevant! To no one's surprise she declared at the 2010 Episcopal Convocation that "There are many roads to God."[30]

- In 2010 The Claremont School of Theology in California, affiliated with the United Methodist Church, announced that it was going to start offering training programs for Muslim Imams and Jewish Rabbis, with the hope of later adding similar clergy programs for Hindus and Buddhists.[31] (After all, if there are many roads to God, what difference does it make which road you take?)

- In 2010 Thomas Nelson Publishers, the world's largest publisher of English language Bibles, announced the publication of *The Remnant Study Bible*, which was advertised on their website as: "The last study Bible you will ever need." What is so distinctive about it? It features the study notes of Ellen G. White, a false prophet whose writings led to the founding of the Seventh Day Adventists.[32]

- In 2011 Adela Yarbro Collins, Buckingham Professor of New Testament Criticism and Interpretation at Yale University, declared that any Jew who has led a good life need not worry about being thrown into the lake of fire at the end of time. She then went even further to state that all people would be judged on the basis of their works and that "those whose names will be erased from the book of life are not those whose beliefs are inadequate. Rather, they are those whose works are not 'full' or 'complete' in the sight of God."[33]

Apostasy Among Evangelicals

These examples of apostasy I have cited thus far are bad enough, but what is more shocking is the apostasy that is currently rampaging among those who claim to be Evangelicals. Consider, for example, the Emergent Church Movement. The leaders among this growing group of churches claim to be Evangelicals, but they are thoroughly post-modern in their thinking, denying the existence of absolute truth and questioning, if not denying the fundamentals of the Christian faith.

Here's what one of their leaders, Brian McLaren, had to say about the abominable *DaVinci Code* book: "I don't think The Da Vinci Code has more harmful ideas in it than the Left Behind novels."[34] And when asked to define his theology, he stated: "I am a missional, evangelical, post/protestant, liberal/ conservative, mystical/poetic, biblical, charismatic/contemplative, fundamentalist/calvinist, anabaptist/anglican, methodist, catholic, green, incarnational, depressed-yet-hopeful, emergent, unfinished Christian."[35] In other words, he is all things to all people because he considers doctrine to be irrelevant.

Another spokesman for the Emergent Church Movement is Rob Bell, pastor of Mars Hill Church in Grand Rapids, Michigan. In his book, *Velvet Elvis*, sub-titled, *Repainting the Christian Faith*, he states, "God is bigger than any religion. God is bigger than any worldview. God is bigger than the Christian faith."[36] Which happens to be one of the mantras of those who believe there are many roads to God.

One of the themes of Bell's book is his low view of Scripture, as illustrated by this statement: ". . . part of the problem [is] continually insisting that one of the absolutes of the Christian faith must be a belief that 'scripture alone' is our guide. It sounds nice, but it is not true . . . When people say that all we need is the Bible, it is simply not true."[37]

And consider his interpretation of one of Jesus' most famous statements: "When Jesus said, 'No one comes to the Father except through Me,' He was saying that His way, His words, His life is our connection to how things truly are at the deepest level of existence."[38] No, what He was really saying was "No one comes to the Father except through Me" (John 14:6).

In one of his newest books, *Love Wins*, Bell reveals that he has become a universalist, believing that all people will ultimately be saved.[39] Although he believes some people will go to Hell, he pictures Hell as a purifying place where people will receive a second chance. He summarizes his position in the preface of his book in the following words:[40]

> . . . A staggering number of people have
> been taught that a select few Christians will
> spend forever in a peaceful, joyous place
> called heaven, while the rest of humanity
> spends forever in torment and punishment
> in hell with no chance of anything better ...
> This is misguided and toxic and ultimately
> subverts the contagious spread of Jesus'
> message of love, peace, forgiveness, and
> joy. . .

Bell reveals the fundamental reason for his apostasy
when he states: "We have to listen to what our inner voice is
saying."[41] Sounds like Oprah or Shirley MacLaine!

Christianity Today Magazine

Another confusing voice among Evangelicals is the
magazine, *Christianity Today*. This is a magazine established
by Billy Graham in 1956. At the time, he said the purpose of
the magazine was "to plant the evangelical flag in the
middle-of-the-road, taking a conservative theological position."[42]

But over the years the magazine has strayed from the
conservative theological path. It has consistently taken a
liberal approach to social issues, it has incorporated Catholic
writers as contributing editors, and it has touted Replacement
Theology with regard to Israel and the Jews.

In the July 2010 issue, the managing editor, Mark Galli,
wrote an editorial that clearly revealed how far the magazine
has veered from its Evangelical roots. It was an article about
the nature of God, and believe it or not, it was titled "The
Divine Drama Queen."[43] The article is so blasphemous, that
I hesitate to quote it, but I feel I must in order to illustrate
how strong the stream of apostasy is that is running through
the Evangelical Movement today. So, hold on to your seat!

I like a tranquil, even-keeled, self-controlled God. A God who doesn't fly off the handle at the least provocation. A God who lives one step above the fray. A God who has that British stiff upper lip even when disaster is looming.

When I read my Bible though, I keep running into a different God, and I'm not pleased. This God says he "hates" sin. Well, He usually yells it. Read the prophets. It's just one harangue after another, all in loud decibels. And when the shouting is over, then comes the pouting . . .

This God is like the volatile Italian woman who, upon discovering her husband's unfaithfulness, yells and throws dishes, refuses to sleep in the same bed, and doesn't speak to him for 40 days and 40 nights . . .

We may think this a crude depiction, except that Jesus – God with us — seems to suffer the same emotional imbalance. He rants about Pharisees and Scribes — or "snakes" and "hypocrites," as He calls them . . . This God knows nothing about being a non-anxious presence. This is a very anxious God indeed.

I'd rather have a God who takes sin in stride. Why can't He relax and recognize that to err is human. I mean, you don't find us flawed humans freaking out about one another's sins. You don't see us wrathful, indignant, and pouting. Why can't God almighty just chill out and realize we're just human?

Can you believe such nonsense was expressed by a so-called Evangelical? What he is saying is, "Why can't God be more like us?" It reminds me of the famous line from the musical, *My Fair Lady* — "Why can't a woman be more like a man?"

Conclusion

There is only one basic defense against the apostasy that is epidemic in the Church today, and that is knowledge of God's Word. Unfortunately, public opinion polls prove that the average professing Christian today is biblically illiterate, and that conclusion applies also to those who consider themselves to be "born-again Evangelicals."[44]

Too many of our churches have surrendered the preaching of the Bible to the proclamation of pop-psychology in an effort to keep from offending anyone, when the reality is that people need to be lovingly confronted with their sins and then pointed to faith in Jesus as their only hope. And they also need to be taught how to test everything by the standard of God's Word, as the Bereans did with the teachings of the Apostle Paul (Acts17:10-11).

The gross apostasy that characterizes the Church today, together with its frightening increase in such a short time, is strong evidence that we are truly living in the season of the Lord's return. And that means we are living on borrowed time.

The Outpouring of the Holy Spirit 12

Reaching the world for Christ.

One hundred years ago, as the 20th Century began, the Holy Spirit was not alive and well in the Church. Christendom was in bondage to the theology of Deism which held that miracles had ceased, all aspects of the supernatural (such as angels and demons) had been laid to rest, and that God was a grand old man in the sky, best identified as "The Great I Was."

A Deceptive Doctrine

The Church had been deceived into adopting a theological argument which had the effect of stifling and quenching the Holy Spirit. The argument was based on a statement in 1 Corinthians 13:10 — "... when the perfect comes, the partial [interpreted as spiritual gifts like tongues] will be done away." It was argued that the "perfect" was the completion of the perfect, inerrant Word of God. Thus, it was argued, all supernatural gifts of the Spirit, as well as other manifestations of the supernatural, ended with the completion of the New Testament canon around 95 AD.

To this was added the argument that gifts of the Spirit could only be passed along to others by the Apostles through the laying on of hands. Therefore, when the last Apostle died (John in about 100 AD), the gifts ceased.

Flawed Arguments

The arguments were so neat. But they were full of holes. For one thing, they flew in the face of experience. Throughout Church history, there is abundant evidence of spiritual gifts being experienced on the part of the small minority who continued to believe in them. There had also been major outbreaks of the supernatural, as in the camp meetings on the American frontier in the early 1800s.

The argument revolving around 1 Corinthians 13:10 was faulty because it denied the contextual meaning of the word "perfect." In context, the word refers to the return of Jesus. This is made clear in verse 12: "For now we see in a mirror dimly, but then [when the perfect comes] face to face; now I know in part, but then I shall know fully . . ." The argument also overlooked the clear teaching of 1 Corinthians 1:7 that all the gifts of the Spirit will continue to be operative until Jesus returns: ". . . you are not lacking in any gift, awaiting eagerly the revelation of our Lord Jesus Christ."

Finally, the argument about the Apostles passing the gifts along to others was a sham because it attempted to convert the gifts of the Spirit into gifts of the Apostles. The Apostles may have been able to lay their hands on people and pray for them to receive certain gifts, but the gifts came from the Holy Spirit, not from the Apostles. Furthermore, every believer receives at least one supernatural gift of the Spirit at the time of his or her salvation (1 Corinthians 12:4-11). Paul put it this way: "To each one is given the manifestation of the Spirit for the common good" (1 Corinthians 12:7).

An Important Prophecy

The anti-Holy Spirit mentality of the Church in 1900 also ignored the clear teaching of Bible prophecy that the end times would be characterized by a great outpouring of God's Spirit. The key passage is found in Joel 2:28-29 —

It will come about after this
That I will pour out My Spirit on all mankind;
And your sons and daughters will prophesy,
Your old men will dream dreams,

Your young men will see visions.
Even on the male and female servants
I will pour out My Spirit in those days.

The Church's position in 1900 was that this prophecy had been fulfilled on the Day of Pentecost in about 30 AD and was no longer applicable. It was argued that the "last days" began at Pentecost when the Church was established (Hebrews 1:2 and 1 Peter 1:20). Also, it was pointed out that the Apostles themselves quoted this passage from Joel when they were asked what was going on as they began "to speak with other tongues" (Acts 2:4).

More Flawed Arguments

But again, these arguments about Joel 2:28-29 ignored the context of the passage. Note that the passage begins with the words, "It will come about after this . . ." After what? If you back up and read verses 18 through 27 you will see that the chapter is talking about the regathering and resettlement of the Jews in the land of Israel — something that did not occur until the 20th Century.

Also, the preceding verses speak of the outpouring of the Spirit symbolically as the "early and latter rain," referring to the two rainy seasons of Israel. In other words, the prophet was saying there will be two great outpourings of the Spirit. The "early rain" was at Pentecost and continued throughout the early history of the Church, as recorded in the book of Acts. The "latter rain" would immediately precede the return of the Messiah in judgment. This is made clear again by the passage itself in verses 30-31: "And I will display wonders in the sky and on the earth, blood, fire, and columns of smoke. The sun will be turned into darkness and the moon into blood, before the great and awesome day of the Lord comes." This is classic language about the Second Coming of the Messiah.

Yes, the Bible speaks of the Church Age as the last days: "He [Jesus] was foreknown before the foundation of the world, but has appeared in these last times for the sake of you" (1 Peter 1:20). But it also speaks of the Lord's return as the last days when it says Christians are being protected "by the power of God through faith for a salvation ready to be revealed in the last time . . . at the revelation of Jesus Christ" (1 Peter 1:5,7).

We have been in the "last times" since the Day of Pentecost. We are now in the latter part of the last times.

Joel 2:28-29 was fulfilled in part on the Day of Pentecost. Its total fulfillment was yet future in 1900, awaiting the "latter rain" that would be one of the signs of the Lord's soon return.

A Move of God

The Church had its jaw set against the Holy Spirit as the 20th Century began. But God was ready to burst on the scene with a great move of the Spirit in order to prepare the way for the return of His Son. That move began at a poverty-stricken school in Topeka, Kansas in January 1901 when a student named Agnes Ozman received the gift of tongues.[1] A year later a great Holy Spirit revival broke out in the English area of Wales, led by a remarkable young man named Evan Roberts.[2] Then, in 1906, the Spirit fell with great power on a home meeting in Los Angeles led by a black preacher named William J. Seymour.[3]

At Seymour's meeting, spiritual gifts were manifested, spectacular healings occurred, people were "slain in the Spirit," and sinners were saved. The meeting grew quickly and had to be moved to a dilapidated building on Azusa Street. It continued for almost four years, with preaching every day, three times a day![4]

The Azusa Street meeting gave birth to the Pentecostal Movement. The latter rain had begun. But it was only a sprinkle in terms of its impact on Christendom at large. The Pentecostals were written off as "Holy Rollers," and their religion was considered appropriate only for the superstitious and uneducated. But they were paving the way for a rediscovery of the Spirit by mainline Christianity.

The Latter Rain

The latter rain did not become a downpour until after the regathering of the Jewish people to the land of Israel (1900-1945) and the re-establishment of the state (May 14, 1948). Then, just as Joel had prophesied, the heavens opened and the downpour began — first, with the anointing of Oral Robert's ministry in 1948 followed by a similar anointing for the ministry of Billy Graham in 1949, and then with the emergence of the Charismatic Movement in the 1960s.

Today, much of Christendom is caught up in the Third Wave Movement that grew out of the Charismatic Movement in the 1970s and 80s. It is made up of churches that fully recognize the ministry of the Holy Spirit, including the significance of Spirit-led worship, the continuing validity of spiritual gifts, the reality of spiritual warfare, and the importance of a Spirit-filled life in winning that warfare. However, unlike the Pentecostals and Charismatics, the Third Wave Movement does not put an emphasis on the gift of tongues as the sign of having been baptized in the Spirit.

Confusion About the Spirit

The 20th Century has been the century of the rediscovery of the Holy Spirit. Yet, widespread ignorance and confusion about the Holy Spirit still characterizes the Church. A 1997 poll by the Barna Research Group showed that only 40% of Americans believe in the existence of the Holy Spirit (as opposed to 90% who believe in the existence of God). But what was even more stunning was the response of "born-again Christians." More than 5 out of 10 born-again Christians (55%) agreed that the Holy Spirit is a symbol of God's presence or power but not a living entity![5] It appears that Christians have been brainwashed into believing that the Holy

Spirit is an impersonal power like "The Force" in Star Wars.

Why is there so much continuing confusion about the Spirit? I think it relates in part to the self-effacing role of the Spirit. As we will see, one of the primary roles of the Spirit is to point people to Jesus as Savior and Lord. He does not draw attention to Himself. He works behind the scenes. Another factor relates to the many symbols that are used of the Spirit in Scripture — things like wind, rain, and fire. These symbols seem to communicate an impersonal force.

Our Creator God has been revealed to us as our Father. That is a concept we can grasp. Jesus took on a human body and lived among us. We have biographies of Him by eye witnesses. But for most people, the Holy Spirit is a shadowy entity difficult to grasp. Trying to get hold of the concept for many is like trying to nail jello to a wall.

The Identity of the Spirit

So, let's look for a moment at the identity of the Holy Spirit. The first thing you need to keep in mind is that the Spirit is never referred to as an "it." The Spirit is not an inanimate object. The Spirit is not, for example, the Bible, as some contend. The Spirit is intimately related to the Bible because it was the Spirit who inspired the biblical writers (2 Timothy 3:16), but the Bible is the "sword of the Spirit," not the Spirit Himself (Ephesians 6:17). The Spirit works through the Bible to draw people to Jesus, although the work of the Spirit is not confined to the testimony of the Scriptures. The Spirit can witness directly to our spirits (Romans 8:16).

The Holy Spirit is a person. The Spirit is always referred to directly in the Scriptures as "He." Referring to the Spirit, Jesus told His disciples that when He left, He would send a "Helper." ("Paracletos" in Greek, meaning a helper or intercessor.) Jesus added, "And He, when He comes, will convict the world concerning sin, and righteousness, and judgment" (John 16:7-8). To Jesus, the Holy Spirit was "He" not "it."

The Bible says the Holy Spirit can be lied to (Acts 5:3-4). It also says the Holy Spirit can be quenched (1 Thessalonians 5:19) and grieved (Ephesians 4:30). These are characteristics of a personality. You cannot lie to a chair, or quench a wall, or grieve a light fixture.

The Holy Spirit is the supernatural presence of God in the world today. Paul put it this way: "The Lord is the Spirit" (2 Corinthians 3:17). Luke stated that the Holy Spirit is "the Spirit of Jesus" (Acts 16:6-7). Peter equated the Holy Spirit with God the Father when he told Ananias and Sapphira that they had lied to the Holy Spirit (Acts 5:3) and then added, "You have not lied to men but to God" (Acts 5:4). Remember that old axiom in geometry: "Things equal to the same thing are equal to each other."

The Holy Spirit is one of the three persons who constitute the One God. That's the reason we are told to be baptized "in the name of the Father and the Son and the Holy Spirit" (Matthew 28:19). As such He is co-equal to Jesus and the Father, but He plays a different role.

The Work of the Spirit

This brings us to the work of the Spirit. The Holy Spirit has two roles — one toward the unbeliever and another within the believer. With regard to the unbeliever, the Holy Spirit is the Father's Evangelist. With regard to the believer, He is the Father's Potter. Let's consider these two roles in detail.

Jesus summarized the work of the Spirit regarding unbelievers. He said that the Holy Spirit would "convict the world concerning sin, and righteousness, and judgment" (John 16:8). Specifically, the Spirit convicts unbelievers of their sinfulness, impresses upon them the righteousness of Jesus, and points them to the judgment of Satan (John

16:9-11). The Bible makes it clear that no person can come to Jesus apart from the testimony of the Holy Spirit. Jesus put it this way: "No one can come to Me, unless the Father who sent Me draws him" (John 6:44). And how does the Father draw unbelievers to Jesus? He does so through the Holy Spirit who bears witness of Jesus as the Father's only begotten Son (John 15:26 and 1 John 5:7).

When a person responds to the witness of the Spirit by accepting Jesus as Lord and Savior, he is "born-again" (John 3:3), and the Father gives that person a very special birthday present — the Holy Spirit! That's right, the Holy Spirit ceases to be on the outside drawing the person to Jesus. Instead, He moves inside the person and takes up residence within him (Romans 8:9). And when He does so, His role changes.

The Spirit in the Believer

Within the believer, the Holy Spirit is the Father's Potter. His role is to shape each believer into the image of Jesus (Romans 8:29 and Galatians 4:19), a process which the Bible refers to as sanctification (Romans 6:22 and 2 Thessalonians 2:13). The Spirit does this by first of all gifting us. Each person, when he or she is born-again, is given at least one gift of the Spirit, and sometimes more than one (1 Corinthians 12:4-11). And if we are good stewards of our gifts, using them to advance the Lord's kingdom, we may be given additional gifts during our spiritual walk with the Lord.

The Spirit also accomplishes His work of sanctification by guiding us (Romans 8:14), comforting us (Acts 9:31), strengthening us (Philippians 4:13 and 1 John 4:4), praying for us (Romans 8:26-27), encouraging us (Romans 15:5), defending us (Luke 12:11-12), and illuminating us as we study the Word (1 John 2:27).

The work of sanctification is life long. It continues until we die or we are raptured to meet the Lord in the sky. The Holy Spirit wants to fine tune us into the image of Jesus because the Father is interested in nothing less than perfection in our lives (James 1:4 and 1 Peter 1:13-16). Yes, He is a God of grace who will accept us in all our imperfections, but He desires that we be perfected (Matthew 5:48).

Think of it this way — when a child takes his first step, his father rejoices. But no father is going to be satisfied with that one step. He will not be satisfied until the child can walk and then run without falling. For this reason, Christians are commanded to "be filled with the Spirit" (Ephesians 5:18).

Prophetic Fulfillment

The end time pouring out of the Spirit that began in the 20th Century and which continues to this day has resulted in an unparalleled advancement of the Gospel around the world, just as Jesus prophesied in Matthew 24:14 when He said, "This gospel of the kingdom shall be preached in the whole world for a witness to all the nations, and then the end will come."

Oral Roberts was a pioneer televangelist, attracting a vast viewership. He began broadcasting his revivals by television in 1954. His television ministry continued with "The Abundant Life" program, which was reaching 80% of the United States by 1957. Through the years, he conducted more than 300 crusades on six continents, and personally laid hands in prayer on more than 2 million people.[6]

Billy Graham's ministry reached even more people. It is estimated that his ministry proclaimed the Gospel to more people than all the rest of the evangelists put together who lived and preached before the 20th Century began. This, of course, was due to modern technology.[7]

For example, consider the impact of a series of sermons that Graham delivered in Puerto Rico in March of 1995. They were broadcast by satellite radio and television to 175 countries across 29 time zones in more than 150 languages.[8]

Other Manifestations

In addition to the rediscovery of the Holy Spirit, the resurfacing of spiritual gifts, and the anointing of the ministries of Graham and Roberts, the end time pouring out of God's Spirit has been manifested in other ways, such as the translation of the Scriptures into many languages, the re-emergence of Messianic Judaism, and the revival of the type of praise worship that characterized the times of King David. Important too is the understanding of prophecies that have never been understood before.

Translations of the Scriptures

Regarding the Scriptures, there was an explosion of translations during the second half of the 20th Century, due mainly to the introduction of computers. Since 1942, the Wycliffe Global Alliance of Bible translators (100 organizations in 60 nations) has produced 830 complete New Testament translations and 35 complete Bibles, potentially impacting around 214 million people speaking 799 languages.[9]

In November 2012, Wycliffe presented statistics that said that Scripture existed in 2,798 languages out of the 6,877 languages currently known to be in use in the world. There are currently 518 languages with a full Bible translation. At least 4.9 billion people (70% of the world's population) have access to a full Bible translation in their first language.[10]

A further 595 million (8.5% of the world's population), representing 1,275 languages, have at least the New Testament in their first language. Also, 1,005 languages (almost 20% of the world's population) have at least one portion of scripture (one or more books) available in their first language. By September 2012, personnel from participating Bible translation organizations were involved in 2,075 active language programs, most of them for tribal groups of 100 thousand or less people.[11]

Messianic Judaism

Another amazing manifestation of the end time pouring out of God's Spirit can be found in the revival of Messianic Judaism.

The very first church was founded in Jerusalem nearly 2,000 years ago when 3,000 people responded to the first gospel sermon that was preached by Peter (Acts 2:14-41). It was a 100 percent Jewish church. And the person who soon emerged as the leader of the Jerusalem church was the Jewish brother of Jesus, named James.

Needless to say, these people did not shed their Jewishness overnight, nor did they build a church with a steeple and an organ. They continued to live as Jews, and they continued to practice the Jewish religion. What set them apart from other Jews was their conviction that they had found the promised Messiah.

The term "Christian" was first applied to Gentile believers at the church in Antioch (Acts 11:26). Prior to that, Christianity was referred to as "the Way" (Acts 9:2), its adherents were called "Nazarenes" (Acts 24:5), and it was considered to be a sect of Judaism.

Over the next 200 years the Church became increasingly Gentile in membership and nature. Greek thought became dominant over the Hebrew worldview, impacting theology, worship, and church practices. The historical record clearly reveals that Messianic Judaism came under attack from both Jews and Christians, and by the 5th Century it was dead.[12] The Church had become Gentilized, and it had become virulently anti-Semitic, dismissing the Jews as having no hope because of their sin of deicide.

What irony! The First Century Messianic Jewish Church had graciously accepted Gentile converts without requiring that they adopt a Jewish lifestyle. Two hundred years later the

Gentile Church was condemning Jews and demanding that Jewish converts give up their lifestyle and become Gentiles.

For the next 1,600 years there were Jewish converts from time to time (often forced to convert), but there was no meaningful outreach to the Jews. The Church became captive to Replacement Theology. Church leaders argued that God had washed His hands of the Jews when they rejected Jesus. The Church had replaced Israel and had inherited the promises and blessings of the Jews. God had no purpose left for the Jews. They were a people without hope, doomed to wander the nations and be persecuted wherever they went.[13]

When the Six Day War began in June of 1967 there was not a single Messianic congregation on planet earth. With the supernatural victory of Israel in that war came a pouring out of the Spirit on young Jews worldwide. They suddenly realized that the hand of God was upon the new state of Israel. Many were driven to the Scriptures where they discovered Bible prophecy and their Messiah, and those who put their faith in Yeshua desired a new way of expressing their Christian faith in a more Jewish style.

The result was the establishment of the first Messianic congregation in Cincinnati, Ohio in 1970. Since that time, the Messianic Movement has spread worldwide, and today there are more than 200,000 Messianic Jews in the United States and over one million worldwide.[14]

Looking back now on the exciting days in the late 1960s and early 1970s, it appears that God was orchestrating a spiritual renewal among Jews worldwide to produce a Jewish first fruits in anticipation of the great harvest of Jewish souls that the Bible says will take place at the end of the Tribulation (Zechariah 12:10).

Messianic Judaism is bringing a great harvest of Jewish souls into the Kingdom. It is reminding the Church of its Jewish roots. It is helping to counter anti-Semitism. It is providing insight into the biblical context of the Christian faith. It is bringing new life to Christian worship. And the movement stands as a clear sign that we are living in the season of the Lord's return.

Jesus Himself said He would not return until the Jewish people are willing to cry out, "Blessed is He who comes in the name of the Lord" (Matthew 23:39). Messianic Judaism, through its proclamation of the Gospel to the Jewish people, is planting the seeds in Jewish hearts that will one day produce the salvation of a great remnant.

The Revival of Davidic Worship

Another manifestation of the outpouring of the Holy Spirit in these end times can be found in the revival of Davidic praise worship, with its hand-clapping, flag-waving, dancing, shouting and praise singing. This revival is prophesied in Amos 9:11-12 where it states that the "tabernacle of David" will be raised up in the end times.

Most Christian have heard of the Tabernacle of Moses, the nomadic temple that the Jews used while wandering in the wilderness, and the temple they continued to use for 400 years after they got settled in their promised land. During that time, it was located in the central highlands in a city called Shiloh.

But few Christians seem to have heard of the Tabernacle of David. It came into being after the Ark of the Covenant was stolen by the Philistines and the Tabernacle at Shiloh was destroyed (1 Samuel 4:1-11 and Jeremiah 7:12).

When plagues afflicted the Philistines every where they took the Ark, they decided to send it back to Israel on an ox cart. It finally came to rest eight miles west of Jerusalem in a town called Kiriath-jearim where it stayed for approximately 70 years (20 years under Samuel's judgeship, 40 years under Saul's kingship, and almost 10 years into David's kingship).

Meanwhile, the Tabernacle of Moses was reconstructed and moved to Nob for a while (1 Samuel 21:1) and then on to Gibeon (about ten miles northwest of Jerusalem) where it remained until the Temple of Solomon was built (2 Chronicles 1:3).

Now note something very important. During this 70 year period of transition between the Judges and the Kings, there was no Shekinah Glory in the tabernacle of Moses located at Gibeon. The Holy of Holies was empty. The priests continued to minister at the tabernacle, offering daily sacrifices, but it was all dead ritual, for the glory had departed.

The astounding thing is that the Ark was located in a farmhouse situated only about five miles from Gibeon. It would have been very easy to restore the Ark to the Tabernacle of Moses, but no one cared enough to do so. The Ark was ignored, and it became a symbol of Israel's apostasy.

Saul did not have a heart for the Lord, so he ignored the estrangement of the Ark from its proper resting place. But when David became king, he was determined to correct this situation, for he was a man after God's own heart (1 Samuel 13:14). David had to wait seven and a half years until he became king of all Israel (he was king of only Judah during his first years in power — see 2 Samuel 5:5).

David was determined to bring God back into the heart of his nation, and he recognized the symbolic significance of the Ark in accomplishing this purpose. He was so determined to provide a proper resting place for the Ark that it became the top priority of his kingship. In this regard, we are told in Psalm 132 that when David became king of all of Israel, he "swore to the Lord" that he would not sleep in a bed until he could provide a proper "dwelling place for the Mighty One of Jacob" (Psalm 132:1-5).

The amazing thing is that David brought the Ark to Jerusalem rather than returning it to the Holy of Holies in the

Tabernacle of Moses at Gibeon. David pitched a tent in Jerusalem (probably on a slope of Mt. Moriah), placed the Ark inside, and instituted a whole new concept of praise worship. Instruments of worship were introduced. Special psalms of praise were written and sung. And, incredibly, special priests were appointed to minister music before the ark continually (1 Chronicles 16:6,37) — whereas, before, only the High Priest had been allowed to minister before the Ark once a year in the Tabernacle of Moses.

David's revolution in worship was very radical. There was no singing or celebration at the Tabernacle of Moses. The worship there was one of solemn ritual focused on sacrifices. The only joy that had ever been evidenced in the worship of the Israelites had occurred spontaneously, as when Miriam danced with a tambourine and rejoiced over the destruction of Pharaoh and his army (Exodus 15).

The Psalms make it clear that the praise worship inaugurated by David was a worship of great joy that was characterized by hand clapping (Psalm 47:1), shouting (Psalm 47:1), singing (Psalm 47:6-7), dancing (Psalm 149:3), hand waving (Psalm 134:2), and the display of banners (Psalm 20:5). The worshipers were encouraged to praise God with every form of musical instrument, from the gentle lyre to the "loud crashing cymbals" (Psalm 150:3,5).

But why? Why did David so radically change the worship of Israel? We are told in 2 Chronicles 29:25 that he did so in response to commands of God given to him through the prophets Nathan and Gad. But why didn't the Lord simply tell David to put the Ark back in the Holy of Holies in Gibeon? Why did God tell him to revolutionize the worship of Israel?

The Bible does not tell us why. We can only guess. My guess is that God wanted to give David a prophetic glimpse of the glorious Church Age to come when animal sacrifices would cease, worshipers would have direct access to God, and worshipers would come before the Lord in rejoicing with a sacrifice of praise.

I think there was also another reason. I believe the Lord wanted to give the Church a model for Spirit-filled worship.

For one generation (about 30 years under David and 12 years into Solomon's reign), two tabernacles existed in Israel. In Gibeon there was the dead, liturgical worship that characterized the Tabernacle of Moses. In Jerusalem, there was the lively, spontaneous worship that characterized the Tabernacle of David. The worship in Gibeon was the performance of ritualistic symbolism. The worship in Zion was the experience of the presence of God. At Gibeon, the priests offered the sacrifice of animals. At Zion, the offering was the sacrifice of praise: "Come before Him with joyful singing . . . Enter His gates with thanksgiving and His courts with praise" (Psalm 100:2,4).

The Tabernacle of David served as a joyous bridge between the spiritual deadness that had come to characterize the Tabernacle of Moses and the Spirit-filled glory that would characterize the Temple of Solomon.

In like manner, since the re-establishment of the nation of Israel in 1948, God has been raising up the Tabernacle of David again to serve as a joyous bridge of transition between the dead worship of mainline Christendom and the glorious worship that will characterize the Millennial Temple of Jesus Christ. God wants His Son to return on a cloud of praise.

Appropriately, God began to focus His revival of the Tabernacle of David in Jerusalem in the early 1980s. It occurred when the International Christian Embassy decided to host a celebration of the Feast of Tabernacles. Zechariah 14 says that during the millennial reign of Jesus the nations will send representatives to Jerusalem each year to celebrate this feast and that any nation that fails to do so will not receive rain. The Embassy decided it would be appropriate for Gentiles to start rehearsing for the Millennium, so they sent out a call worldwide for Christians to come to Jerusalem to celebrate the feast and to show their support of Israel.

The Embassy also decided to give an emphasis to Davidic praise worship which was springing up all over the world at that time through a sovereign move of the Holy Spirit. They brought together Christendom's best practitioners of celebratory worship.

The result was an explosion of Davidic worship all over the world as the thousands of Christians who came to Jerusalem took what they had experienced back home with them in their hearts and on videos. The Embassy's celebration has continued to this day, with 4,000 to 6,000 Christians attending annually from every continent.

In fulfillment of prophecy, renewal in worship is sweeping Christendom worldwide. It is a move of the Spirit, and it is a mark of the end times. It is a sign of the soon return of Jesus.

Understanding End Time Prophecies

Another spiritual sign of the end times is the understanding of prophecies that have never been understood before. God told the prophet Daniel that this would happen in the end times.

Daniel complained to God that He had given him prophecies that he did not understand. God responded by telling Daniel that they were not for him to understand because they related to "the end time" (Daniel 12:8-9). Their understanding would have to await historical and technological developments.

That time of understanding arrived in 1970 when Hal Lindsey published his book, *The Late Great Planet Earth*.[15] It became an instant best seller and remained so for ten years! It hit a nerve because it used historical and technological developments to explain prophecies that had never been understood before. Let's take an in-depth look in the next chapter at this important sign that we are living on borrowed time.

The Impact of Change   13

Understanding baffling prophecies through historical and technological developments.

Whenever I present an overview of the signs of the times that point to the soon return of Jesus, I am often confronted by someone — often a professing Christian — who will say, "Come on David, these signs you are talking about have always existed in one degree or another, so what else is new?"

They will then proceed to point out that there have always been wars and rumors of war, there have always been natural calamities, and throughout history Christians have always been persecuted. Then comes the inevitable challenge: "Show me something really new and unique that clearly points to our day and time as the season of the Lord's return."

The challenge is understandable, but it is not entirely legitimate. That's because Jesus said the end time signs would be like "birth pangs" (Matthew 24:8). In other words, the signs would increase in frequency and intensity as the time draws near for Jesus to return. There would be more earthquakes, and more intense ones. Wars would be more frequent and more horrible in their degree of devastation. And that, of course, is exactly what began happening in the 20th Century. All the signs have been increasing exponentially in both frequency and intensity.

But still, it is legitimate to ask if there are any signs that are truly unique to our day and time — signs that have never existed before. Are there new signs that clearly point to this period of history as the time of the Lord's return? The answer is yes.

A Key Prophecy

A verse that immediately comes to mind in this regard is found in Daniel 12. Daniel was given many prophecies by the Lord. Those relating to his day and time he clearly understood. He even seemed to understand prophecies that the Lord gave him relating to distant times, such as the succession of Gentile empires that would ultimately lead to the establishment of the Roman Empire. But when it came to prophecies about the end times — the period leading up to the Lord's return as King of kings and Lord of lords — Daniel did not understand what was revealed to him.

He wrestled mightily with the prophecies and finally cried out to the Lord in despair. "I have heard," he said, "but I do not understand! What do these events mean?" (Daniel 12:8). The Lord, in effect, responded by saying, "Cool it, Daniel, because it is not for you to understand!" The Lord's actual words were: "Go your way, Daniel, for these words are concealed and sealed up until the end time" (Daniel 12:9). It was Daniel's responsibility to deliver the prophecies, not understand them.

Note that Daniel was told the prophecies would not be understood "until the end time." In fact, in the very next verse the Lord told Daniel that at the proper time "those who have insight will understand" (Daniel 12:10).

Accordingly, there are many end time prophecies that have never been understood until now, either because their understanding depended on historical events or because they were dependent upon technological developments. The fact that these prophecies have become understandable in recent years for the first time ever is proof positive that we are living in the end times. Let's look at some examples from the book of Revelation.

Revelation Examples

1) The Tribulation Slaughter — Revelation 6 says that the Tribulation will begin with a series of judgments that will result in the death of one-fourth of Mankind. The world's population is approaching 7 billion. If one billion are taken out in the Rapture, that means that one-fourth of 6 billion, or 1½ billion people will die in the initial judgments, reducing the world's population to 4.5 billion. The next series of judgments, recorded in Revelation 8 and 9, will kill another third of Mankind. One-third of 4.5 billion is another 1½ billion. Thus, in the first 3½ years of the Tribulation, a total of 3 billion people will die. That's half the population of the world!

Is this possible apart from the use of nuclear weapons? Only if it is a supernatural intervention of God. But God normally works through natural processes.

The unparalleled carnage of the Tribulation seems to me to point to nuclear weapons. Revelation 8 speaks of one-third of the earth being burned and one-third of the seas being polluted (Revelation 8:7-8). Later in the Tribulation, near the end, we are told that people will suffer from "loathsome and malignant sores" (Revelation 16:2). That sounds like one of the effects of radiation poisoning.

The advent of nuclear weapons makes possible for the first time the overwhelming Tribulation carnage portrayed in Revelation. I think nuclear power was what Jesus referred to in His Olivet discourse when He said that the end times will be characterized by "men fainting from fear and the expectation of the things which are coming upon the world; *for the powers of the heavens will be shaken"* (Luke 21:26, emphasis added).

The prophecies concerning the Tribulation carnage have clearly depended upon a major technological breakthrough for their understanding. We are living in the time of that breakthrough.

2) The Army of 200 Million — Chapters 9 and 16 of Revelation state that an army of 200 million soldiers will march "from the east" toward Israel. Daniel 9 indicates that this will be an army representing nations in revolt against the Antichrist.

Demographers estimate that the total population of the world at the time the Apostle John wrote Revelation (95 AD) was only 200 million. How could an army that size march out of the east? It made no sense. In fact, it took 1,650 years for the world's population to double to 400 million! At the beginning of the 20th Century the total world population was only 1.6 billion, still too small for an army of 200 million to march from the east.

But the 20th Century witnessed an exponential increase in population. The population count is now at almost 7 billion, and just one country to the east of Israel — namely, China — could field an army of 200 million.

Here we have a clear example of a prophecy about the end times that could never be understood apart from historical developments.

3) The Two Witnesses — Revelation 11 reveals that two great witnesses of God will preach in the city of Jerusalem during the first 3½ years of the Tribulation. Then, in the middle of that terrible period, the Antichrist will kill them.

We are further told that their dead bodies will lie in the streets of Jerusalem for 3½ days and that all the people of the world will look upon them. How could that be? Prior to 1957 that prophecy was not understandable in natural terms. There was just no way that all the people of the world could look upon two dead bodies in the streets of Jerusalem.

All that changed on October 4, 1957 when the Russians sent up the first satellite, called Sputnik. Today, our planet has many man-made satellites circling it, making possible all sorts of instantaneous communication.

When those two prophets lie dead in the streets of Jerusalem, all someone will have to do is point a TV camera at them, send the signal up to a satellite, and all the world will be able to look upon them. Once again, modern technology has made an ancient prophecy understandable for the first time.

4) The Nation of Israel — Revelation 12 focuses on the nation of Israel. It makes clear that in the middle of the Tribulation, Satan will motivate and empower the Antichrist to annihilate the Jewish state and its people. A remnant of the Jews will flee into the "wilderness" where they will be supernaturally protected by the Lord (Revelation 12:14).

At the time the book of Revelation was written, Jerusalem had already been destroyed by the Romans and the worldwide distribution of the Jews had begun. Until the 20th Century, there was never any prospect that the nation of Israel would ever exist again. There were, of course, prophetic scholars who pointed to the many promises in Scripture that say the Jews will be regathered in the end times and the nation of Israel will be reestablished once more. But people laughed at these scholars and wrote them off as "dreamers" who were out of touch with reality.

Then, on May 14, 1948 the "dream" came true. The independence of the nation of Israel was proclaimed, and the Jewish state came back into existence for the first time in almost 2,000 years.

All the end time prophecies of the Hebrew Scriptures make it clear that the Lord will return when the Jews are back in the land (Ezekiel 37) and back in their capital city of Jerusalem (Zechariah 12). Jesus emphasized these two events in

His teaching. He pointed to the re-establishment of the state in His fig tree parable (Matthew 24:32-35), and He stressed the importance of the re-occupation of Jerusalem in His Olivet discourse (Luke 21:24). He stated point blank that when Jerusalem is no longer under Gentile control, all the end time events would take place. Jerusalem ceased to be under Gentile control on June 7, 1967.

The central piece of the end time world political puzzle is now in place for the first time.

5) The Image of the Beast — Revelation 13 says that the Antichrist's religious leader, the False Prophet, will make an image of the Antichrist that will appear to come alive and speak. This trickery will amaze most of the world's population and will cause many of them to give their allegiance to the Antichrist.

What is the explanation of this event? Many have concluded that Satan will empower the False Prophet to give the image life. But Satan does not have the power to create life. Satan is a liar and a deceiver.

So, again, how can the False Prophet give an image life? I don't see any way for him to do it apart from modern technology. The illusion can be created through the use of modern robotics.

In 1967 I took my family to Disneyland. We went into a theater where we saw a man who looked exactly like Abraham Lincoln get up out of his chair in stage center, walk to the edge of the stage, grab the lapels of his jacket, and proceed to quote the Gettysburg Address. When he finished, a lady behind me exclaimed, "Wasn't he a good actor!" He was not an actor. The "actor" was a robot. That was over 40 years ago. Think what could be done today with the advances that have since occurred in computer technology, robotics and holograms.

6) The Mark of the Beast — Another prophecy in Revelation 13 that is dependent on modern technology is the famous one that states the Antichrist will control the world's economy by requiring people to bear his mark or name on their hand or forehead in order to buy or sell anything.

Again, how could this be possible before the invention of laser and computer technology?

The Uniqueness of our Age

After reviewing the prophecies listed above, I don't think we need any handwriting on the wall to indicate to us that we are living in a unique age. Historical developments and technological inventions are making it possible for us to understand many end time prophecies for the first time.

Nor is the list above an exhaustive one. I could name many other signs unique to our day and time — such as the reunification of Europe, the exponential increase in travel and knowledge, and the preaching of the Gospel to the whole world.

Even the phenomenal success of Hal Lindsay's book, *The Late Great Planet Earth,* is a unique sign of the times. Keep in mind that this book was the number one best seller in the world, with the sole exception of the Bible, for ten consecutive years, from 1970 to 1980 (as authenticated by *Time Magazine*). What was it that the Lord told Daniel? "Seal it up to the end of time when those who have insight will understand."

The bottom line, my friends, is that we are living on borrowed time, because Jesus is coming soon!

The Accelerator Principle   14

Living in the age of birth pangs.

Have you noticed how almost everything in life seems to be accelerating? Knowledge has exploded. We are traveling faster and farther than ever before. Instant, world-wide communication has become common place. And the power at our disposal is mind boggling.

A Sign of the Times

The Bible teaches that this acceleration of life which we are experiencing will be a sign of the end times — a sign that will signal the soon return of the Lord. Consider Daniel 12:4. In this verse the Lord tells Daniel that one of the signs of the end times will be an acceleration of travel and knowledge. Here's how the verse reads in *The Living Bible* paraphrase: "Daniel, keep this prophecy a secret . . . Seal it up so that it will not be understood until the end times when travel and education shall be vastly increased."

The same concept of end time acceleration is found in the New Testament. Jesus spoke about it when He talked with His disciples about the signs of the end times that would herald His return (Matthew 24:5ff). He mentioned a great variety of signs — spiritual, natural, societal and world politi-cal — and then He said these signs would be like "birth pangs" (Matthew 24:8).

Any mother knows that as the birth of a baby approaches, the birth pangs increase two ways. They increase in frequency and intensity. Thus, Jesus was saying that the closer we get to the time of His return, the more frequent and intense the signs will become. There will be more earthquakes and more intense ones. Likewise things like famine, pestilence and war will increase in frequency and intensity.

The Mathematical Concept

In mathematics this acceleration is called an "exponential curve." This term comes from what happens when rapid growth is plotted on a chart. When graphing the growth or decline of anything, the rate of change becomes exponential when it starts increasing or decreasing so fast that the plot line becomes vertical.

Now, the point is that the Bible indicates that the exponential curve will be one of the signs of the end times, and my thesis is that we are living in the midst of the exponential curve. Therefore, we are living in the end times.

Examples of the Curve

The 20th Century was the century of the exponential curve. Let's consider some examples.

1 **Population** — Demographers estimate that the population of the world at the time of Jesus was only 200 million.[1] It took 1,650 years for the world's population to double! But thereafter it began to double very rapidly because the Industrial Revolution produced modern medicine, which, in turn, reduced infant mortality rates and increased longevity. As the statistics below indicate, the rate of doubling has now reached exponential proportions.[2]

Time of Christ		200 million
1650	1650 years	400 million
1850	200 years	1.3 billion
1950	100 years	2.5 billion
1980	30 years	4.5 billion
2000	20 years	6.0 billion

Again, the key to this phenomenal growth has been modern medicine. Most people do not realize how modern our medicine really is and how radically it has affected our lives. For example, the life expectancy in the United States in 1900 was 47 years.[3] At the end of the 20th Century it was 77 years. That's an increase of 30 years in life expectancy over a one hundred year period of time!

Many health problems today that are considered minor were deadly as recently as the 19th Century — appendicitis being a good example. During the horrible Flu Pandemic of World War I (1918-1919) over 40 million people died because the flu usually developed into pneumonia, and there was no guaranteed way for treating pneumonia. That's because the very first anti-biotic, penicillin, was not discovered until 1928.[4]

Life before the 20th Century was short and brutal — often filled with suffering. If you are 35 years of age or older, you have lived longer than the vast majority of humanity.[5] Here's an amazing fact: Two-thirds of all the people who have lived to the age of 65 are alive today![6]

2 Knowledge — Another area that is increasing exponentially is knowledge. The prophet Daniel was specifically told that knowledge would vastly increase in the end times (Daniel 12:4), and it has. In fact, we have become so overwhelmed with the flood of new information that it is difficult to find wisdom anymore, because wisdom comes from reflection on knowledge.

It is estimated that 80% of all scientists who have ever lived are alive today. Every minute they add 2,000 pages to man's scientific knowledge, and the scientific material they produce every 24 hours would take one person five years to read.[7] The scientific journals cannot publish all the academic articles that are being written. Many have to limit the articles to one page abstracts, and even then most articles are rejected for a lack of space.

Consider how rapidly knowledge is increasing:[8]

From Jesus to 1500 it doubled	(1,500 years)
1500 to 1750 it doubled again	(250 years)
1750 to 1900 it doubled again	(150 years)
1900 to 1950 it doubled again	(50 years)

Today, knowledge is doubling every 12 months!

That means encyclopedias are out of date before they can be printed, which is the reason they are no longer printed. Britannica stopped printing in 2010 after 244 years.[9]

I read recently where a research organization had determined that one Sunday issue of the New York Times contains more information than the normal person in the 19th Century was exposed to in a lifetime![10]

The most amazing thing to me in the area of information is the World Wide Web that can be accessed through the Internet. Using it, I can access the documents of the Vatican in seconds, and then in a matter of moments, I can go to the Israel Museum in Jerusalem, or I can dart back to the Library of Congress in Washington, D.C. In short, I can access information all over the world without ever leaving my office.

3 **Transportation** — In 1900 the major means of transportation was what it had always been throughout history — namely, walking and riding a horse. The bicycle had been invented, and the steam engine had been applied to ships and trains. But steam powered transportation was too expensive for most people.

I have a photograph of 5th Avenue in New York City in 1905. The photo was taken from a tall building and shows the avenue for several city blocks. The only means of transportation visible is the horse-drawn carriage.

I have a similar photo that was taken in my home town of Waco, Texas in 1912. It shows the city square, and like the New York City photo, all that can be seen are horse-drawn wagons and carriages.

Today we have automobiles (usually two or more to a family!) and airplanes. We have bullet trains that travel 150 miles per hour and planes that travel faster than the speed of sound. And then, of course, there are rocket ships that take astronauts into orbit around the earth.

In 1866 Mark Twain traveled to the Holy Land. It took him three months to get there. Today, a group can get on a jet plane in New York and be in Tel Aviv in 13 hours (and most will complain about how long the trip took!).

During the 19th Century, the average number of miles traveled per year by a person in the United States was 500. Many lived and died and never got outside the county they were born in! By 1900 the average number of miles traveled per year by a person inside the United States had risen to 1,000. Today it is 25,000 miles per year, and many of us put twice that much mileage on an automobile in a year's time.[11]

4 **Communications** — At the beginning of the 20th Century the telegraph had sped up communications considerably, and the telephone had been invented. But the fundamental means which most people used to get information was still the newspaper.

Today our communication resources are overwhelming. We have telephones, radio and television. We have exotic devices like fax machines, pagers and cellular phones. And we can communicate worldwide through satellites.

I never cease to be amazed when I see someone use a credit card at an Arab shop in the Old City of Jerusalem. The shop may be nothing but a primitive hole in the wall, but over in some dark corner there will be a machine where the merchant can swipe the card. A few moments later he receives an authorization. During those few moments, the card number has been transmitted to Tel Aviv, from Tel Aviv to New York by satellite, from New York to the credit card processing center somewhere in the States, and then back to the Arab shop in Jerusalem!

I am equally amazed at the way I can sit down at a computer at my home or office and use the Internet to send a letter in seconds to almost any place in the world. In 1995 when I got on the Internet, there were only 16 million people using it. Three years later, in 1998, there were 150 million. Today there are 2.2 billion users worldwide![23]

Once again, we have the exponential curve.

5 **Computers** — Computer technology has contributed to the rapid acceleration of many aspects of life, and, of course, the exponential curve applies to the development of computers as well. Anyone who tries to stay on the cutting edge of what is new in computer equipment knows that it is a never-ending battle that requires a lot of money. Advances are so rapid that equipment is out of date within a few months.

In 1970 I was a professor at a college where we bought an IBM computer for $100,000. It operated off punch cards, it was so large that it filled a room, and it generated so much heat that we had to have the room equipped with additional air conditioning. The computer's memory was 64K!

Now, if you are not a computer buff, that may not mean much to you, but keep reading because I'm going to make it understandable; and in the process, I'm going to illustrate how rapidly computer technology has developed.

Ten years later in 1980, the ministry I established bought one of the first desktop computers made. It was a Tandy TRS 80, Model II. It cost $4,800 (equivalent to $12,500 today!).

When I turned it on, I was astounded by the first thing that appeared on the screen: "64K Memory." In ten years' time we had gone from a computer that weighed more than a ton to one that sat on a desk top, and the price had dropped 95%. But the memory was the same!

Ten years later in 1990, I went to Radio Shack and bought an electronic Rolodex small enough to fit into the palm of my hand. It cost $90. And when I turned it on, guess what? The first message that appeared on the screen was "64K Memory."

Today, you can purchase a computer with 4 gigs of memory and a 1 terabyte hard drive operating at 2.7 gigahertz for less than $500!

The exponential curve also applies to data storage units. The first floppy disk that we used in the TRS 80 was 8" in size. It held 300,000 bytes of information. A few years later the 5¼" disk appeared. It would hold 700,000 bytes. Then came the 3½" disk. Its capacity was 1.4 million bytes! The next hottest thing to come along was the CD Rom disk. I recently read an advertisement for a CD that contained 134,000 pages of theological documents — the equivalent of 1,400 pounds of books!

Today, my data storage device of choice is a tiny thumb drive or flash drive that holds 30 gigabytes!

6 **Military Power** — Throughout most of recorded history, the maximum power at man's disposal consisted of bows and arrows, spears, and catapults. Even at the beginning of the 20th Century, war was still primitive. World War I turned into a stagnant war of attrition because neither side had sufficient power to break out of the trenches.

Eighty years later, we had air power, armored power, nuclear weapons, and sophisticated bacteriological and chemical weapons. We have ICBM's that can deliver a nuclear payload halfway around the world. We have laser-guided missiles that can guide a bomb down a smoke stack hundreds of miles away. And we have nuclear submarines that can circle the globe without surfacing. Incredibly, just one of those subs today has more firepower than all the bombs dropped in World War II![13] It is no wonder the Bible says that in the end times "men will faint with fear" over the expectation of "the things which are coming upon the world" (Luke 21:26).

7 **Violence** — I don't think I have to emphasize that violence and lawlessness have been increasing. But it is hard to comprehend how rapid the increase was during the 20th Century.

It is estimated by experts that the number of people killed in all the wars fought from the time of Jesus until 1900 was 40 million. In the 20th Century 231 million people died in wars, making it a century of unparalleled carnage.[14]

There are currently a total of 38 wars or civil wars raging worldwide.[15] And then, of course, there has been the advent of international terrorism, resulting in the loss of tens of thousands of lives. In 2011 alone there were 10,283 terrorist attacks worldwide.[16]

Within the United States, violent crime increased 430% between 1960 and 2010. During the same period, the country's population increased only 67%.[17]

8 **Society** — The disintegration of society has multiplied in speed as violence, wickedness and immorality have increased exponentially. Jesus prophesied this would happen when He said that end time society would be like it was in the days of Noah (Matthew 24:37-39), when violence and immorality prevailed (Genesis 6:11).

Paul prophesied about the disintegration of society in 2 Timothy 3:1-5 where he wrote that in the end times people would be lovers of self, lovers of money, and lovers of pleasure. The love of self is Humanism, and it is the religion of the world today, masquerading under many different labels. The love of money is Materialism, and money is the god of these times. The love of pleasure is Hedonism, and that is the prevalent lifestyle of today.

But God cannot be mocked or deceived. When a society makes Humanism its religion, Materialism its god, and Hedonism its lifestyle, there is always a payoff, and that is Nihilism, or despair. And thus it is no accident that we see societies around the world wallowing in despair.

I have witnessed the exponential decaying of society with my own eyes. I was born in 1938. When I was born:

- Abortionists were sent to prison.

- Pregnancy out of wedlock was thought of as scandalous.

- Homosexuality was considered unnatural and immoral.

- Pornography was despised as a perversion.

- Marriage was sacred. Living together was taboo.

- Divorce was a disgrace.

- Homemaking was honored, and daycare was provided by mothers in their homes.

- Child abuse was unheard of.

- Ladies did not curse or smoke.

- "Damn" was considered flagrant language in a movie. (A 1992 film called, "Glengarry Glen Ross," had the "f-word" in it 138 times in 100 minutes!)[18]

I could go on and on about the many ways in which our society (and societies around the world) have decided to "call evil good and good evil" (Isaiah 5:20). But the most dramatic way I can think of to illustrate how rapid the deterioration of society has become in America is to consider the results of two polls concerning public school discipline problems, one taken in the 1940s and the other in the 1980s. Both were taken in the Fullerton, California School District. Consider the drastically different results (and weep!):

The Top Public School Discipline Problems

Mid-'40s	Mid-'80s
1) Talking	1) Drug Abuse
2) Chewing gum	2) Alcohol Abuse
3) Making noise	3) Pregnancy
4) Running in the halls	4) Suicide
5) Getting out of turn in line	5) Rape
6) Wearing improper clothing	6) Robbery
7) Not putting paper in wastebaskets	7) Assault

(Source: *Time Magazine,* February 1, 1988)

The disintegration of society has multiplied in speed as violence, wickedness and immorality have increased exponentially.

9 **Natural Disasters** — The Bible says that natural disasters will also be increasing exponentially in the end times, and that is exactly what is happening.

Consider these statistics for natural disasters within our nation between October 1991 and November 2004, a period of 13 years:[19]

9 of the 10 largest insurance events in US history.
5 of the costliest hurricanes in US history.
3 of the 4 largest tornado swarms in US history.

And all that was before Hurricane Katrina in 2005!

Putting together all types of natural disasters worldwide, you can see on the chart below how rapidly they are increasing, from an average of 300 per year in the 1980s to almost 1,000 in 2010.

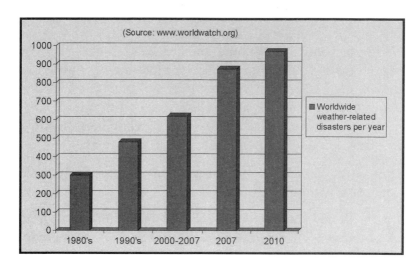

Incidentally, this is a better way of considering natural disasters, as opposed to plotting individual types of disasters. That's because one type of natural disaster can restrain another type.

Let me illustrate what I mean. During 2012 our nation experienced its worst drought in modern history, with over 61% of our nation affected.

One side effect of the drought is that we experienced the lowest number of tornados in 60 years. After all, you can't have tornados without thunderstorms. The drought also greatly reduced the amount of flooding.

10 **The Economy** — This brings us to a man-made disaster — namely the out of control spending that has come to characterize the modern welfare state. Accordingly, our national debt is on the exponential curve.

It took over 200 years for our nation's debt to reach one trillion dollars in 1980. Thirty years later, in 2010, it had soared to 14 trillion. In mid-2013, it was rapidly advancing toward 17 trillion. It is increasing at the rate of 150 million per hour. The interest alone is accumulating at the rate of 50 million an hour.[20]

A good way of illustrating the impact of this overwhelming debt is to consider how much it represents per person in the United States. At a Tea Party Rally in 2010, a little girl about 4 years old was seen wearing a sign that read: "I'm already $38,375 in debt, and I only own a doll house!" Since that time, our individual share has increased to $53,284.[21]

In short, our nation is bankrupt, and our economy could collapse any minute.

11 **World Evangelism** — Not all the exponential curves are bad. Modern technology has made it possible for the Gospel to be preached to billions of people through the use of such media as short wave radio, motion pictures, and satellite television.

And, again, this phenomenal development is a fulfillment of Bible prophecy. Jesus Himself said: "This gospel of the kingdom shall be preached in the whole world for a witness to all the nations and then the end shall come" (Matthew 24:14).

Consider translations of the Bible. In 1800 there were 71 in whole or in part. By 1930 that number had risen to 900. Today there are 2,798 with 1,900 in progress.[22]

Incidentally, those statistics are a little misleading because they leave the impression that many people still do not have a Bible in their language. The fact is that the existing translations cover all the major languages of the world, representing more than 90% of the world's population. The translations currently in progress are for tribal languages spoken by 100,000 or less people.

In March of 1995 Billy Graham broadcast a gospel message from Puerto Rico that was carried by 37 satellites to 175 countries and territories in a total of 150 different languages! Over 1.5 billion people viewed the program. It is estimated that more people heard that one sermon than had heard the Gospel since it was first proclaimed by the Apostle Peter 2,000 years ago![23]

With regard to world mission activity, I attended a mission conference in the mid-1990s where one of the key speakers told us that 70% of all mission work in history had been done since 1900, and 70% of that since 1945, and 70% of that since 1985 — all due, of course, to the implementation of modern technology.[24] The results have been overwhelming:

There were 10 million Christians in Africa in 1900.
Today: 516 million.[25]

There were 700 thousand Christians in China in 1949.
Today: 70 million.[26]

There were 50 thousand Evangelical Christians in Latin America in 1900.
Today: 60 million.[27]

And, according to Muslim sources, every day 16,000 Muslims convert to Christianity, for a total of 6 million per year![28]

Worldwide, the number of Christians has nearly quadrupled in the last 100 years, from about 600 million in 1910 to more than 2 billion in 2010, constituting one-third of the world's population.[29]

The conversion rate is on the exponential curve:[30]
    1800 100 per day
    1900 1,000 per day
    1950 4,000 per day
    1980 20,000 per day
    1990 86,000 per day
    1995 100,000 per day
    2010 175,000 per day

12 **World Politics** — The exponential curve also applies to world events. Habakkuk 1:5 is as relevant today as if it were written yesterday: "The Lord replied, 'Look, and be amazed! You will be astounded at what I am about to do! For I am going to do something in your own lifetime that you will have to see to believe.'"

I took a Sabbatical in 1987 and wrote a book called *Trusting God*. Seven years later, in 1994, I took another Sabbatical and completely rewrote that book. The exercise gave me an opportunity to reflect back over the seven years between the two Sabbaticals. I was astounded — even overwhelmed — by the rapid and stupendous nature of world events.

Who could have dreamed in 1987 that within the next seven years any of the following events would have occurred? —

- The tearing down of the Berlin Wall.

- The peaceful liberation of Eastern Europe from Communism.

- The collapse of the Soviet Union.

- The reunification of Germany.

- The resurgence of Islam and its emergence as the greatest threat to world peace.

- The sending of 500,000 American troops to the other side of the world to defend a country most Americans had never heard of (Kuwait).

- The handshake between Rabin and Arafat that has led to Israel surrendering portions of its heartland to the PLO.

In 1987 if you had predicted any of these developments, you would have been written off as "nuts." The rapidity of these events and their radical nature is breathtaking. They underscore the possibility of the impossible. And they certainly reveal that man is not in control.

The Significance of the Curve

So, what does all this mean to you and me? I would mention at least three things.

First, the exponential curve is proof positive that Bible prophecy is true. The Lord has told us what He is going to do in the end times, and we had better pay attention to what He has said.

Second, the fulfillment of prophecy related to the exponential curve shows that God is in control. Even when it appears that everything on this earth is out of control, we can be assured that God is orchestrating all the chaos to the ultimate triumph of His Son in history (Psalm 2).

Third, the exponential curve is very strong evidence that we are living on borrowed time. It points to the fact that Jesus is at the very gates of Heaven, waiting for the command of His Father to return.

A Warning and an Illustration

I want to conclude by issuing a strong warning against taking time for granted.

Many people are doing that today. They are saying, "I'm going to get serious about the Lord when I get out of school;" or "after I get a job;" or "after I'm established in my career;" or "after I get married;" or "after I get my children raised." Time is precious. There is very little left. Now is the time to get serious about the Lord.

Let me illustrate how critical the timing is by returning to the exponential curve. Suppose you put one bacterium in a jar, and assume it doubles every second. How many bacteria do you think would exist in the jar at the end of 30 seconds? The answer, incredibly, is 1,073,741,824. That's more than a billion in thirty seconds! That's the *ferocity* of the exponential curve.

Now, let's carry the illustration a step further. If at the end of 30 seconds the jar is half full, how much longer will it take for the jar to become full? The answer is one second (because it will double in the next second). That is the *suddenness* of the exponential curve.

That's what the Bible means when it says that people will be saying, "Peace and safety!" when "sudden destruction" will come upon them (1 Thessalonians 5:3).

A Call to Action

Are you taking time for granted? Don't do it. The Exponential Curve is just one of many signs God is giving us to warn of the soon return of His Son. The Bible says that the only reason Jesus has not returned is because God does not wish that any should perish. 2 Peter 3:9 says:

> The Lord is not slow about His promise, as some count slowness, but is patient toward you, not wishing for any to perish but for all to come to repentance.

In other words, the lovingkindness of God has restrained Him from sending His Son back to this earth. But that restraint is soon coming to an end for our God is a God of justice, and as such, He must deal with the sinful rebellion of this world.

The signs of the times are shouting from the heavens that Jesus is returning soon to pour out the wrath of God on those who have rejected His love and grace. Are you ready for His return? Have you placed your faith in Jesus as your Lord and Savior? Do you understand that God deals with sin in only one of two ways?

Consider John 3:36 — "He who believes in the Son has eternal life; but he who does not obey the Son shall not see life, but the wrath of God abides on him."

Are you under grace or wrath? God deals with sin in one of those two ways. It is a glorious thing to be under the grace of God. It is a dreadful thing to be subject to His wrath.

Do not turn a deaf ear to the signs of the times. The time to act is now. If you are not a Christian, then reach out in faith and receive Jesus as your Lord and Savior. If you have already done that, then commit your life to holiness and evangelism. You are living on borrowed time!

The Decay of Society   15
Watching the restoration of Noah's day.

One of the key signs of the end times that the Bible tells us to watch for is the deterioration of society. Jesus emphasized this sign in His Olivet Discourse when He stated that He would return at a time when society becomes like it was in "the days of Noah" (Matthew 24:37). If you take a look at Genesis 6 where Noah's society is described, you will see that its two fundamental characteristics were violence and immorality (Genesis 6:11).

The Apostle Paul also emphasized this sign in his writings. In 2 Timothy 3:1 he prophesied that the end time society would be one characterized by "perilous times" (KJV) or "terrible times" (NIV) or "difficult times" (NASB). He proceeded to describe the end time society as one where "men will be lovers of self" (Humanism), "lovers of money" (Materialism), and "lovers of pleasure" (Hedonism). The result will be a society engulfed in despair (Nihilism).

Worldwide today we are witnessing the fulfillment of these prophecies as societies "slouch toward Gomorrah."[1] As in the days of Noah, immorality and violence are reigning supreme. And that observation certainly applies to the United States.

Our Nation's Rejection of God

An outline of our course to depravity can be found in the writings of the Apostle Paul. In Romans chapter one he states that the road to destruction for a nation begins when its institutions decide to "suppress the truth in unrighteousness," an action that will ultimately lead to people worshiping the creation rather than the Creator (Romans 1:18,25).

The decade of the 1960s proved to be the turning point for America. But the cultural revolution against God that characterized that decade was rooted in developments that occurred early in the 20th Century. The two most influential were intellectual tides that swept into America from Europe. They arrived almost simultaneously.

One was Darwinism with its atheistic attack on the very concept of God. The origin and purpose of Man was called into question. Man was reduced to a mere animal, a product of chance with no particular purpose.

The other was the German School of Higher Criticism which challenged the Bible as the infallible revelation of God. The Bible was viewed instead as Man's search for God and was therefore considered to be full of myth, legend and superstition.

The Christian worldview suddenly came under attack from without and within the Church. The faith of many was shattered.

Embracing Moral Relativism

As the authority of God's Word was undermined, and Man's purpose became meaningless, moral relativism gradually took center stage. People began to challenge traditional concepts of right and wrong. As in the days of the Judges of Israel, people began to do what was right in their own eyes (Judges 21:25). They called it, "different strokes for different folks." Each man became a god unto himself, able to determine for himself his own values and ethics, if any. And anyone who would dare judge someone else's actions was declared "intolerant."

By the 1980s America had reached the point referred to in Judges 2:10 — we had produced a whole generation "who did not know the Lord . . ."

We had "suppressed the truth in unrighteousness" by banning prayer from public schools, prohibiting the posting of the Ten Commandments, and declaring that evolution was the only theory that could be taught about the origin of the universe.

Suddenly government was actively promoting all sorts of abominable activity such as gambling, abortion, and homosexuality. Eastern religions and mystical intellectual philosophies like the New Age Movement began to penetrate Christianity.

Earth Day became a national celebration. People gathered to worship "Mother Earth" rather than the Father God who created the earth. They joined hands and hummed to get synchronized with the rhythm of "Mother Earth." They further celebrated their new religion by hugging a tree or stroking a salmon.

Millions of people paid hundreds of dollars each to attend self-discovery seminars of various types. What they all had in common was the teaching that God resides in each of us, and that we must learn how to release our "god power."

A Pagan and Secular Society

By the 1990s, America had fulfilled Paul's prophecy in 2 Timothy 3:1-5. Humanism (the worship of Man) had become our national religion, Materialism (the love of money) was our god, and our national lifestyle had become one of Hedonism (the love of pleasure). The result, as prophesied, is that our society began wallowing in despair.

Today, our television news reports reflect in detail the society that Paul said would characterize the end times. The reports are full of stories about boastful, arrogant revilers who are ungrateful and unholy — as well as stories about rebellious children and reckless, conceited haters of good. And we are constantly bombarded with the opinions of those "professing to be wise" but who in reality are fools (Romans 1:22).

America, like the rest of the world, is thumbing its nose at God, and in the process we are begging for judgment, for God cannot be mocked (Galatians 6:7).

The fact of the matter is that America is finished. We as a nation have turned our back on God. We have kicked Him out of our schools and out of the public arena. We have declared Him to be off-limits.

Our only hope has been repentance. But instead, we have set our jaw against God, determined to go our own way and do our own thing.

This attitude was manifested in the incredible proclamation issued by President Bill Clinton in June of 2000 when he called for Americans to "celebrate" homosexuality. He declared June 2000 to be "Gay and Lesbian Pride Month."[2] I responded by sending him an email message in which I asked, "What will you ask us to 'celebrate' next? Will you proclaim Adultery Pride Month? What about a month honoring prostitutes or pedophiles?" President Obama resumed this practice of designating the month of June to celebrate sexual perversion, but he expanded it to include the LGBT community (lesbian, gay, bi-sexual and transgendered).

Our Rejection of God

We have given the boot to the very One who made us great and showered us with blessings. We are in the process of becoming a thoroughly secular and pagan nation. And in the process, we are courting the wrath of God.

- Since 1973 we have murdered our babies in their mothers' wombs at the rate of 4,000 per day, totaling nearly 60 million, and their blood cries out for vengeance.[3]

- We consume more than one-half of all the illegal drugs produced in the world, yet we constitute only 5% of the world's population.[4]

- We spend $2.8 billion dollars per year on Internet pornography, which is more than half the worldwide total of $4.9 billion.[5]

- Our rate of cohabiting partners has increased tenfold since 1960, totaling over 12 million unmarried partners today.[6]

- Our divorce rate is the highest of any nation in the world.[7]

- Forty percent of all our children are born to unmarried women.[8]

- We spend over $100 billion per year on gambling.[9]

- Our number one drug problem is alcohol, producing over 17.6 million adults who are alcoholics or who have alcohol problems.[10]

- Our nation has become a debt junkie, leading the world in both government debt and personal debt.[11]

- Blasphemy of God's name, His Word, and His Son has become commonplace in our media.[12]

- We are the moral polluter of planet earth through the distribution of our immoral, violent and blasphemous television programs and movies.

- We have forsaken the nation of Israel, demanding that they surrender their heartland and divide their capital city.

The Consequences of Rebellion

We have become a nation that calls good evil and evil good (Isaiah 5:20). And we are paying the price:

- Our schools have become arenas of deadly violence.

- Our prison population is increasing exponentially, from 500,000 in 1980 to over 2.5 million today. Over 7.2 million of our people are under some form of correctional supervision.[13]

- Over 1.5 million of our women are reported victims of domestic violence each year, and it is estimated that the majority of cases are never reported.[14]

- We are currently averaging over 3 million child abuse cases each year, involving 6 million children.[15]

- We experience more than 12 million crimes every year, more than any other nation in the world.[16]

- Teen violence has increased exponentially, with youngsters killing each other over tennis shoes.[17]

- Gangs are terrorizing our cities.

- Even the nicest of our neighborhoods are no longer safe, requiring us to protect our homes with security systems and weapons.

- Our money is becoming increasingly worthless.

- Our economy is being choked to death by a pile of debt that is beyond comprehension.

- Our major corporations and labor unions are in bondage to greed.

- Our society has become deeply divided, splintered among competing groups defined by racial, religious and economic factors.

- Our families are being destroyed by an epidemic of divorce.

- Our entertainment industry consists of vulgarians amusing barbarians.

- One of our fastest growing businesses is the pagan practice of tattooing and body piercing.

- Our universities and media outlets are controlled by radical leftists who hold God in contempt.

- Our federal government has become top-heavy with bureaucrats who are insensitive to taxpayers.

- Our politicians have become more concerned with power than service.

- All levels of government have become increasingly oppressive, seeking to regulate every aspect of our lives.

- Taxation has become confiscatory in nature.

- Our legal system has been hijacked by activists who desire to impose their will on the people, regardless of what the people desire.

- Our freedom of speech is being threatened by "hate crime" legislation.

- Our forms of sports are becoming increasingly violent, reminiscent of the gladiators of ancient Rome.

- Our society has become star-stuck, more interested in celebrities than people of integrity.

- Our churches are caught up in an epidemic of apostasy as they set aside the Word of God in an effort to cozy up to the world and gain its approval.

- We are experiencing one major natural disaster after another in unprecedented volume and ferocity.

- We have become afflicted with a plague of sexual perversion, producing an army of hard core militant homosexuals.

In summary, we are a people who have become desensitized to sin, and in the process, we have forgotten how to blush (Jeremiah 6:15).

Persecution and Alienation

Another negative characteristic of our society is that true Bible-believing Christians are being alienated from society and are being increasingly subjected to persecution. The speed at which this has happened in recent years is breathtaking.

Jim Garlow is a Nazarene minister who pastors the Skyline Church in La Mesa, California. He is considered to be an expert on Church history. In a recent presentation to the National Religious Broadcasters, Pastor Garlow presented a sweeping overview of the relationship between Bible-believing Christians and American society:[18]

1607 - 1833	— The Establishment (236 years)
1833 - 1918	— The Predominant Force (85 years)
1918 - 1968	— The Sub-dominant Force (50 years)
1968 - 1988	— A Sub-culture (20 years)
1988 - 1998	— A Counter Culture (10 years)
1998 - 2008	— An Antithetical Culture (10 years)
2008 - Present	— A Persecuted Culture

Cultural Christianity

An overwhelming majority of Americans (85%) claim to be Christians, but the evidence of Christianity in the lives of most of them is almost nil. They purchase lottery tickets, frequent R-rated movies, watch trash shows on TV, purchase pornography, idolize crude and vulgar musicians, frequent abortion clinics and compile a divorce rate that equals non-Christians.

They are what might be called "Cultural Christians" — born into a Christian family, raised going to church, but without any personal relationship with Jesus.

Another characteristic of Cultural Christians is that they rarely (if ever) read the Bible. This has resulted in gross biblical ignorance and the un-doing of doctrine.

Evangelical Christianity

Ignorance of God's Word has even become true of Evangelical Christians, the very people whose identity in the past was linked to their reliance on the Bible for their ultimate authority in all things.

Surveys by the Barna Group reveal that among those claiming to be Evangelicals today:[19]

19% are living with a partner outside of marriage.

37% do not believe the Bible to be totally accurate.

45% do not believe Jesus was sinless.

52% do not believe Satan is real.

57% do not believe Jesus is the only way to eternal life.

57% believe that good works play a part in gaining eternal life.

As you can see from these survey results, the term, Evangelical, has lost its meaning.

Christian Confusion

It is no wonder we have professing Christians voting for candidates who promote homosexuality, same-sex marriage, abortion, and casino gambling. Or professing Christians who vote out of greed for the candidate who offers to give them the most, regardless of the person's wretched lifestyle or beliefs about social and moral issues. Or professing Christians who vote on the basis of race or ethnicity, regardless of a candidate's viewpoints concerning vital moral issues.

Public opinion polls concerning the fundamental beliefs of Christianity consistently reveal that the number of true Bible-believing Christians in America today is less than 10%.[20] It's no wonder that during the past 50 years our society has secularized and paganized so rapidly.

We are a nation shaking its fist at God. We are literally crying out for God's judgment. God has been very patient with us, as He always is. Consider the words of the prophet Nahum:

> A jealous and avenging God is the LORD;
> The LORD is avenging and wrathful.
> The LORD takes vengeance on His adversaries,
> And He reserves wrath for His enemies.
> The LORD is slow to anger and great in power,
> And the LORD will by no means leave the
>   guilty unpunished. (Nahum 1:2-3a)

Yes, God has been patient, but His patience is wearing thin. He has sent prophetic voices to call us to repentance. When we turned a deaf ear, He began sending remedial judgments. But our faces have become harder than stone (Jeremiah 5:3). The result is that we are now wallowing in immorality, violence and greed.

The Steps to Destruction

The first chapter of Romans reveals how God deals with a rebellious nation. He will step back, lower the hedge of protection and allow evil to flourish. The first result of this action will be the outbreak of a sexual revolution which occurred in this nation in the 1960s (Romans 1:24-25).

If the nation refuses to repent, God will take a second step back, lower the hedge again, and a plague of homosexuality will be unleashed (Romans 1:26-27). That happened in our nation in the 1980s, and it accelerated in the 1990s.

If the nation continues in its sin with no sign of repentance, God will step back a third time, lower the hedge again, and the society will be delivered over to a "depraved mind" that will result in its destruction (Romans 1:28-32).

The time has come for God to deliver us over to a depraved mind — to deliver us from judgment to destruction. We have reached the point of no return, which is identified by the biblical prophets as the point where "the wound cannot be healed" (Jeremiah 30:12, Micah 1:9, and Nahum 3:19).

Our Prophetic Type

Only one other nation in history has been as blessed as ours, and that was ancient Judah. Like us, they rebelled against the God who had blessed them so richly. And as with us, God sent prophets to call them to repentance. When they refused, He hammered them with remedial judgments.

When they persisted in their rebellion, God delivered them from judgment to destruction, allowing the Babylonians to conquer them and take them away from their homeland into captivity.

The fate of Judah prompted two of the saddest verses in the Bible:

> The LORD, the God of their fathers, sent word to them again and again by His messengers, because He had compassion on His people and on His dwelling place; but they continually mocked the messengers of God, despised His words and scoffed at His prophets, until the wrath of the LORD arose against His people, until there was no remedy. (2 Chronicles 36:15-16)

We may experience a temporary revival, as ancient Judah did when the righteous king Josiah succeeded the monster king Manasseh (2 Chronicles 34-35). But when Josiah was killed, the nation plunged right back into spiritual darkness and soon ceased to exist (2 Chronicles 36). Evil had simply become too ingrained in the fabric of the nation.

Like ancient Judah, our fate is sealed. Our collapse will be just as sudden and overwhelming. Why should God treat us any differently? We can be assured that He will not. We are living on borrowed time.

Living on Borrowed Time

Part 4
Challenges to the Church
and Christians

Challenging the Church to get serious
about the Lord's return.

Jesus is about to return, and the Church at large seems to be oblivious to the fact.

In the Church today, Bible prophecy is neglected, abused or scorned. Most pastors simply ignore it as irrelevant or too controversial. Many abuse it by spiritualizing it to mean anything they please. Some just write it off as nonsensical gobbledygook.

Prophetic Irony

The irony is that all this is a fulfillment of end time Bible prophecy, pointing to the fact that we are truly living in the season of the Lord's return:

> Know this first of all, that in the last days mockers will come with their mocking, following after their own lusts, and saying, "Where is the promise of His coming? For ever since the fathers fell asleep, all continues just as it was from the beginning of creation." (2 Peter 3:3-4)

I used to think this prophecy referred to unbelievers — but they could care less about the return of Jesus. To them the whole concept is an absurd myth.

It is Christian leaders who are mocking and scoffing. Some are liberals who are Christians in name only. To them,

ction or evangelism, or a combina-
tion of the two, and that the Church will then rule over the
earth for a thousand years. At the end of this reign, the
Church will surrender the kingdom to Jesus who will trans-
port the Church to Heaven and burn up the earth.

Few concepts could be more unbiblical! The Bible makes
it clear that the vast majority of humanity will always reject
the Gospel (Matthew 7:13-14). And the Bible makes it
equally clear that as we approach the end of the Church Age,
society will grow increasingly evil rather than increasingly
righteous (Matthew 24:9-12, 36-39).

Furthermore, Postmillennialism is based upon the Hu-
manist assumption of inevitable progress which, in turn, is
based upon a belief in the essential goodness of Man. Again,
this is a very unbiblical concept. The Bible teaches that Man
is born with a sin nature that makes him inherently evil
(Jeremiah 17:9).

Man cannot elevate himself by his own effort. Nor can
Man be perfected by education or the revolution of society.
God will prove this during the upcoming millennial reign of
Jesus. During that time, all the world will be flooded with
peace, righteousness and justice. Yet, at the end, when Satan
is loosed, he will be able to lead a worldwide revolt against
Jesus.

Jesus' rule with a rod of iron (Psalm 2:8-9 and Revelation 2:26-27) may produce outward conformity, but inwardly, there will be boiling resentment that will explode into open rebellion. Man will not be transformed by life in a paradise on earth. And that's because people can only be truly transformed by the indwelling of the Holy Spirit that comes through faith in Jesus as Lord and Savior (2 Corinthians 3:17-18).

The Amillennial Viewpoint

The end time viewpoint that is held by the Catholic Church and the majority of Christian denominations today is Amillennialism. It is the strange concept that the Millennial reign of Jesus began at the Cross and continues to this day. Like the Postmillennial view, this view is based on a spiritualization of Scripture — which is a nice way of saying that it is based on an outright denial of what the Scriptures plainly state.

Logic alone is sufficient to destroy the Amillennial viewpoint. The Bible teaches that during the Millennium, the earth will be flooded with peace, righteousness and justice (Isaiah 11:3-9 and Micah 4:1-7). Can anyone truly argue with a straight face that such an atmosphere prevails today?

The Bible says that during the Millennium, Satan will be bound so that he can no longer deceive the nations of the world (Revelation 20:1-3). Is that a present reality? Of course not. All the nations of the world, without exception, are deceived and exist in a state of rebellion against God.

The Bible says six times in the book of Revelation that the Millennium will last 1,000 years (Revelation 20:2-7). Amillennialists say the Millennium began at the Cross and will continue indefinitely until the return of Jesus. Who is correct? The Bible or the Amillennialists?

The Premillennial Viewpoint

A literal reading of end times prophecies, seeking the plain sense meaning, will produce what is called the Premillennial viewpoint.

According to this view, society will disintegrate in the end times (2 Timothy 3:1-5), becoming as immoral and violent as in the days of Noah (Matthew 24:37-39). The Church will be taken out of the world in an event called the Rapture (1 Thessalonians 4:13-18), and then God will begin to pour out His wrath during a seven year period called the Tribulation (Revelation 6-18).

At the end of the Tribulation, Jesus will return (Revelation 19:11-16). A great remnant of the Jews will accept Him as their Messiah (Zechariah 12:10, Romans 9:27 and Romans11: 25-27). Jesus will regather these believing Jews to Israel (Deuteronomy 30:1-9) and establish them as the prime nation of the world (Zechariah 8:22-23).

Jesus will then begin His thousand year reign from Jerusalem during which time the earth will experience peace, righteousness and justice (Micah 4:1-7 and Revelation 20:4-6).

Replacement Theology

This clear meaning of the Scriptures has been rejected by the Church ever since 400 AD due to anti-Semitism. The Jews were classified as "Christ-killers," and the argument was made that God had "washed His hands of them." Further, it was argued that the Church had replaced Israel and had thus become the heir of the promises which God had given the Jews.

The wretched theology that developed from these unbiblical assumptions came to be known as Replacement Theology. It contends that the Church has replaced Israel and God has no further purpose for the Jews. Accordingly, the advocates of this theology argue that God's promise to the Jews of a future kingdom (Acts 1:1-9) has been annulled and has been transferred to the Church.

Paul's Refutation

Replacement Theology is thoroughly unbiblical, as any reading of Romans 9-11 will clearly prove. In these chapters Paul affirms the Old Testament prophecies that God will save a great remnant of the Jews in the end times (Romans 9:27), and He will fulfill for them all the promises that He has made to the Jewish people (Romans 11:36).

Paul specifically addresses the issue of Replacement Theology in two places in Romans. In the third chapter he asks this rhetorical question concerning the Jewish people: "If some did not believe, their unbelief will not nullify the faithfulness of God, will it?" For almost 1,600 years, ever since 400 AD, the Church has answered, "Yes!" But Paul answers his question in a directly opposite manner by declaring, "May it never be! Rather, let God be found true, though every man be found a liar . . ." (Romans 3:3-4).

In Romans 11, Paul addresses the issue again, once more using a rhetorical question: "I say then, God has not rejected His people, has He?" (Romans 11:1). And once again, the Church has always answered, "Yes!" But Paul responds by saying, "May it never be! . . . God has not rejected His people whom He foreknew" (Romans 3:1-2).

An Absolute Truth

Whether Church leaders like it or not, God has promised the Jews that one day the Messiah will establish a kingdom for them and through that kingdom He will reign over all the earth (Isaiah 2:1-4).

There is no excuse for the Church to be covetous of the promises God has made to the Jewish people. God has also made some marvelous promises to the Church. One, of course, is the Rapture. Another is the promise that we will reign with Jesus over all the Gentile nations of the earth (Daniel 7:13-14,18,27 and Revelation 2:26-27).

Getting Serious About Prophecy

It is time to stop playing games with God's Prophetic Word. There is too much at stake to simply say, "Every man to his own opinion."

Jesus is about to return. This Church Age is about to come to a screeching halt. The world is on the threshold of the most horrendous time in human history — the Great Tribulation — when God will pour out His wrath on this God-hating world, (Revelation 6-18) and one half of humanity and two-thirds of the Jews will be killed in a period of only seven years (Zechariah 13:7-9).

Yet, despite this impending horror, Church leaders are lulling people into believing that the return of Jesus is some far distant possibility that is a current "distraction" to Christian living. What garbage!

> The Word says the return of Jesus could occur at any moment (Matthew 24:36-44).
>
> The Word says that we are to live looking for the return of Jesus (Titus 2:11-14).
>
> The Word says that living with the expectation and hope of the Lord's return will produce holiness in our lives (1 John 3:2-3 and 1 Peter 1:13-16).
>
> The Word provides signs we are to watch for that will signal the season of the Lord's return (Hebrews 10:25 and Matthew 24:33).

Today, one would have to be spiritually blind to not discern the fact that the future has arrived. The ancient prophecies pointing to the season of the Lord's return are being fulfilled before our very eyes. The signs are literally shouting the Lord's soon return. And yet most Church leaders seem to be blind to the signs.

The Preservation and Regathering of the Jews

How, for example, can a person ignore the supernatural regathering of the Jewish people back to their homeland from the four corners of the earth? This regathering in unbelief is the most prolific prophecy in the Old Testament (See Isaiah 11:10-12 as an example). It is always pictured in an end time context (Ezekiel 36:22-38).

Jeremiah proclaims two times that when history is done, the Jewish people will look back and consider the current regathering to be a greater miracle than their deliverance from Egyptian captivity! (Jeremiah 16:14-15 and 23:7-8)

This regathering began in the late 1890s and continues to this day — from 40,000 Jews in Israel in 1900 to over 6 million today.

> No other people in history have been so widely scattered all over the world.

> No other people in history have been so hated and so systematically persecuted.

> No other people have been submitted to such an unspeakable atrocity as the Holocaust.

> No other people have been so devoid of hope.

Yet, God miraculously preserved them, as He said He would (Jeremiah 30:11, Jeremiah 31:35-37, Isaiah 49:14-16 and 2 Samuel 7:24). And He has regathered them, just as He said He would (Isaiah 11:10-12 and Ezekiel 36:22-24). But Christian leaders write-off these miracles of their preservation and regathering as an "accident of history" with "no prophetic significance." Incredible!

We are blessed to be the generation that is witnessing the fulfillment of these prophecies, and yet the average Christian seems unaware of them, and even worse, many who are aware of them have the unmitigated audacity to deny that they are a fulfillment of prophecy or that they have any spiritual significance.

Other End Time Signs

Twenty-five hundred years ago the prophet Daniel said that in the end times the last great Gentile empire — the Roman Empire — would be revived and that the Antichrist would rise out of it (Daniel 2:31-45). Is the revival of the Roman Empire today, in the form of the European Union, an accident of history?

The prophet Zechariah said that in the end times the nation of Israel would come back into existence and that all the nations of the world would come against it (Zechariah 12:1-3). Is the rebirth of the state of Israel in May of 1948 an accident? What about the way in which all the nations of the world are currently coming together against Israel over the issue of who will control Jerusalem?

The prophet Ezekiel said that in the end times all the Arab nations would attempt to take the land of Israel (Ezekiel 35-36). Are their attempts today an accident of history?

Jesus said we were to watch Jerusalem. He prophesied that the city would be destroyed and the Jews dispersed, but He also prophesied that in the end times the Jews would return and re-occupy the city (Luke 21:24). Was the re-occupation of the city of Jerusalem by the Jews in June of 1967 (for the first time in 1,897 years) an accident of history?

New Testament prophets warned that one of the foremost signs of the end times would be an epidemic of apostasy in the Church (2 Thessalonians 2:3, 1 Timothy 4:1, 2 Timothy 3:5 and 2 Timothy 4:1-4). Is the present gross apostasy we are experiencing today an accident of history?

Spiritual Blindness

What's the problem with the Church today? Why are so many Christians and their leaders ignoring the fact that Jesus is at the very gates of Heaven waiting for His Father's command to return? Why is the Church so spiritually blind? Why are so many pastors more focused on church growth than on sounding the alarm that Jesus is coming soon?

Again, the lackadaisical attitude that prevails about the Lord's imminent return is a fulfillment of end time prophecy:

> For the time will come when they will not endure sound doctrine; but wanting to have their ears tickled, they will accumulate for themselves teachers in accordance to their own desires, and will turn away their ears from the truth and will turn aside to myths (2 Timothy 4:3-4).

Satan's Deception

We have arrived at the end of the end times which began with the establishment of the Church on the Day of Pentecost (Acts 2:14-42, Hebrews 1:2 and 1 Peter 4:7). Again, we are living on borrowed time. And Satan is working overtime to camouflage the fact.

> He is deceiving people into believing that the end times prophecies do not mean what they say.

> He is motivating well-meaning people to set dates for the Lord's return in order to discredit Bible prophecy.

> He is convincing pastors that Bible prophecy is pie-in-the-sky, with no relevance to the here and now.

He is convincing both Christians and their leaders that Bible prophecy is a Chinese puzzle that no one can understand, and thus it is a waste of time to study it.

In short, there is a Satanic conspiracy to keep the truths of Bible prophecy in the dark. Satan does not want anyone to know that Jesus is about to return. Nor does he want anyone to know that Bible prophecy reveals that when Jesus returns, Satan will be totally defeated and Jesus will be gloriously victorious and completely vindicated in history.

Realities We Need to Face

What pastors need to understand is two fundamental truths about Bible prophecy. The first is that the preaching of Bible prophecy can be a great evangelistic tool, as it was in the first Gospel sermon which Peter preached on Pentecost (Acts 2:14-36). Read that sermon. It is nothing but the recitation of one Messianic prophecy after another, followed by assertions that Jesus fulfilled each prophecy.

The second truth is that the preaching of Bible prophecy can serve as a great tool of sanctification, for if you can ever convince a Christian that Jesus really is coming back and that He could return at any moment, that person will be motivated to holiness and evangelism.

Let's face it: the average Christian no more believes in the imminent return of Jesus than he believes in Santa Claus or the Easter Bunny. He may believe it intellectually, but he does not believe it with his heart. It is only when a proposition moves from the mind to the heart that it is truly believed and will start having an impact on our minds and actions.

The three most urgent facts of our time that need to be proclaimed from every pulpit in America are:

1) Jesus is coming back to pour out the wrath of God and to reign over all the

earth.

2) The return of Jesus could occur at any moment — there is not one prophecy that must be fulfilled for the Rapture of the Church to occur.

3) The signs of the times indicate that we have arrived at the time of the Lord's return.

These truths arc like a two-edged sword. To unbelievers, they are a call to flee from the wrath that is to come by fleeing into the loving arms of Jesus now. To the believer they are a call to holiness and evangelism.

The Message for the Unbeliever

The unbeliever needs to face the fact that our Creator God is a God of Justice (Psalm 89:14). Accordingly, He must deal with sin — otherwise life has no meaning. And God deals with sin in one of two ways — either grace or wrath (John 3:36).

Every person on this planet is living under either the grace of God or His wrath. It is a terrible thing to be subject to God's wrath. The Bible says that when Jesus returns, the unsaved will crawl into holes in the ground and cry out for the mountains to fall upon them, so great will be the wrath of God (Isaiah 2:19).

The most tragic thing about this scenario is that all a person must do to move from wrath to grace is reach out in faith, confess that he or she is a sinner, and receive Jesus as Lord and Savior. Salvation is a free gift of God's grace through faith in His Messiah, Jesus. You cannot earn your salvation (Ephesians 2:8-10), and anyone who even implies that you can is an agent of Satan.

The Message for Believers

For believers, the imminent return of Jesus is a call to evangelism — to share the Gospel with as many people as possible, as quickly as possible.

The Lord's imminent return is also a call to believers to commit themselves to holiness. In practical terms, this means making Jesus the lord of everything in your life — your money, your job, your food, your entertainment — *everything.*

The Message for Pastors

And for those pastors who argue that prophecy is pie-in-the-sky, with no practical relevance, I ask, "What could be more relevant than a message that propels unbelievers to Jesus and motivates believers to holiness and evangelism?"

And that brings me to another point concerning pastors. It relates to the number one cop-out that pastors use for ignoring the teaching and preaching of God's Prophetic Word. It is often expressed in this manner: "I'm not Premillennial or Amillennial or Postmillennial — I'm Panmillennial because I believe it will all pan-out in the end."

Let me give you a translation of that comment. What the pastor is really saying is that he is too lazy to study prophecy to discover its truths, so he has decided to set aside one-third of God's Word and simply ignore it. And that is truly tragic!

The Meaning of a Promise

"Jesus is coming soon!" That's the promise given by the prophets of the Bible. It's a promise made to Jesus' disciples by angels on the day He ascended into Heaven (Acts 1:9-11). And it is the last promise Jesus made in the last words He spoke on this earth when He appeared to the Apostle John on the island of Patmos some 65 years after His death and resurrection (Revelation 22:12,20).

That promise means all, or it means nothing at all. To the world, it means nothing. To the average Christian, it is something that has been consigned to the indefinite future. To a true believer, it means everything.

True believers yearn daily with all their hearts for the Lord's return. They share the Gospel at every opportunity, and they live with a commitment to holiness.

And because they live with a yearning for the Lord's return, they will be candidates to receive a special Crown of Righteousness when they stand before the Lord on their day of judgment:

> I have fought the good fight, I have finished the course, I have kept the faith; in the future there is laid up for me the crown of righteousness, which the Lord, the righteous Judge, will award to me on that day; and not only to me, but also to all who have loved His appearing (2 Timothy 4:7-8).

Challenging Believers to yearn for the Lord's soon return.

Many scholars believe that one of the earliest prayers of the Church was "Maranatha!" (1 Corinthians 16:22).

That word is actually an Aramaic phrase that means "Our Lord come!" This prayer expresses a fact that is confirmed by many other scriptures; namely, that the First Century Church had an ardent desire for the soon return of Jesus.

The Yawning of the Church

As I pointed out in the last chapter, the 21st Century Church seems to have lost that desire. The average Christian today does not pray "Maranatha!" He does not yearn for the return of the Lord.

Instead of yearning, he is yawning. Christendom at large is caught up in apathy regarding the return of Jesus. And that is sad, for the Word says that the return of the Lord is our "Blessed Hope" (Titus 2:13).

Also, we are constantly admonished in the Scriptures to watch for the Lord's coming and to be ready. As Jesus Himself put it, "Be dressed in readiness, and keep your lamps alight" (Luke 12: 35).

Reasons for Yearning

There are at least six reasons why every Christian should earnestly desire the soon return of Jesus:

1 **Jesus** — When Jesus returns He will get what He deserves — honor, glory and power.

When Jesus came the first time, He was rejected by His home town, spurned by His family and repudiated by the Jews. He was persecuted by the religious leaders, betrayed by a friend, denied by another friend, deserted by His disciples, and mocked by the masses. He had no place to lay His head. His only possession was a robe.

He was born in a stable, raised in poverty, nailed to a tree, and buried in a borrowed tomb. Today, people scoff at Him and ridicule Him. His name is used as a curse word.

That is not what He deserves!

It is going to be different when He returns. The first time He came as a gentle and helpless baby. He is going to return as a mighty warrior. He came the first time as a suffering lamb to die for the sins of the world, but He will return as a conquering lion who will pour out the wrath of God on those who have rejected the love, mercy and grace of God. His first coming was marked by compassion, humility, and a willingness to be judged and to die. He will return in triumph and in wrath to judge and make war against the enemies of God. He came the first time as a Servant; He is returning as a Monarch.

Jesus was humiliated in history. I want to see Him vindicated and glorified in history. And He will be because His Father has promised Him that He will reign over all the earth (Psalm 2:7-9). He has also been promised that He will manifest His glory before His saints (Isaiah 24:21-23) and before the nations of the earth (Isaiah 66:18 and Psalm 22:27-31). Paul says He is returning "to be glorified in His saints . . . and to be marveled at among all who have believed" (2 Thessalonians 1:10).

2 Satan — When Jesus returns, Satan will receive what he deserves — defeat, dishonor and humiliation.

I'm sick of Satan. I'm tired of his plots and schemes and lies and deceptions. I'm fed up with his sicknesses and temptations. I'm weary of his physical, emotional and spiritual pollution. I'm disgusted with his wrecking of marriages and homes. I loath his wars and terrorism. I despise His ceaseless attacks on the Church.

I often feel like the martyrs portrayed in Revelation who cry out day and night before the throne of God, "How long, O Lord, holy and true, will You refrain from judging and avenging our blood?" (Revelation 6:10). Like Isaiah, I want to cry out to God, "Oh, that You would rend the heavens and come down!" (Isaiah 64:1).

The fate of Satan was sealed by the Cross, but his nefarious activities will not cease until the Lord returns. At that time, the Word says that God will deal with Satan decisively. Luke 18:7 says that God will vindicate His elect who cry out to Him day and night by providing them justice. Romans 16:20 says that Satan will be "crushed." The book of Revelation says he will then be thrown into the lake of fire where he "will be tormented day and night forever and ever" (Revelation 20:10 — see also, Isaiah 14:12-17).

But Satan doesn't want to go to Hell alone. He's working overtime to take as many people with him as he can. And I want that work stopped! I want Satan to get what he deserves.

3 The Creation — When Jesus returns, the creation will receive what it has been promised — restoration.

The material universe was originally created in beauty and perfection. There were no poisonous plants or animals, nor were there any meat eating animals. There were no natural cataclysms like earthquakes and tornados. Mankind lived in perfect harmony with nature.

But when Man rebelled against God, one of the consequences of his sin was that God placed a curse on the creation. Poisonous plants and animals suddenly appeared. The animal kingdom turned against itself and Man as some of the animals became meat eaters. And the natural cataclysms began to take their toll. Man now had to strive against nature to survive.

But the moment God placed the curse on the creation, He promised that one day it would be lifted through "the seed of woman" (Genesis 3:15). That promise is repeated throughout the Scriptures. For example, in Isaiah 11, the prophet says that when the Messiah comes to reign, "the wolf will dwell with the lamb" and "the lion will eat straw like the ox." He further states that "the nursing child will play by the hole of the cobra" because snakes will no longer be poisonous.

Paul reaffirms this promise in the New Testament in the eighth chapter of Romans. He pictures the whole creation as being like a pregnant woman gripped by birth pains, crying out for the moment of delivery. He says that moment will come when "the sons of God are revealed." In other words, it will occur at the resurrection when the Lord returns (Romans 8:18-23).

On the day the Lord returns, the earth will be renovated by earthquakes and supernatural phenomena in the heavens (Revelation 6:12-17). The result will be a refreshed and beautified earth. The destructive forces of nature will be curtailed. Deserts will bloom. The plant and animal kingdoms will be redeemed. Poisonous plants and animals will cease to be poisonous. The carnivorous animals will become herbivorous. All of nature will cease to strive against itself. Instead, it will work together harmoniously to the benefit of Man. (Isaiah 11:6-9; Isaiah 35:1-10; Isaiah 65:17-25; Acts 3:19-21; and Romans 8:18-23)

4 **The Nations** — When Jesus returns, the nations will receive what they have been promised — peace, righteousness and justice.

People have dreamed of world peace throughout history. Disarmament treaties have been negotiated, peace treaties have been signed, international organizations have been created, but true peace has remained elusive.

The Bible says that permanent world peace will never be achieved until the Prince of Peace, the Messiah, returns. Both Isaiah and Micah prophesied that when the Lord returns, the nations "will hammer their swords into plowshares and their spears into pruning hooks" and that "nation will not lift up sword against nation, and never again will they train for war" (Isaiah 2:4 and Micah 4:3).

The hope of the world for peace will never be realized in summit conferences between heads of state. The only hope is the return of Jesus, the Prince of Peace, who will rule the world with "a rod of iron" (Psalm 2:9 and Revelation 2:26-27).

5 **The Jews** — When Jesus returns, the Jews will receive what they have been promised — salvation and primacy.

God has made many wonderful promises to His chosen people, the nation of Israel. Most of these are unfulfilled and will not be fulfilled until a remnant of the Jews turn to Jesus and accept Him as their Messiah. The prophetic scriptures tell us this will happen at the end of the Tribulation when the Jews who are left alive have come to the end of themselves and decide to turn to God.

Zechariah says this remnant will "look upon Him whom they have pierced and will mourn for Him as one mourns for an only son" (Zechariah 12:10). The prophet also says that on that day of repentance, "a fountain of salvation will be opened for the house of David and for the inhabitants of Jerusalem, for sin and for impurity" (Zechariah 13:1).

This believing remnant will then be regathered to the land of Israel to receive the blessings that God has promised the nation. Those incredible blessings are described in great detail in chapters 60 through 62 of Isaiah. God's Shekinah glory will return (60:2) to a rebuilt Temple (60:7). The nations will send all kinds of assistance (60:10), including their wealth (60:5). The land of Israel will be reclaimed (60:13), the nation will receive respect (60:15), the people will enjoy peace (60:18), and the Messiah will live in their presence (60:13,19). All the ruins will be rebuilt (61:4) and the land will be filled with joy (61:7-8) and praise (61:10-11). The nation will be a beacon of righteousness, and its glory will be witnessed all over the world (62:1-3).

To sum it up, Isaiah says the nation of Israel will be "a crown of beauty in the hand of the Lord, and a royal diadem in the hand of God" (62:3).

In effect, the world will be turned upside down regarding its relationship to the Jews. Today the Jewish people are despised and persecuted. They are the butt of jokes and ridicule. But a day is coming when all that will cease. Zechariah says that during the Lord's millennial reign the Jewish people will be so honored that when a Jew walks by, ten Gentiles will grab his clothing and say, "Let us go with you, for we have heard that God is with you" (Zechariah 8:23).

6 **The Saints** — Some of the promises to the Saints — to those who are members of the Lord's Church — will be fulfilled at the time of the Rapture. The Rapture is an event that could occur any moment. It will precede the Second Coming.

At the Rapture, the dead in Christ will be resurrected and the living will be translated to meet Him in the air (1 Thessalonians 4:13-18). It is at this time that both the living and dead in Christ will receive their glorified bodies. These will be immortal, perfected bodies — like the body that Jesus had after His resurrection (1 Corinthians 15:42-53 and Philippians 3:21).

When Jesus returns to this earth, the Saints who have died will come with Him and will witness His glorious victory over the Antichrist and his forces (Revelation 19:11-21). The Saints will then receive what they have been promised — a redeemed earth and ruling power over the nations (Matthew 5:5 and Revelation 2:26-27).

Jesus will reign from Mount Zion in Jerusalem as King of kings and Lord of lords (Isaiah 24:21-23). David in his glorified body will reign as king of Israel (Jeremiah 30:9 and Ezekiel 34:23-24). The Saints in their glorified bodies will be scattered all over the world to assist with the Lord's reign (2 Timothy 2:12 and Revelation 2:26-27). Some will serve as administrators (mayors, governors, presidents, and kings), others will serve as judges, but most will serve as teachers, for the entire educational system of the world will be in the hands of glorified Saints. It will be their responsibility to teach those who are in the flesh about the Lord. There will be no legislators (thank God!), for Jesus Himself will give the law. (See Isaiah 2:1-4; Isaiah 66:19-21; Jeremiah 3:12-18; and Luke 19:11-27.)

These six reasons make it clear that every Christian should be earnestly desiring the return of the Lord. Yet apathy prevails. Why?

Yawning about Jesus

I have found four reasons for the apathy and indifference that characterize the Christian community concerning the return of Jesus: unbelief, ignorance, fear, and carnality.

Unbelief

Regarding unbelief, many professing Christians simply do not believe that Jesus will ever return. Most of these are people with a liberal view of Scripture. They have spiritualized away the meaning of the Second Coming, just as they have spiritualized the virgin birth and the miracles. To them, the Second Coming is nothing more than a fairy tale.

In 2 Peter 3:3-4 we are told that the end times will be characterized by scoffers who will mock the Lord's promise to return. The tragedy is that many of these are people who profess to be Christians.

Ignorance

I think most of the Christians who are apathetic about the Lord's return are just ignorant about what will happen when He comes back. As a result, they cannot get excited about an event they know nothing about. I was in this category for 30 years. Although I attended church faithfully, my church ignored the teaching and preaching of God's Prophetic Word. I didn't have the foggiest idea about what would happen when the Lord came back, and the result was apathy about His return.

But when I began studying Bible prophecy and learned what is in store for believers when the Lord returns, I started jumping pews and shouting "Maranatha!" I have never been apathetic since that time.

Fear

The apathy of some Christians is due to the fact that they fear the Lord's return. Because of that fear, they try to repress the thought that He might break from the heavens at any moment.

These people fear He might return on one of their "bad" days or when they have an "unconfessed sin" on their conscience. These people are caught up in works salvation. They do not understand that they are saved by grace and that "there is no condemnation for those who are in Christ Jesus" (Romans 8:1).

Carnality

Finally, there are many carnal Christians who cannot get excited about the coming of the Lord because they are in love with the world. They are walking with one foot in the church and one foot in the country club.

Their attitude about the Lord's return is, "I want Him to return, but . . ." They want the Lord to come, but they want Him to come after they have made a million dollars, or written the great novel, or built the huge church. They want the Lord to come, but they want Him to come after they are 80 years old and have experienced all that this world has to offer. In other words, they want Him to come, but they don't want Him to mess up their lives.

A Seventh Reason

There is a seventh reason I want to see the Lord return, and it is rather personal in nature. It has to do with the fact that when you love someone, you want to be with them.

My wife and I have been married for over 50 years. When I have to be on the road, my desire is to be with her. I call her every day and tell her that I love her. I send her cards, and when I have to be gone a long time, I arrange for flowers to be delivered to her. I love to talk with her on the phone and send her cards and flowers, but these things are no substitute for being with her.

Likewise, I love to fellowship with Jesus in worship, in prayer, and in His Word. But these forms of fellowship are no substitute for being with Him. I love Him, and therefore . . .

> I want to be with Him.
> I want to bask in the presence of
> His love and holiness.

I want to see the glory of God in
    His face.
I want to kiss His nail-scarred
    hands and say, "Thank you!"
        for dying for me,
        for forgiving me,
        for changing me,
        for guiding me,
        for comforting me,
        for giving my life
        meaning and purpose.
And I want to join the Saints and
the Heavenly Host in singing,
    "Worthy is the Lamb!"

MARANATHA!

Living on Borrowed Time

Part 5
The Question of Timing

The Return of Jesus 18

Looking for Jesus today.

Could Jesus return today? I am probably asked this question more than any other one pertaining to Bible prophecy.

The Question of Timing

The answer to the question depends upon the meaning of the word, "return." That's because the return of Jesus is going to be in two stages.

First, He will appear in the heavens to take His Church out of this world in an event known as the Rapture (1 Thessalonians 4:13-18).

Then, later, He will return to this earth to pour out the wrath of God on those who have rejected His love, grace, and mercy (Revelation 19:11-16). He will then begin his thousand year reign over all the earth from Jerusalem. (Revelation 20:1-10).

The Rapture vs. The Second Coming

The Rapture is an event that could occur any moment. There are no prophecies that have to be fulfilled before it happens. It could certainly occur today.

The Second Coming cannot occur until a number of prophecies are fulfilled. Here is a partial list:

- A treaty is signed that will allow Israel to live in peace and rebuild its Temple (Daniel 9:27).

- Two miracle-working witnesses appear in Jerusalem to call the world to repentance (Revelation 11:3-6).

- The Antichrist leader based in Europe launches a war to take over the entire world, resulting in the death of half the world's population (Revelation 6:8-9).

- The Antichrist goes to Jerusalem, kills the two witnesses, enters the rebuilt Temple, and declares himself to be god (Revelation 11:7, Revelation 13:1-7, and 2 Thessalonians 2:3-4).

- The Jews in the Jerusalem area flee into the Jordanian wilderness where they are supernaturally sheltered from harm (Revelation 12:13-17 and Daniel 11:41).

- The Antichrist vents his fury by killing two-thirds of the Jews in the rest of the world (Zechariah 13:8).

- The kingdom of the Antichrist is totally destroyed supernaturally by God in one hour of one day (Revelation 18:8-10).

Knowing the Date

The Bible tells us over and over that no one can know the date of the Lord's return (Matthew 24:36,42,44 and 25:13). These warnings must apply to the Rapture and not the Second Coming, because the date of the Second Coming can be calculated precisely once the Tribulation begins.

The book of Revelation tells us that the Tribulation will last exactly 2,520 days after the treaty is signed that marks the start of that terrible period (Revelation 11:3 and 12:6). Another way of stating this time period is seven years, based on prophetic years of 360 days each.

The current day signs of the times point to the beginning of the Tribulation and the Second Coming of Jesus. Although the Rapture could occur at any moment, we can know for sure that it is near when we see signs that we are on the threshold of the Tribulation. That's because the best inference of the Scriptures is that the Rapture will occur before the Tribulation begins.

The Rapture is not the event that marks the beginning of the Tribulation, since there could be a time period between the Rapture and the Tribulation, but it is most likely to occur in close proximity to the start-up of the Tribulation.

Think of it like this: When you see Christmas decorations going up in early November, you know they are specifically pointing to Christmas Day, but they are also an indicator that Thanksgiving Day is right around the corner!

So, the very day you are reading this book could very well be the day of the Rapture, but not the day of the Second Coming.

The Crucial Question

The crucial question that only you can answer is, "Are you ready for the Lord's return?"

When Jesus appears in the heavens to rapture His Church out of this world, He will appear either as your Blessed Hope or your Severe Disappointment. You will either be taken out or left behind to face the horrors of the Antichrist and the Tribulation.

If you have accepted Jesus as your Lord and Savior, you will be taken out of this world and return with Him to Heaven. In the process, you will be glorified, as your body is translated from mortal to immortal.

If, on the other hand, you have rejected Jesus as your Lord and Savior, you will suffer the severe disappointment of being left behind on this planet to experience the Antichrist and the acute tribulation he will inflict upon the earth.

During the seven year Tribulation that will follow, a great host of people left behind at the Rapture will turn their hearts to Jesus and accept Him as their Savior (Revelation 7:9-17). But the vast majority will double up their fists, shake them at God and continue to reject Him and His Son (Revelation 9:20-21).

The Tribulation Judgment

During the Tribulation, one-half of all Gentiles on earth will die (Revelation 6:8 and Revelation 9:15) and two-thirds of the Jews will be killed (Zechariah 13:8). Only a small number of people will survive to the end, and most of these will be unbelievers.

When the Second Coming occurs at the end of the Tribulation, Jesus will return to earth as either a Gracious Deliverer or a Stern Judge. The Gentiles who have put their faith in Him during the Tribulation, and who survive to the end of that horrendous period, will respond in joy. They will "go forth and skip about like calves released from a stall" (Malachi 4:2). They will be allowed to enter the millennial reign of Jesus in the flesh.

All the Jews who live to the end of the Tribulation will have come to the end of themselves and will respond to the appearance of their Messiah by looking upon Him "whom they have pierced, and they will mourn for Him, as one mourns for an only son, and they will weep bitterly over Him, like the bitter weeping over a first-born" (Zechariah 12:10). They too will be allowed to enter the Millennium in the flesh (Isaiah 10:22, Romans 9:21 and Romans 11:25-26).

The remaining Gentiles who have persisted in their rejection of God and His Son will be judged, condemned and consigned to Hell (Matthew 25:31-46).

The Crucial Question Again

What will be your fate? In a sermon delivered by John the Baptist, he proclaimed: "He who believes in the Son has eternal life; but he who does not obey the Son will not see life, but the wrath of God abides on him" (John 3:36).

This passage is very clear. Our Holy God is going to deal with sin, and He does so in one of two ways — either grace or wrath.

It is a glorious thing to live under the grace of God, knowing that your sins have been forgiven and forgotten through faith in Jesus. It is a terrible thing to exist under the wrath of God, considering the fact that you may die any moment, or that Jesus may return any day.

On the day that Jesus returns to this earth, you will either go forth in joy like a calf released from a stall (Malachi 4:2) or you will crawl into a hole in the ground and pray for the mountains to fall on you (Isaiah 2:12-19).

It is so easy to move from wrath to grace. All you have to do is repent of your sins and receive Jesus as your Savior. You cannot earn salvation (Ephesians 2:8-10). It is a gift of God's grace through faith in His Son.

An Illustration of God's Grace

Many years ago, my wife and I read a story during our morning devotional time that greatly impacted my soul — to the point that I vowed to share the story with as many people as possible until I died or was taken in the Rapture. I want to conclude this book by sharing that story with you now. It is one of the clearest explanations I have ever encountered of the meaning of the death of Jesus and the grace of God.

In 1848 gold was discovered in California. In the following years, over 300,000 Americans made the long and perilous journey to California in search of a fortune in gold. Some traveled by boat around the tip of South America, but most went overland in wagon trains.

The people who participated in these wagon trains were mainly city-slickers who did not know how to survive in the wilderness. Their fate was in the hands of the wagon masters who served as their guides and protectors.

We know from the logs that were kept by the wagon masters that there were many things they feared — things like Indian attacks, polluted or dried-up water sources, plagues and natural calamities like blizzards. One particularly fearsome threat was the prairie fire.

When the wagon master would spot smoke on the horizon (probably from a fire started by lightning) he knew he had only minutes to protect the wagon train because the prairie fires often traveled as fast as 40 miles per hour, depending on how hard the wind was blowing.

But there is no record of a wagon train being lost to a prairie fire. The reason is that there was a crafty way of protecting the wagons from the fire.

What the wagon master would do is start a fire downwind of his wagons and wait for it to burn away. Then he would circle the wagons in the burned-out area, take down the cloth tops, and wait for the prairie fire to arrive. When it did arrive, the fire would simply burn around the circled wagons and move on.

How does this story relate to the death of Jesus? As He was hanging on the Cross as the only sinless and totally innocent man who had ever lived, all the sins we have ever committed, and will ever commit, were placed upon Him, and the wrath of God, which we deserve, was poured out on Him.

When you accept Jesus as your Lord and Savior, you step into the area where the fire of God has already fallen, and you become immune to God's wrath.

Praise the Lord!

What a merciful God, that He would send His only begotten Son to die for our sins. And what a glorious Savior, that

He would be willing to leave the glories of Heaven to take on human flesh, assume our sins, and submit Himself to the wrath of God in our behalf. He took the wrath that we deserve, and by doing so, He made it possible for those who put their faith in Him to be reconciled to their Creator.

I am reminded of the song by Joe Pace entitled, "He Paid the Price:"[1]

> What can I say, how can I repay
> the sacrifice He made for me ?
> He died upon the cross,
> paid the cost,
> so I wouldn't be lost.
> Now I have the victory.

> Jesus shed His blood for me
> way back on Calvary,
> washed all my sins away.
> Now I've got a right to the tree of life.
> Because He lives, I'm alive today.

> Chorus:
> He died that I might have life
> and have life more abundantly.
> Sacrificed, He paid the price for me .

> Bridge:
> *Jesus paid a debt He did not owe*
> *I owed a debt I could not pay.*
> It was my soul that He saved
> when He rose from the grave.
> What a sacrifice He made!

References

Chapter 4 — The Signs of the Return

1) Robert Longley, "FEMA's List of Top 10 U.S. Natural Disasters," http://usgovinfo.about.com.

2) Wikipedia, "Agnes Ozman," http://en.wikipedia.org/wiki/Agnes_Ozman.

3) Wikipedia, "Evan Roberts (Minister)," http://en.wikipedia.org/wiki/Evan_Roberts_(minister).

4) Wikipedia, "William J. Seymour," http://en.wikipedia.org/wiki/William_J._Seymour.

5) Frank Bartleman, *Azuza Street: An Eyewitness Account*, (Gainesville, FL: Bridge-Logos Publishers, 2001).

Chapter 5 — The Future is Now

1) Theodor Herzl, *Der Judenstaat* (published in Leipzig and Vienna in 1896). Modern versions are available from several publishers under the name, *The Jewish State.*

2) Robert St. John, *The Life Story of Ben Yehuda: Tongue of the Prophets* (Noble, OK: Balfour Books, 2013). Originally published in 1952 by Doubleday as *Tongue of the Prophets: The Life Story of Eliezer Ben Yehuda.*

3) GFP, "Countries Ranked by Military Strength (2013)," http://www.globalfirepower.com/countries-listing.asp.

Chapter 7 — The Re-establishment of Israel

1) Arthur Koestler, *Promise and Fulfillment* (New York: Macmillan, 1949) p. 7.

2) Howard M. Sachar, *A History of Israel* (New York: Knopf, 1976) p. 99.

3) William L. Hull, *The Fall and Rise of Israel* (Grand Rapids: Zon-

dervan, 1954) p. 124.

4) Fredrick A. Tatford, *The Midnight Cry: The Story of Fifty Years of Witness* (Eastbourne, Sussex: Bible and Advent Testimony Movement, 1967) pp. 17-18.

5) Ibid., p. 19.

6) Ibid., p. 35.

7) The website of The Prophetic Witness Movement International can be found at http://www.pwmi.org.

8) Hull, p. 208.

Chapter 8 — The Revival of the Roman Empire

1) Kenneth Humphries, "Relating the EU to Bible Prophecy," *Lamplighter* magazine published by Lamb & Lion Ministries, May-June 2001, page 4.

2) Eurocorps, "One of the main things missing . . ." (www.eurocorps. org/site/index.php?language=en&content=home).

3) Pascal Fontaine, "Seven Key Days in the Making of Europe," http://ec.europa.eu/archives/publications/archives/booklets/move/16/txt_en.htm (1997).

4) Kenneth Humphries, "Europe in Bible Prophecy," http://www.treasuredtruthtoday.org/article/khsa/prophetic_series/ps-003.php.

5) Ibid.

6) Humphries, "Relating the EU to Bible Prophecy," page 5.

7) Alan Franklin, "The New Unholy Roman Empire, *Lamplighter* magazine published by Lamb & Lion Ministries, May-June 2001, page 8.

8) Remarks of Leon Marchal that were reported by Dr. William Crampton, executive director of The Flag Institute in York, England. The remarks were made in 1973.

9) Ibid.

10) "Building Europe Together," a pamphlet published by the European Union, Brussels, Belgium, 1997.

11) Alan Franklin, "The New Unholy Roman Empire," page 9.

12) Ibid.

13) Ibid.

14) Ibid.

15) The CIA World Factbook, "The European Union," https://www. cia.gov/library/publications/the-world-factbook/geos/ee.html.

16) This is a frequently quoted remark attributed to Paul-Henri Spaak. However, its original source is uncertain.

Chapter 9 — The Proliferation of Cults

1) *The Catholic Encyclopedia*, "Gnosticism," http://www.newadvent. org/cathen/06592a.htm.

2) "The Church of Jesus Christ of Latter-Day Saints," home website, http://mormon.org.

3) Dr. Paul M. Elliott, "Evangelicals' Romance with Mormonism," Teaching the Word Ministries, http://www.teachingtheword.org/ apps/articles/?articleid=82453&columnid=5441.

4) Rick Miesel, "Robert Schuller: General Teachings/Activities," Computer Discernment Notebook of Biblical Discernment Ministries, January 1999, http://www.rapidnet.com/~jbeard/bdm/expo ses/schuller/general.htm, p. 5. Schuller's support of the Unity Church is also documented in an article by Dave Hunt published in the CIB Bulletin, January 1988. In a letter to the author, dated January 24, 2000, Dave Hunt states that he has a tape recording of the speech that Schuller delivered to the Unity pastors about church growth principles.

5) Wikipedia, "Iglesia ni Cristo," http://en.wikipedia.org/wiki/ Iglesia_ ni_Cristo.

6) All About Cults, "Jose Luis de Jesus Miranda – Million-Dollar Messiah," http://www.allaboutcults.org/jose-luis-de-Jesus- miranda. htm.

Chapter 10 – The Convulsion of Nature

1) William Koenig, *Eye to Eye: Facing the Consequences of Dividing Israel* (Washington, D.C.: About Him Publishers, 2006).

2) Based on a personal conversation with Bill Koenig.

3) Matthew Henry, *Matthew Henry Commentary on the Whole Bible: Complete and Unabridged* (Peabody, MA: Hendrickson Publishers, 2008).

4) Koenig, *Eye to Eye*, revised and updated edition, 2008, pp. 40-41.

5) Koenig, pp. 41-42.

6) Ibid., pp. 71-72.

7) Ibid., pp. 76-77.

8) Ibid., pp. 84-85.

9) Ibid., p. 111.

10) Ibid., 114-115.

11) Robert Longley, "FEMA's List of Top 10 U.S. Natural Disasters," http://usgovinfo.about.com.

12) International Christian Embassy Jerusalem, "In Brief: Rice says it cannot be 'Gaza Only,'" http://nir.icej.org/news/headlines/brief-rice-says-it-cannot-be-%C2%B4gaza-only%C2%B4.

13) William Koenig in a television interview on "Christ in Prophecy," the television program of Lamb & Lion Ministries, April 2005.

14) LifeSiteNews.com, "Maybe God is Going to Cleanse Us," http://www.blowthetrumpet.org/KillerKatrinaGodsJudgement.htm.

15) Linda Feldmann, "Another side to disaster relief: prayer," *The Christian Science Monitor*, http://www.csmonitor.com/2005/0919/p03s01-ussc.html.

16) LifeSiteNews.com, "New Orleans City Council President: 'Maybe God's Going To Cleanse Us,'" September 1, 2005, http://www.life sitenews.com/news/archive//ldn/2005/sep/05090111.

17) Abraham Lincoln, "Proclamation — Fasting Humiliation Prayer —1863," http://www.wallbuilders.com/LIBissuesArticles.asp?id= 131332.

18) USGS, "Global Earthquake Search" http://earthquake.usgs.gov/earthquakes/eqarchives/epic.

19) WorldWatch.org, "Worldwide Weather-Related Disasters per year," www.worldwatch.org.

Chapter 11 — The Growth of Apostasy

1) Wikipedia, "Harry Emerson Fosdick," http://en.wikipedia/wiki/Harry_Emerson_Fosdick.

2) Christian History, "Harry Emerson Fosdick: Liberalism's Popu-

larizer," www.christianitytoday.com/ch/131christians/pastorsand preachers/fosdick.html.

3) InPlainSight.org, "Norman Vincent Peale: Apostle of Self-Esteem," www.inplainsight.org/html/norman_vincent_ peale.html.

4) Dave Hunt, "Revival or Apostasy," *The Berean Call*, October 1997, page 2.

5) Rick Miesel, "Robert Schuller: General Teachings/Activities," Computer Discernment Notebook of Biblical Discernment Ministries, January 1999, http://www.rapidnet.com/~jbeard/bdm/ expo ses/schuller/general.htm, p. 8. See also his article on Norman Vincent Peale at the same website: http://www.rapidnet.com/ ~jbeard/bdm/Psychology/guidepo/peale.htm.

6) Robert Schuller, *Self Esteem: The New Reformation,* (Waco, Texas: Word Books, 1982), p. 39. An insightful review of Schuller's writings can be found in an article by Joseph P. Gudel entitled "A New Reformation?" It was published in *Passport Magazine*, January-February 1988. It is available on the Internet at http://www.issue setc.org/resource/archives/guide12.htm. There are other excellent summaries of Schuller's thought that can be found on the Internet. One is an article by David W. Cloud entitled "Evangelicals and Modernist Robert Schuller" (http://cnview.com/on_line_resources/ evangelicals_and_modernist_robert_schuller.htm). Another good analysis is entitled, "The God of the Bible Versus the God of Multi-level Marketing: Positive Thinking," (http://www.users.fast.net/ ~gospeltruth/positive.htm).

7) Schuller, *Self Esteem*, page 19.

8) Ibid., page 80.

9) Ibid., page 14.

10) Ibid., page 68.

11) Robert Schuller, "Dr. Schuller Comments," (letter to the editor), *Christianity Today*, October 5, 1984, pages 12-13.

12) Richard Stengel, "Apostle of Sunny Thoughts," *Time*, March 18, 1985, page 70.

13) *The Phil Donahue Show*, transcript 08120, August 12, 1980, page 10.

14) Robert Schuller, *Possibilities Magazine*, Summer 1986, page 12.

15) Miesel, page 5. Schuller's support of the Unity Church is also docu-

mented in an article by Dave Hunt published in the *CIB Bulletin*, January 1988. In a letter to the author, dated January 24, 2000, Dave Hunt states that he has a tape recording of the speech that Schuller delivered to the Unity pastors about church growth principles.

16) Dave Hunt, "What's Happening to the Faith?" *The Berean Call*, May 1998, page 1.

17) John Shelby Spong, *Rescuing the Bible from Fundamentalism: A Bishop Rethinks the Meaning of Scripture* (San Francisco, California: Harper, 1992). Another revealing book by Bishop Spong is *Why Christianity Must Change or Die: A Bishop Speaks to Believers in Exile* (San Francisco, California: Harper, 1999). A good summary of Bishop Spong's views can be found on the Internet in his "Call for a New Reformation," http://www.diocese ofnewark.org /jsspong/reform.htm.

18) Dave Hunt, "What's Happening to the Faith?" *The Berean Call*, May 1998, page 1. Dr. Godsey's views can be found in the book, *When We Talk About God, Let's Be Honest*, (Macon, Georgia: Smyth & Helwys Publishing Co., 1996).

19) R. Albert, "The Immoderator," *World Magazine*, March 1998, page 18.

20) "The Jesus Seminar: The Search for Authenticity," http://home. fireplug.net/~rshand/reflections/messiah/seminar.htm.

21) In April 1996, *Time* magazine featured the Jesus Seminar on its cover under the title "The Search for Jesus." The cover article presented a comprehensive survey of the seminar's organization, methodology, and conclusions. See David Van Biema, "The Gospel Truth? — The iconoclastic and provocative Jesus Seminar argues that not much of the New Testament can be trusted. If so, what are Christians to believe?" *Time*, April 8, 1996.

22) Craig L. Blomberg, "The Seventy-Four 'Scholars:' Who Does the Jesus Seminar Really Speak For?"*Christian Research Journal*, Fall 1994, page 32. Also available on the Internet at http://www.rim.org /muslim/jesusseminar.htm.

23) Robert W. Funk and Roy W. Hoover, *The Five Gospels* (San Francisco, California: Harper, reprint edition, 1997). A good review of this book can be found in an article by D. A. Carson entitled "Five Gospels, No Christ." The article appeared in *Christianity Today*, April 25, 1994, pages 30-33.

24) ReligiousTolerance.org, "The United Church of Canada and Homosexuality," www.religioustolerance.org/hom_ ucc.htm.

25) Mark Tooley, "Church Gathering Features Radical Speakers," *AFA Journal*, June 1997, page 19. See also, Jackie Alnor, "Invasion of the Sophia Women," *Christian Sentinel*, Spring 1999, pages 24-25.

26) *Daily Mail*, "Bishop gives up Bible for Lent," February 14, 1997.

27) *Daily Mail*, "Archbishop of Canterbury: Doubts Resurrection of Jesus," August 4, 1999.

28) Wikipedia, "Gene Robinson," http://en.wikipedia.org/wiki/Gene_Robinson.

29) Shaila Dewan, "United Church of Christ Backs Same-Sex Marriage," *The New York Times*, July 5, 2005.

30) George Conger, "'Jesus is not the only way to God,' says Presiding Bishop," www.religiousintelligence.co.uk/news/?NewsID=4282.

31) Albert Mohler, "The Amazing Technicolor Multifaith Theology School," www.albertmohler.com/2010/06/11/claremont-and-the-amazing-technicolor-multifaith-theology-school.

32) Thomas Nelson Publishers, "The Remnant Study Bible: The Last Study Bible You'll Ever Need," www.theremnantstudybible.com/component/content/article/3-newsflash/4-news flash-3.html.

33) Adela Yarbro Collins, "Is Hershel Doomed to the Lake of Fire?" *Biblical Archaeology Review*, January/February 2011, page 26.

34) Denny Burk, "Brian McLaren: DaVinci Code Not As Dangerous as Left Behind," www.dennyburk.com/brian-mclaren-davinci-code-not-as-dangerous-as-left-behind/?cat=6.

35) Brian McLaren, "A Generous Orthodoxy," www.brianmclaren.net/archivesbooks/brians-books/a-generous-orth.html.

36) Rob Bell, *Velvet Elvis: Repainting the Christian Faith* (Grand Rapids, MI: Zondervan, 2006), page 27.

37) Ibid., page 68.

38) Ibid., page 21.

39) Rob Bell, *Love Wins: A Book About Heaven, Hell, and the Fate of Every Person Who Ever Lived* (New York, NY: HarperOne, 2011).

40) Ibid., page viii.

41) Bell, *Velvet Elvis*, page 118.

42) Wikipedia, "Christianity Today," http://en.wikipedia.org/wiki/Chr istianity_Today#cite_note-Press-1.

43) Mark Galli, "The Divine Drama Queen," *Christianity Today*, July 2010.

44) For evidence of the overwhelming biblical illiteracy that exists among professing Christians today, including Evangelicals, see the polls conducted by the Barna Group. They can be found on the Internet at www.barna.org.

Chapter 12 — The Outpouring of Holy Spirit

1) Wikipedia, "Agnes Ozman," http://en.wikipedia.org/wiki/Agnes_ Ozman.

2) Wikipedia, "Evan Roberts (Minister)," http://en.wikipedia.org/ wiki/Evan_Roberts_(minister).

3) Wikipedia, "William J. Seymour," http://en.wikipedia.org/wiki/ William_J._Seymour.

4) Frank Bartleman, *Azuza Street: An Eyewitness Account*, (Gaines-ville, FL: Bridge-Logos Publishers, 2001).

5) *Toledo Blade* newspaper, Toledo, Ohio, May 24, 1997, "Holy Spirit, Satan, lose out in recent poll," http://news.google.com/news papers?nid=1350&dat=19970524&id=huo0AAAAIBAJ&sjid=P Q4EAAAAIBAJ&pg=6238,8151365.

6) David Edwin Harrell, Jr., *Oral Roberts: An American Life*, (Bloom-ington, IN: Indiana University Press, 1985).

7) William Martin, *A Prophet with Honor: The Billy Graham Story,* (New York, NY: Harper Perennial, 1992).

8) Billy Graham Evangelistic Association, "Biography of Billy Gra-ham," http://www.billygraham.org/biographies_show.asp?p=2d=1. See also: *Los Angeles Times,* Associated Press, "Technology Will Give Billy Graham Crusade a Worldwide Audience," February 25, 1995, http://articles.latimes.com/1995-02-25/local/me-35843_1_ billy-graham-crusade.

9) Wycliffe Global Alliance, "2012 Scripture Access Statistics," http:// www.wycliffe.net/resources/scriptureaccessstatistics/tabid/ 99/Default.aspx.

10) Wycliffe Bible Translators, "Translation Statistics," http://www. wycliffe.org/About/Statistics.aspx.

11) Ibid.

12) Jacob Jocz, *The Jewish People and Jesus Christ*, 3rd ed. (Grand Rapids: Baker Book House, 1979) p. 199.

13) For an in-depth discussion of Christian anti-Semitism see the author's article, "Anti-Semitism: Its Roots and Perseverance," *Lamplighter* magazine, Sept-Oct 2007, pp. 3-9.

14) About.com, "What is Messianic Judaism?" http://christianity.about.com/od/messianicjewishmovement/a/What-Is-Messianic-Judaism.htm.

15) Hal Lindsey with Carole C. Carlson, *The Late Great Planet Earth* (Grand Rapids, MI: Zondervan, 1970).

Chapter 14 — The Accelerator Principle

1) The National Academies Press, "World Population Problems: The Growth of World Population," www.nap.edu/openbook.php?record_id95438page=8.

2) Worldmeters, "World Population Statistics," www.worldmeters.info/world-population, pages 3-4.

3) Laura B. Shrestha, "Life Expectancy in the United States," http://aging.senate.gov/crs/aging1.pdf, page 10.

4) Infoplace, "Medical Advances Timeline," www.infoplace.com/ipa/Ao932661.html, pages 1-4.

5) Michael D. Lemonick, "Working Stiffs," *Time* magazine, April 6, 1998, pages 60-61.

6) Edwin J. Pittock, "Is Living Longer More Than We Bargained For? America's Crisis in Aging," www.csa.us/SeniorPopulationGrowth.aspx.

7) Seven-Minute Sermons, "Sustainable Knowledge at Work," http://sevenminutesermons.wordpress.com/2012/02/17/sustainable-knowledge-at-work.

8) "Knowledge Doubling," http://epoq.wikia.com/wiki/Knowledge_doubling.

9) Julie Bosman, "After 244 Years, Encyclopaedia Britannica Stops the Presses," *The New York Times*, March 13, 2012, http://media decoder.blogs.nytimes.com.

10) For a very good study of transportation in America, see: "Transportation: Past, Present and Future," by The Henry Ford Organization,

http://www.thehenryford.org/education/erb/TransportationPast PresentAndFuture.pdf.

11) Oakton Community College 24/7 Library Research guide and Webletter, "Are You Information Savvy?" www.oakton.edu/user/4/ jmayzel/247/savvy.htm, page 1.

12) Sam Nurmi, "Internet 2011 in Numbers," http://royal.pingdom.com/ 2012/01/17/internte-2011-in-numbers, page 4.

13) PBS, "Ship Guide: USS George Washington," www.pbs.org/wnet/ warship/submarines/guide8.html.

14) Milton Leitenberg, "Deaths in Wars and Conflicts in the 20th Century," www.cissm.umd.edu, page 4.

15) Wikipedia, "List of Ongoing Military Conflicts," http://en.wiki pedia.org/wiki/List_of_ongoing_military_ conflicts, pages 1-4.

16) Haaretz, "Terrorist Attacks Drop Nearly 12% Worldwide in 2011, U.S. Report Shows," http://haaretz.com.

17) The Disaster Center, "United States Crime Rates 1960-2010," www.disastercenter.com/crime/uscrime.htm.

18) Brian Rentschler, "Review: Glengarry Glen Ross," http://screen rant.com/review-glengarryglen-ross-brian-385, page 3.

19) Robert Longley, "FEMA's List of Top 10 U.S. Natural Disasters," http://usgovinfo.about.com.

20) "U.S. Debt Clock," www.usdebtclock.org.

21) Ibid.

22) Wycliffe Bible Translators, "The Worldwide Status of Bible Trans-lation," www.wycliffe.org/About/Statistics.aspx.

23) Sherwood Eliot Wirt, "A Personal Look at Billy Graham," http:// www.ccel.us/billy.ch27.html, page 4.

24) From notes taken by the author.

25) Charles Colson, "How Christianity is Growing Around the World," www.cbn.com.

26) Bible Probe, "The New Church: Miracles and Conversions, China and More," http://proregeforum.com/ messages/414.html.

27) John L. Allen, Jr., "The Dramatic Growth of Evangelicals in Latin America," National Catholic Reporter, August 18, 2006, http:// neronline.org.

28) Ali Sina, "Islam in Fast Demise," www.faithfreedom.org/oped/sina31103.htm, page 1.

29) The Pew Forum, "Global Christianity: A Report on the Size and Distribution of the World's Christian Population," www.pewforum.org/Chritian/Global-Christianity-exec.aspx, page 1.

30) World Hopper Ministry Travel, "Facts About Missions," www.worldhopperministry.com/why/html.

Chapter 15 — The Decay of Society

1) Robert H. Bork, *Slouching Towards Gomorrah: Modern Liberalism and American Decline* (New York, NY: Harper Perennial, 2003).

2) Wikipedia, "Gay Pride," http://en.wikipedia.org/wiki/Gay_pride.

3) Steven Ertelt, "54,559,615 Abortions Since Roe vs. Wade Decision in 1973," www.lifenews.com/2012/01/23/54559615-abortions-since-roe-vs-wade-decision-in-1973.

4) Michael's House, "Drug Addiction Facts and Statistics," www.michaelshouse.com/drug-addiction/drug-addictionstatistics.

5) OnlineSchools, "The Stats on Internet Pornography," www.onlinemba.com/blog/stats-on-internet-pornography.

6) Unmarried.org, "Statistics on Marriage," www.unmarried.org/statistics.html.

7) NationMaster.com, "Divorce rate (most recent) by country," www.nationmaster.com/graph/peo_div_rat-people-divorce-rate.

8) FirstThings.org, "Out of Wedlock Pregnancy Fact Sheet," http://firstthings.org/page/research/out-of-wedlock-pregnancy-fact-sheet.

9) James Quinn, "American's Gambling $100 Billion in Casino's Like Rats in a Cage," www.casinowatch.org/commentary/like_rats_in_a_cage.html.

10) MedlinePlus, "Alcoholism," http://www.nlm.nih.gov/medlineplus/alcoholism.html.

11) US Debt Clock.org, http://www.usdebtclock.org.

12) Richard Corliss, "Show Business: X Rated," *Time* magazine, May 7, 1990.

13) Wikipedia, "Incarceration in the United States," http://en.wikipedia.org/wiki/Incarceration_in_the_United_States.

14) NCADV Public Policy Office, "Domestic Violence Facts," www. ncadv.org/files/DomesticViolenceFactSheet(National).pdf.

15) ChildHelp.org, "National Child Abuse Statistics," www.childhelp. org/pages/statistics.

16) EndOfTheAmericanDream.com, "10 Facts About Crime In The United States That Will Blow Your Mind," http://endoftheamerican dream.com/archives.

17) Center for Disease Control, "Understanding School Violence," www.cdc.gov/violenceprevention.

18) Jim Garlow, Presentation at the National Religious Broadcasters' Convention in 2010.

19) Barna Group, "Survey Explores Who Qualifies As an Evangelical," http://www.barna.org/culture-articles/111-survey-explores-who-qualifies-as-an-evangelical?q=evangelicals.

Chapter 18 — The Return of Jesus

1) Joe Pace, "He Paid the Price," http://www.lyriczz.com/lyrics/joe-pace/ 22941-he-paid-the-price.

Dr. Reagan's Comprehensive Book About Bible Prophecy

What is the destiny of planet earth?

What is going to be the fate of mankind?

Dr. David R. Reagan

We don't have to guess. The Bible spells out God's plan for the ages in great detail through prophecies given thousands of years ago.

In this book Dr. Reagan presents a panoramic survey of the fundamentals of Bible prophecy, with a focus on the prophecies that relate to the end times. In the process, he reveals God's plan for the redemption of mankind and the restoration of the creation.

The book is written in a down-to-earth, easy-to-understand style. Although all the chapters relate to the overall theme, each chapter is designed to stand alone. This makes it possible for you either to read the book straight through or to skip around, reading only those chapters whose topics appeal to you.

The book is divided into five parts:

> Prophetic Significance
> Prophetic Issues
> Prophetic Viewpoints
> Prophetic Signs
> Prophetic Hope

There is a Prophetic Epilogue in which Dr. Reagan presents an in-depth, verse by verse explanation of Psalm 2, one of the Bible's greatest passages about the Second Coming of the Lord.

The book contains 42 chapters and runs 415 pages in length. It sells for $20, including the cost of shipping. You can order a copy by calling 972-736-3567, Monday through Friday, 8am to 5pm Central time. You can also purchase the book through the Lamb & Lion website at www.l amblion.com.

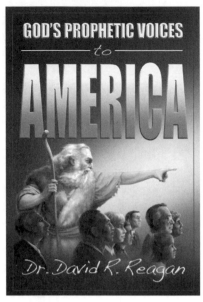

America's Prophetic Voices

This book begins with an in-depth description of the major enemy of Christianity in America today — namely, the philosophy of Humanism, which Dr. Reagan claims is the religion of Satan.

He then launches into the presentation of summaries of the messages of 13 prophetic voices God has anointed to speak out against Humanism and to warn our nation of its danger. These are voices that have also alerted us to our sins and have called us to repentance.

Four of the voices are from the past. The other nine are currently active. The four voices from the past are Peter Marshall, David Wilkerson, Aleksandr Solzhenitsyn and Francis Schaeffer.

The nine current voices are Donald Wildmon, Erwin Lutzer, David Jeremiah, William Koenig, Jan Markell, Albert Mohler, Jr., Franklin Graham, Robert Jeffress and Jonathan Cahn.

The book concludes with an essay by Dr. Reagan in which he addresses the crucial question: "Is America Doomed?"

This is a book with a hard-hitting, jolting message about America's rebellion against God and how it is leading to the pouring out of God's wrath on our nation.

The book is illustrated throughout with full color photographs. It runs 287 pages in length. It sells for $20, including the cost of shipping.

You can order the book through the ministry's website at lamb lion.com or by calling the ministry's office at 972-736-3567 Monday through Friday, 8am to 5pm Central time. ✜